All Authority

Les Dorman

Copyright Information

Copyright 2014 Les Dorman. All rights reserved. No part of these materials may be reproduced or transmitted in any form or by any means, electronic or mechanical, including photocopying and recording, or by any information storage or retrieval system, except as may be expressly permitted in writing from the publisher.

Unless otherwise noted scripture quotations are taken from the *World English Bible*. The World English Bible (WEB) is a public domain (no copyright) modern English translation of the Holy Bible. That means that anyone may freely copy it in any form, including electronic and print formats. The World English Bible is based on the *American Standard Version* of the Holy Bible first published in 1901.

Scripture quotations marked *NASB* are taken from the *New American Standard Bible*. New American Standard Bible Copyright 1960, 1962, 1963, 1968, 1971, 1972, 1973, 1975, 1977, 1995 by The Lockman Foundation, A Corporation Not for Profit, La Habra, California. All Rights Reserved

Photos of scriptures are taken from the King James Version of the Bible.

It is the author's opinion that most of the newer Bible translations have a remarkable harmony in their translations and can be trusted to deliver God's word with clarity and integrity.

Published February, 2015.

ISBN: 978-0-578-15896-9

Available in print at Amazon.com
and also available for Amazon Kindle

All Authority

STRUCTURE:

Questions to be asked

Paradoxes and Precepts
to be examined

Parables to be grasped

Author's opinion in light of Scripture

Contents

All Authority	iii
Introduction	1
Chapter 1	**9**
How should we embrace the Biblical mysteries?	9
Author's Opinion	12
Paradoxes to be examined	15
One God in three persons	15
The Word	18
Virgin birth	21
Grace	23
Parables to be grasped	27
The Parable of the Mustard Seed	27
Author's Opinion	27
Parable of the Rich Man and Lazarus	30
Author's Opinion	30
Parable of the Hidden Treasure	32
Author's Opinion	32
Parable of the Pearl of Great Price	32
Author's Opinion	33
Chapter 2	**35**
Why is the Bible hard to understand?	35
Author's Opinion	39
Paradoxes to be examined	41
Creation	41
False Teaching	43
Stumbling Blocks	45
Scandal (Shame)	48
Parables to be grasped	50
The Parable of the Sower	50
Author's Opinion	51

- The Parable of the Leaven. ... 53
- Author's Opinion ... 53
- The Parable of the Wicked Vinedressers ... 55
- Author's Opinion ... 55
- The Parable of the Great Supper ... 58
- Author's Opinion ... 58
- The Parable of the Barren Fig Tree ... 59
- Author's Opinion ... 60

Chapter 3 ... 63

- Why did God create man?. ... 63
- Author's Opinion ... 65
- Paradoxes to be examined ... 67
- Worship 67
- Predestination ... 70
- Faith 72
- Soul ... 74
- Parables to be grasped 76
- The Parable of the Lamp and Salt. ... 76
- Author's opinion ... 76
- The Parable of the Lost Sheep 77
- Author's opinion ... 78
- The Parable of the Good Samaritan 80
- Author's Opinion ... 80
- The Parable of the Expedient Servant ... 81
- Author's Opinion ... 82
- The Parable of the Marriage Feast ... 83
- Author's Opinion ... 84

Chapter 4 ... 87

- What does a Child of God believe? ... 87
- Author's Opinion ... 89
- The Short Answer 96
- The thief on the cross ... 96
- The woman at the well ... 97
- The Long Answer 97

Apostles' Creed. 98

The Distinction between
Orthodox and Unorthodox Beliefs 100

Paradoxes to be examined 109

Divisions 109

The fall or depravity of man 111

Man's sin nature 112

Parables to be grasped. 116

The Parable of the Pharisee
and the Tax Collector 116

Author's Opinion 116

The Parable of the Wheat and Tares 118

Author's Opinion 119

The Parable of the Faithful Servant 125

Author's Opinion 126

The parable of the Ten Virgins 129

Author's Opinion 130

Chapter 5 133

Does God's Word
need to change with the times? 133

Author's Opinion 136

Paradoxes to be examined 138

Eternal Life 138

Fairness of God's Law 140

Resurrection 143

Parables to be grasped 145

The Parable of the householder 145

Author's Opinion 146

Parable of the foolish man
who builds his house on the sand. 147

Author's Opinion 147

The Parable of the fig tree 150

Author's Opinion 150

The Parable of the absent householder 153

Author's Opinion 153

Chapter 6 155

How are we to approach God? 155
Author's Opinion 159
Paradoxes to be examined 160
Repentance 160
Hope 164
Man's choice 166
Judgment 170
Parables to be grasped 175
The Parable of the Prodigal Son 175
Author's Opinion 177
The Parable of the Unprofitable Servant 179
Author's Opinion 179
The Parable of the Unforgiving Servant 181
Author's Opinion 181
The Parable of the Ten Minas 182
Author's Opinion 184
The Parable of the Dragnet 185
Author's Opinion 185

Chapter 7 187

Where are the right answers to be found? 187
Author's Opinion 189
Paradoxes to be examined 193
Church 193
Inerrancy of Scriptures 196
Death 198
Satan 200
Parables to be grasped 203
The Parable of the Growing Seed 203
Author's Opinion 203
The Parable of the Unshrunk Cloth
on Old Garment 205
Author's opinion 205
The Parable of the New Wine in Old Wineskins 207

Author's Opinion 207

The Parable of the Two Sons 209

Author's opinion 209

Chapter 8 211

What choice do we have? 211

Author's Opinion 214

Paradoxes to be examined 215

Pride 215

Hypocrisy 217

Hell 219

Heaven 220

Parables to be grasped 222

The Parable of the Laborers 222

Author's Opinion 223

The Parable of the Woman and the Judge 224

Author's Opinion 225

The Parable of the Cost of Discipleship 226

Author's Opinion 227

The Parable of the Rich Fool 228

Author's Opinion 229

The Parable of the Unjust Servant 230

Author's Opinion 231

Chapter 9 235

How do we know God is faithful? 235

Author's Opinion 239

Paradoxes to be examined 241

Redemption 241

Salvation 244

Born again 246

Spirit 247

Parables to be grasped 250

The Parable of the Talents 250

Author's Opinion 251

The Parable of the Persistent Friend 253

Author's Opinion	254
The Parable of the Lost Coin.	255
Author's Opinion	255
The Parable of the Creditor and Two Debtors	256
Author's Opinion	257
Everyone has a need to know that Jesus saves!	258

Chapter 10 267

What must I do to be saved?	267
Author's Opinion	268

Appendix 269

Parables in Alphabetical Order .	269
Paradoxes in Alphabetical Order	270

Introduction

> 8 He hath ᵐshewed thee, O man, what *is* good; and what doth the LORD require of thee, but ⁿ to do justly, and to love mercy, and to †walk humbly with thy God?
> 9 The LORD's voice crieth unto the city, and ‖ *the man of* wisdom shall see thy name: hear ye the rod, and who hath appointed it.

Informed decisions are always better than uninformed decisions! Everyone has a need to know, but who will dare to tell the people the rules that come from the whole counsel of God as recorded by Jesus' words of truth the Bible. Biblical paradoxes are not being examined, and Jesus' parables need to be grasped with clarity in order to fully understand their true meaning and relevance in today's society. On every continent, there are generations of well-educated people who have virtually no knowledge of God. People all around the world are living their lives in a dry and thirsty land, alone without any consideration of God's precepts or His love and Grace. Today, in this abundant information age, the priceless wisdom of God is available just for the taking. How can it be that people have not yet heard and understood, the Gospel? It seems ironic that the leadership of far too many churches is unconcerned about repeating the age-old message of Jesus' free gift of Grace. The mysteries of these paradoxes and parables can be clearly seen in the scripture. Are you captivated by a pressing need to know if you are included in the family of God? This book will attempt to make clear God's mercy and Grace as described by Jesus' Word of truth. Jesus is the author and creator of all creation, including His Holy Word, the Bible.

As you will see, the Parables spoken by Jesus are remarkably timeless, and are as applicable in today's modern world as they were in the past. These parables contain spiritual truths from God's perspective, told with simplicity and clarity. They relate to our everyday life experiences and yet capture our imagination of unseen conflicts and ultimate triumph over our sin-filled world. The first nine chapters deal with these parables along with this author's opinions, which are not to be confused with Jesus' own words. Each chapter starts with a question; Bible verses that follow help clarify the answers to these questions. The parable and paradoxes shown in these chapters may or may not relate directly to the chapter question. All of these paradoxes and parables have spiritual value, some of the parables have repetitive themes, but all need to be included for our complete understanding.

To live and thrive in any environment requires an understanding of the major influences that govern that environment. Who is in control? Man or God? This is the question. Jesus has been given all authority, and He has given man authority to go and bear witness to His words of truth and Grace to all the nations. This book, *All Authority,* examines and declares the glory of God and His rightful authority in our lives.

Matthew 28: 18-19

₁₈ Jesus came to them and spoke to them, saying, "All authority has been given to me in heaven and on earth. ₁₉ Go and make disciples of all nations, baptizing them in the name of the Father and of the Son and of the Holy Spirit,

John 12: 48-50

₄₈ He who rejects me, and doesn't receive my sayings, has one who judges him. The word that I spoke, the same will judge him in the last day. ₄₉ For I spoke not from myself, but the Father who sent me, he gave me a commandment, what I should say, and what I should speak. ₅₀ I know that his commandment is eternal life. The things therefore which I speak, even as the Father has said to me, so I speak."

My objective is to encourage a serious consideration of these spiritual issues. If used properly, the reader will be equipped to find the written source of God's wisdom. It will greatly increase understanding of God's purpose for our lives and further provide the groundwork for the reader to feel comfortable finding answers to his or her own questions. *All Authority* will show that the entirety of the Scriptures, from Genesis to Revelations was designed to proclaim the Divinity of Jesus Christ and his sacrificial provision of Grace for all mankind to see. Jesus is the inspiring author of the Bible and has given us a living commentary that guides and makes possible our reconciliation with the Lamb of God.

Hebrews 12: 1-2

₁ Therefore let us also, seeing we are surrounded by so great a cloud of witnesses, lay aside every weight and the sin which so easily entangles us, and let us run with perseverance the race that is set before us, ₂ looking to Jesus, the author and perfecter of faith, who for the joy that was set before him endured the cross, despising its shame, and has sat down at the right hand of the throne of God.

This book is an attempt to show that Jesus' Words of Truth provides us with answers that can be found in the scriptures. This is the appropriate time to state that I am not a preacher or scholar. I am not an expert or an authority. My words stated in the "author's opinions" should be considered as a lubricant to get the reader from one question to the next and to provide answers that are just waiting to be understood by all who have eyes to see and ears to hear. The wisdom, authority and power that we all seek must be seen as coming from the Scriptures. The author's opinion should be seen as an effort to be a faithful witness, with a clear and consistent voice, as to what these Bible verses have to say. Hopefully the readers will take mental and spiritual possession of Jesus' teaching, trusting and claiming His priceless wisdom as their own. The Word of God will accomplish its intended purpose for those who trust in the Lord.

1 Corinthians 2: 14-16

> 14 Now the natural man doesn't receive the things of God's Spirit, for they are foolishness to him, and he can't know them, because they are spiritually discerned. 15 But he who is spiritual discerns all things, and he himself is judged by no one. 16 "For who has known the mind of the Lord, that he should instruct him?" But we have Christ's mind.

Romans 10: 13-17

> 13 For, "Whoever will call on the name of the Lord will be saved. 14 How then will they call on him in whom they have not believed? How will they believe in him whom they have not heard? How will they hear without a preacher? 15 And how will they preach unless they are sent? As it is written: "How beautiful are the feet of those who preach the Good News of peace, who bring glad tidings of good things!" 16 But they didn't all listen to the glad news. For Isaiah says, "Lord, who has believed our report?" 17 So faith comes by hearing, and hearing by the word of God.

When one dares to approach the subject of God's wisdom and Satan's influence on today's visible Church (hopefully to make it better), we should do so with hat in hand and in fearful humility. I am not so afraid that others will have honest disagreements with my opinions. I fear that people will make the mistake of thinking that my opinion or any other author's opinion has the same weight and authority of God's Word.

James 3: 1-2

> 1 Let not many of you be teachers, my brothers, knowing that we will receive heavier judgment. 2 For in many things we all stumble. If anyone doesn't stumble in word, the same is a perfect man, able to bridle the whole body also.

1 John 4: 17

> 17 To him therefore who knows to do good, and doesn't do it, to him it is sin.

A common complaint for using scripture to address an issue is that specific verses can be taken out of context. I have made every effort to avoid this problem by searching for Bible verses that deal with individual subjects or issues and let the verses stand alone for consideration. I invite the reader to search not only the reference verse but to read the complete Bible chapter to acquire accurate sense of the issue in question. With such a wide and opposing spectrum of teaching on doctrinal issues available today, not everyone can be right and still hold such opposing views at the same time. *All Authority's* goal is to challenge the reader to search the Scriptures for the true answers. The "Author's Opinion" is here to highlight and focus on Jesus' words of truth, in today's context, but not to justify any particular denominational theology. Chapter 4 deals, at some length, with orthodox and unorthodox doctrinal views, an example of stark contrasting opinions. If the correctness of an issue is in question or offends, search the scriptures to confirm your point of view. Error is inevitable if we find ourselves in opposition to God's Word. Personal introspection must come first, followed by prayer to the Holy Spirit for help in finding the answers we seek if we are to truly have hope of making a change in the direction of our lives. While my words or any other mortal human's will fall short compared to the glory of God's Word, it is hoped that my opinions on the subject at hand will ring true to the reader and be consistent with God's Word. Religious opinions from any source should be first evaluated for consistency with the scriptures, and then only considered as food for thought, on our personal journey to know God's wisdom better. His Holy Word the Bible has the highest authority and possesses the ultimate in righteousness and power.

John 16: 13

> 13 However when he, the Spirit of truth, has come, he will guide you into all truth, for he will not speak from himself; but whatever he hears, he will speak. He will declare to you things that are coming.

Ephesians 1: 21-23 (NASB)

> 21 far above all rule and authority and power and dominion, and every name that is named, not only in this age but also in the one to come. 22 And He put all things in subjection under His feet, and gave Him as head over all things to the church, 23 which is His body, the fullness of Him who fills all in all.

The first order of finding answers starts by asking the correct question, *for faith does not preclude us from having questions.* All have questions. But even before we ask the question, we must recognize that there is also "attitude." God sees the attitude; sometimes our attitudes speak louder than our question. Questions that challenge God's authority and/or are designed to excuse oneself may not be received well. But if we humble ourselves and seek to know Him better, He will receive us and our questions with open arms.

Each chapter has a question that all of us should be asking ourselves. The answers can be found in Bible verses, and also in Jesus' Parables that have been "feeding the hungry a bountiful feast of wisdom" for thousands of years. Parables are short stories told by Jesus that show us the difference between God's perspective and man's perspective. Jesus said, "Blessed are the people that hear and understand my parable." Through His illustrations we are able to get a glimpse at how God views and deals with man. Not every one can grasp their full meaning, but the attempt should be made. At the same time we will be looking at Biblical Paradoxes and precepts. Paradoxes are seemingly contradictory statements that the Bible claims to be nonetheless true. They are often stumbling blocks because they can offend one's sense of reason. It is important to acknowledge that one man's paradox may be another man's precept.

Chapter 1

How should we embrace the Biblical mysteries?

The following verses address some of the unseen mysteries that can challenge man's reason and comprehension.

Matthew 13: 10-15

> 10 The disciples came, and said to him, "Why do you speak to them in parables?" 11 He answered them, "To you it is given to know the mysteries of the Kingdom of Heaven, but it is not given to them. 12 For whoever has, to him will be given, and he will have abundance, but whoever doesn't have, from him will be taken away even that which he has. 13 Therefore I speak to them in parables, because seeing they don't see, and hearing, they don't hear, neither do they understand. 14 In them the prophecy of Isaiah is fulfilled, which says, 'By hearing you will hear and will in no way understand; Seeing you will see, and will in no way perceive: 15 for this people's heart has

grown callous, their ears are dull of hearing, they have closed their eyes; or else perhaps they might perceive with their eyes, hear with their ears, understand with their heart, and would turn again; and I would heal them.'

1 Corinthians 2: 6-7

6 We speak wisdom, however, among those who are full grown; yet a wisdom not of this world, nor of the rulers of this world, who are coming to nothing. 7 But we speak God's wisdom in a mystery, the wisdom that has been hidden, which God foreordained before the worlds for our glory,

1 Corinthians 4: 1-5

1 So let a man think of us as Christ's servants, and stewards of God's mysteries. 2 Here, moreover, it is required of stewards, that they be found faithful. 3 But with me it is a very small thing that I should be judged by you, or by man's judgment. Yes, I don't judge my own self. 4 For I know nothing against myself. Yet I am not justified by this, but he who judges me is the Lord. 5 Therefore judge nothing before the time, until the Lord comes, who will both bring to light the hidden things of darkness, and reveal the counsels of the hearts. Then each man will get his praise from God.

1 Corinthians 13: 1-3

1 If I speak with the languages of men and of angels, but don't have love, I have become sounding brass, or a clanging cymbal. 2 If I have the gift of prophecy, and know all mysteries and all knowledge; and if I have all faith, so as to remove mountains, but don't have love, I am nothing. 3 If I give away all my goods to feed the poor, and if I give my body to be burned, but don't have love, it profits me nothing.

Ephesians 3: 8-13 (NASB)

8 To me, the very least of all saints, this grace was given, to preach to

the Gentiles the unfathomable riches of Christ, 9 and to bring to light what is the administration of the mystery which for ages has been hidden in God who created all things; 10 so that the manifold wisdom of God might now be made known through the church to the rulers and the authorities in the heavenly places. 11 This was in accordance with the eternal purpose which He carried out in Christ Jesus our Lord, 12 in whom we have boldness and confident access through faith in Him. 13 Therefore I ask you not to lose heart at my tribulations on your behalf, for they are your glory.

Ephesians 5: 14-21

14 Therefore he says, "Awake, you who sleep, and arise from the dead, and Christ will shine on you." 15 Therefore watch carefully how you walk, not as unwise, but as wise; 16 redeeming the time, because the days are evil. 17 Therefore don't be foolish, but understand what the will of the Lord is. 18 Don't be drunken with wine, in which is dissipation, but be filled with the Spirit, 19 speaking to one another in psalms, hymns, and spiritual songs; singing, and making melody in your heart to the Lord; 20 giving thanks always concerning all things in the name of our Lord Jesus Christ, to God, even the Father; 21 subjecting yourselves to one another in the fear of Christ.

1 Timothy 3: 8-10

8 Servants, in the same way, must be reverent, not double-tongued, not addicted to much wine, not greedy for money; 9 holding the mystery of the faith in a pure conscience. 10 Let them also first be tested; then let them serve if they are blameless.

2 Timothy 2: 1-7

1 You therefore, my child, be strengthened in the grace that is in Christ Jesus. 2 The things which you have heard from me among many witnesses, commit the same to faithful men, who will be able to teach others also. 3 You therefore must endure hardship, as a good soldier of Christ Jesus. 4 No soldier on duty entangles himself

in the affairs of life, that he may please him who enrolled him as a soldier. 5 Also, if anyone competes in athletics, he isn't crowned unless he has competed by the rules. 6 The farmer who labors must be the first to get a share of the crops. 7 Consider what I say, and may the Lord give you understanding in all things.

2 Peter 3: 14-18

14 Therefore, beloved, seeing that you look for these things, be diligent to be found in peace, without defect and blameless in his sight. 15 Regard the patience of our Lord as salvation; even as our beloved brother Paul also, according to the wisdom given to him, wrote to you; 16 as also in all of his letters, speaking in them of these things. In those, there are some things that are hard to understand, which the ignorant and unsettled twist, as they also do to the other Scriptures, to their own destruction. 17 You therefore, beloved, knowing these things beforehand, beware, lest being carried away with the error of the wicked, you fall from your own steadfastness. 18 But grow in the grace and knowledge of our Lord and Savior Jesus Christ. To him be the glory both now and forever. Amen

Luke 24: 44-47

44 He said to them, "This is what I told you, while I was still with you, that all things which are written in the law of Moses, the prophets, and the psalms, concerning me must be fulfilled." 45 Then he opened their minds, that they might understand the Scriptures. 46 He said to them, "Thus it is written, and thus it was necessary for the Christ to suffer and to rise from the dead the third day, 47 and that repentance and remission of sins should be preached in his name to all the nations, beginning at Jerusalem.

Author's Opinion

The question is how we should we embrace Biblical Mysteries. You cannot see, feel or taste spiritual issues, but instinctively you know they are real. How we deal with these strange and seemly unreasonable Bible mysteries can changes our lives and our eternal destiny. If a person does not like or understand something, is that alone reason enough to disbelieve or question Biblical authority? God made man in His image and gives him the ability to choose what he or she believes. Believing in the "Big Bang Theory" takes as much faith as does belief in the Creation story. Generally speaking most of us decide what we want to believe and then build theories to accommodate those beliefs. People who whole-heartily embrace these biblical paradoxes as truth tend to be the ones who have grown up in a religious environment and/or are people who are in need of finding peace and harmony with God.

John 1: 12

> 12 But as many as received him, to them he gave the right to become God's children, to those who believe in his name:

Please know this, the children of God find great joy and fulfillment in reading the Scriptures, but the ones who are rebellious to God find the scriptures fearful and full of dread. Within our person is a God given spirit that cries out to be at peace with God. But also within our inner man is a self-reliant spirit that resists God.

Daniel 7: 9

> 9 "I watched until thrones were placed, and one who was ancient of days sat. His clothing was white as snow, and the hair of his head like pure wool. His throne was fiery flames, and its wheels burning fire.

God knows the beginning and end of our inner man struggles. The question is, Do you know the end of your own story? Therein lies the spiritual issue of finding Grace, as revealed in the Bible. Some are destined to believe and find Grace and some are not.

Proverbs 20: 27 (NASB)

> 27 The spirit of man is the lamp of the Lord, Searching all the innermost parts of his being.

If a person chooses to deny these eternal unseen mysteries of God, they are considered to be in spiritual denial. Unlike animals, man instinctively knows the difference between right and wrong, good and evil. We can know and love God, much like a child trusts and loves their parents without question. To embrace and believe in the Bibles mysteries will require a child-like faith and obedience. In *Isaiah 1: 18* it says *"Let us reason together, Says the Lord…"* But "reasoning with God" does not mean we are equal with God. Only the arrogant and foolish think they can match wits with God and/or deny His existence. If we desire wisdom without doubting or without a contentious attitude, God will give us His wisdom without reproach.

Matthew 18: 3

> 3 and said, "Most certainly I tell you, unless you turn, and become as little children, you will in no way enter into the Kingdom of Heaven.

Hebrews 4: 1-2

> 1 Let us fear therefore, lest perhaps anyone of you should seem to have come short of a promise of entering into his rest. 2 For indeed we have had good news preached to us, even as they also did, but the word they heard didn't profit them, because it wasn't mixed with faith by those who heard,

James 1: 5-6

> 5 But if any of you lacks wisdom, let him ask of God, who gives to all liberally and without reproach; and it will be given to him. 6 But let him ask in faith, without any doubting, for he who doubts is like a wave of the sea, driven by the wind and tossed.

Paradoxes to be examined

One God in three persons

Exodus 20: 3

3 "You shall have no other gods before me.

Deuteronomy 32: 4

4 The Rock, his work is perfect, for all his ways are just. A God of faithfulness who does no wrong, just and right is he.

Isaiah 45: 22

22 "Look to me, and be saved, all the ends of the earth; for I am God, and there is no other.

Isaiah 53: 10-12 (NASB)

10 But the Lord was pleased To crush Him, putting Him to grief; If He would render Himself as a guilt offering, He will see His offspring, He will prolong His days, And the good pleasure of the Lord will prosper in His hand. 11 As a result of the anguish of His soul, He will see it and be satisfied; By His knowledge the Righteous One, My Servant, will justify the many, As He will bear their iniquities. 12 Therefore, I will allot Him a portion with the great, And He will divide the booty with the strong; Because He poured out Himself to death, And was numbered with the transgressors; Yet He Himself bore the sin of many, And interceded for the transgressors.

Matthew 3: 16-17

16 Jesus, when he was baptized, went up directly from the water: and behold, the heavens were opened to him. He saw the Spirit of God descending as a dove, and coming on him. 17 Behold, a voice out of the heavens said, "This is my beloved Son, with whom I am well pleased."

Matthew 16: 16

16 Simon Peter answered, "You are the Christ, the Son of the living God."

Matthew 27: 51-54

51 Behold, the veil of the temple was torn in two from the top to the bottom. The earth quaked and the rocks were split. 52 The tombs were opened, and many bodies of the saints who had fallen asleep were raised; 53 and coming out of the tombs after his resurrection, they entered into the holy city and appeared to many. 54 Now the centurion, and those who were with him watching Jesus, when they saw the earthquake, and the things that were done, feared exceedingly, saying, "Truly this was the Son of God."

Matthew 28: 19-20

19 Go and make disciples of all nations, baptizing them in the name of the Father and of the Son and of the Holy Spirit, 20 teaching them to observe all things that I commanded you. Behold, I am with you always, even to the end of the age." Amen.

Luke 1: 32

32 He will be great, and will be called the Son of the Most High. The Lord God will give him the throne of his father, David,

1 John 5: 7-8

7 For there are three who testify: 8 the Spirit, the water, and the blood; and the three agree as one.

1 Corinthians 12: 4-6

4 Now there are various kinds of gifts, but the same Spirit. 5 There are various kinds of service, and the same Lord. 6 There are various kinds of workings, but the same God, who works all things in all.

2 Corinthians 13: 14

14 The grace of the Lord Jesus Christ, God's love, and the fellowship of the Holy Spirit, be with you all. Amen.

Philippians 2: 9-11

9 Therefore God also highly exalted him, and gave to him the name which is above every name; 10 that at the name of Jesus every knee should bow, of those in heaven, those on earth, and those under the earth, 11 and that every tongue should confess that Jesus Christ is Lord, to the glory of God the Father.

1 Peter 1: 2

2 according to the foreknowledge of God the Father, in sanctification of the Spirit, that you may obey Jesus Christ and be sprinkled with his blood: Grace to you and peace be multiplied.

2 Peter 1: 16-17

16 For we did not follow cunningly devised fables, when we made known to you the power and coming of our Lord Jesus Christ, but we were eyewitnesses of his majesty. 17 For he received from God the Father honor and glory, when the voice came to him from the Majestic Glory, "This is my beloved Son, in whom I am well pleased."

Jude 1: 20-21

20 But you, beloved, keep building up yourselves on your most holy faith, praying in the Holy Spirit. 21 Keep yourselves in God's love, looking for the mercy of our Lord Jesus Christ to eternal life.

Revelation 1: 17-18

17 When I saw him, I fell at his feet like a dead man. He laid his right hand on me, saying, "Don't be afraid. I am the first and the last, 18 and the Living one. I was dead, and behold, I am alive forever and ever. Amen. I have the keys of Death and of Hades.

The Word

John 1: 1-18

1 In the beginning was the Word, and the Word was with God, and the Word was God. 2 The same was in the beginning with God. 3 All things were made through him. Without him was not anything made that has been made. 4 In him was life, and the life was the light of men. 5 The light shines in the darkness, and the darkness hasn't overcome it. 6 There came a man, sent from God, whose name was John. 7 The same came as a witness, that he might testify about the light, that all might believe through him. 8 He was not the light, but was sent that he might testify about the light. 9 The true light that enlightens everyone was coming into the world. 10 He was in the world, and the world was made through him, and the world didn't recognize him. 11 He came to his own, and those who were his own didn't receive him. 12 But as many as received him, to them he gave the right to become God's children, to those who believe in his name: 13 who were born not of blood, nor of the will of the flesh, nor of the will of man, but of God. 14 The Word became flesh, and lived among us. We saw his glory, such glory as of the one and only Son of the Father, full of grace and truth. 15 John testified about him. He cried out, saying, "This was he of whom I said, 'He who comes after me has surpassed me, for he was before me.'" 16 From his fullness we all received grace upon grace. 17 For the law was given through Moses. Grace and truth were realized through Jesus Christ. 18 No one has seen God at any time. The one and only Son, who is in the bosom of the Father, he has declared him.

Proverbs 30: 5

5 "Every word of God is flawless. He is a shield to those who take refuge in him.

John 14: 24

24 He who doesn't love me doesn't keep my words. The word which you hear isn't mine, but the Father's who sent me.

John 17: 14-19

14 I have given them your word. The world hated them, because they are not of the world, even as I am not of the world. 15 I pray not that you would take them from the world, but that you would keep them from the evil one. 16 They are not of the world even as I am not of the world. 17 Sanctify them in your truth. Your word is truth. 18 As you sent me into the world, even so I have sent them into the world. 19 For their sakes I sanctify myself, that they themselves also may be sanctified in truth.

Psalm 119: 11

11 I have hidden your word in my heart, that I might not sin against you.

Psalm 119: 50

50 This is my comfort in my affliction, for your word has revived me.

Acts 13: 48

48 And when the Gentiles heard this, they began rejoicing and glorifying the word of the Lord, and as many as were appointed to eternal life believed.

Ephesians 5: 25-30 (NASB)

25 Husbands, love your wives, just as Christ also loved the church and gave Himself up for her, 26 so that He might sanctify her, having cleansed her by the washing of water with the word, 27 that He might present to Himself the church in all her glory, having no spot or wrinkle or any such thing; but that she would be holy and blameless. 28 So husbands ought also to love their own wives as their own bodies. He who loves his own wife loves himself; 29 for no one ever

hated his own flesh, but nourishes and cherishes it, just as Christ also does the church, 30 because we are members of His body.

Philippians 2: 16

16 holding up the word of life; that I may have something to boast in the day of Christ, that I didn't run in vain nor labor in vain.

Hebrews 1: 3

3 His Son is the radiance of his glory, the very image of his substance, and upholding all things by the word of his power, who, when he had by himself purified us of our sins, sat down on the right hand of the Majesty on high;

Hebrews 4: 12-16

12 For the word of God is living and active, and sharper than any two-edged sword, piercing even to the dividing of soul and spirit, of both joints and marrow, and is able to discern the thoughts and intentions of the heart. 13 There is no creature that is hidden from his sight, but all things are naked and laid open before the eyes of him to whom we must give an account. 14 Having then a great high priest, who has passed through the heavens, Jesus, the Son of God, let us hold tightly to our confession. 15 For we don't have a high priest who can't be touched with the feeling of our infirmities, but one who has been in all points tempted like we are, yet without sin. 16 Let us therefore draw near with boldness to the throne of grace, that we may receive mercy, and may find grace for help in time of need.

1 Peter 1: 22-25

22 Seeing you have purified your souls in your obedience to the truth through the Spirit in sincere brotherly affection, love one another from the heart fervently: 23 having been born again, not of corruptible seed, but of incorruptible, through the word of God, which lives and remains forever. 24 For, "All flesh is like grass, and all of man's glory like the flower in the grass. The grass withers, and its flower falls;

25 but the Lord's word endures forever." This is the word of Good News which was preached to you.

2 Peter 3: 5-7

5 For this they willfully forget, that there were heavens from of old, and an earth formed out of water and amid water, by the word of God; 6 by which means the world that then was, being overflowed with water, perished. 7 But the heavens that now exist, and the earth, by the same word have been stored up for fire, being reserved against the day of judgment and destruction of ungodly men.

1 John 5: 7-8

7 For there are three who testify: 8 the Spirit, the water, and the blood; and the three agree as one.

Revelation 19: 11-16

11 I saw the heaven opened, and behold, a white horse, and he who sat on it is called Faithful and True. In righteousness he judges and makes war. 12 His eyes are a flame of fire, and on his head are many crowns. He has names written and a name written which no one knows but he himself. 13 He is clothed in a garment sprinkled with blood. His name is called "The Word of God." 14 The armies which are in heaven followed him on white horses, clothed in white, pure, fine linen. 15 Out of his mouth proceeds a sharp, double-edged sword, that with it he should strike the nations. He will rule them with an iron rod. He treads the wine press of the fierceness of the wrath of God, the Almighty. 16 He has on his garment and on his thigh a name written, "KING OF KINGS, AND LORD OF LORDS."

Virgin birth

Luke 1: 26-35

26 Now in the sixth month, the angel Gabriel was sent from God to a

city of Galilee, named Nazareth, 27 to a virgin pledged to be married to a man whose name was Joseph, of David's house. The virgin's name was Mary. 28 Having come in, the angel said to her, "Rejoice, you highly favored one! The Lord is with you. Blessed are you among women!" 29 But when she saw him, she was greatly troubled at the saying, and considered what kind of salutation this might be. 30 The angel said to her, "Don't be afraid, Mary, for you have found favor with God. 31 Behold, you will conceive in your womb, and give birth to a son, and will call his name 'Jesus.' 32 He will be great, and will be called the Son of the Most High. The Lord God will give him the throne of his father, David, 33 and he will reign over the house of Jacob forever. There will be no end to his Kingdom." 34 Mary said to the angel, "How can this be, seeing I am a virgin?" 35 The angel answered her, "The Holy Spirit will come on you, and the power of the Most High will overshadow you. Therefore also the holy one who is born from you will be called the Son of God.

Isaiah 7: 13-14

13 He said, "Listen now, house of David. Is it not enough for you to try the patience of men, that you will try the patience of my God also? 14 Therefore the Lord himself will give you a sign. Behold, the virgin will conceive, and bear a son, and shall call his name Immanuel.

Galatians 4: 4-5

4 But when the fullness of the time came, God sent out his Son, born to a woman, born under the law, 5 that he might redeem those who were under the law, that we might receive the adoption of children.

John 1: 14

14 The Word became flesh, and lived among us. We saw his glory, such glory as of the one and only Son of the Father, full of grace and truth.

Philippians 2: 5-11

5 Have this in your mind, which was also in Christ Jesus, 6 who, existing in the form of God, didn't consider equality with God a thing to be grasped, 7 but emptied himself, taking the form of a servant, being made in the likeness of men. 8 And being found in human form, he humbled himself, becoming obedient to death, yes, the death of the cross. 9 Therefore God also highly exalted him, and gave to him the name which is above every name; 10 that at the name of Jesus every knee should bow, of those in heaven, those on earth, and those under the earth, 11 and that every tongue should confess that Jesus Christ is Lord, to the glory of God the Father.

Grace

Nehemiah 9: 17 (NASB)

17 "They refused to listen, And did not remember Your wondrous deeds which You had performed among them; So they became stubborn and appointed a leader to return to their slavery in Egypt. But You are a God of forgiveness, Gracious and compassionate, Slow to anger and abounding in loving kindness; And You did not forsake them.

Psalm 84: 8-12 (NASB)

8 O Lord God of hosts, hear my prayer; Give ear, O God of Jacob! Selah. 9 Behold our shield, O God, And look upon the face of Your anointed. 10 For a day in Your courts is better than a thousand outside. I would rather stand at the threshold of the house of my God. Than dwell in the tents of wickedness. 11 For the Lord God is a sun and shield; The Lord gives grace and glory; No good thing does He withhold from those who walk uprightly. 12 O Lord of hosts, How blessed is the man who trusts in You!

Psalm 103: 6-18 (NASB)

6 The Lord performs righteous deeds And judgments for all who are oppressed. 7 He made known His ways to Moses, His acts to the sons of Israel. 8 The Lord is compassionate and gracious, Slow to anger and abounding in loving kindness. 9 He will not always strive with us, Nor will He keep His anger forever. 10 He has not dealt with us according to our sins, Nor rewarded us according to our iniquities. 11 For as high as the heavens are above the earth, So great is His loving kindness toward those who fear Him. 12 As far as the east is from the west, So far has He removed our transgressions from us. 13 Just as a father has compassion on his children, So the Lord has compassion on those who fear Him. 14 For He Himself knows our frame; He is mindful that we are but dust. 15 As for man, his days are like grass; As a flower of the field, so he flourishes. 16 When the wind has passed over it, it is no more, And its place acknowledges it no longer. 17 But the loving kindness of the Lord is from everlasting to everlasting on those who fear Him, And His righteousness to children's children, 18 To those who keep His covenant And remember His precepts to do them.

Psalm 145: 8-9 (NASB)

8 The Lord is gracious and merciful; Slow to anger and great in loving kindness. 9 The Lord is good to all, And His mercies are over all His works.

Luke 19: 10

10 For the Son of Man came to seek and to save that which was lost."

John 1: 15-18

15 John testified about him. He cried out, saying, "This was he of whom I said, 'He who comes after me has surpassed me, for he was before me.'" 16 From his fullness we all received grace upon grace. 17 For the law was given through Moses. Grace and truth were

realized through Jesus Christ. 18 No one has seen God at any time. The one and only Son, who is in the bosom of the Father, he has declared him.

John 1: 29

29 The next day, he saw Jesus coming to him, and said, "Behold, the Lamb of God, who takes away the sin of the world!

Romans 5: 1-2

1 Being therefore justified by faith, we have peace with God through our Lord Jesus Christ; 2 through whom we also have our access by faith into this grace in which we stand. We rejoice in hope of the glory of God.

Romans 5: 12-17

12 Therefore as sin entered into the world through one man, and death through sin; and so death passed to all men, because all sinned. 13 For until the law, sin was in the world; but sin is not charged when there is no law. 14 Nevertheless death reigned from Adam until Moses, even over those whose sins weren't like Adam's disobedience, who is a foreshadowing of him who was to come. 15 But the free gift isn't like the trespass. For if by the trespass of the one the many died, much more did the grace of God, and the gift by the grace of the one man, Jesus Christ, abound to the many. 16 The gift is not as through one who sinned: for the judgment came by one to condemnation, but the free gift came of many trespasses to justification. 17 For if by the trespass of the one, death reigned through the one; so much more will those who receive the abundance of grace and of the gift of righteousness reign in life through the one, Jesus Christ.

2 Corinthians 5: 21

21 For him who knew no sin he made to be sin on our behalf; so that in him we might become the righteousness of God.

Ephesians 2: 4-10

4 But God, being rich in mercy, for his great love with which he loved us, 5 even when we were dead through our trespasses, made us alive together with Christ (by grace you have been saved), 6 and raised us up with him, and made us to sit with him in the heavenly places in Christ Jesus, 7 that in the ages to come he might show the exceeding riches of his grace in kindness toward us in Christ Jesus; 8 for by grace you have been saved through faith, and that not of yourselves; it is the gift of God, 9 not of works, that no one would boast. 10 For we are his workmanship, created in Christ Jesus for good works, which God prepared before that we would walk in them.

Galatians 1: 3-4

3 Grace to you and peace from God the Father, and our Lord Jesus Christ, 4 who gave himself for our sins, that he might deliver us out of this present evil age, according to the will of our God and Father—

1 Peter 1: 18-19

18 knowing that you were redeemed, not with corruptible things, with silver or gold, from the useless way of life handed down from your fathers, 19 but with precious blood, as of a lamb without blemish or spot, the blood of Christ;

Titus 2: 11-13

11 For the grace of God has appeared, bringing salvation to all men, 12 instructing us to the intent that, denying ungodliness and worldly lusts, we would live soberly, righteously, and godly in this present age; 13 looking for the blessed hope and appearing of the glory of our great God and Savior, Jesus Christ;

Parables to be grasped

The Parable of the Mustard Seed

Luke 13: 18-19

> 18 He said, "What is God's Kingdom like? To what shall I compare it? 19 It is like a grain of mustard seed, which a man took, and put in his own garden. It grew, and became a large tree, and the birds of the sky live in its branches."

Author's Opinion

The Parable of the Mustard Seed is about Christ's influence on the world. The Mustard seed is very small. It looks insignificant but when planted in the garden or the right environment, it will grow into a large tree. It will provide a resting place to all that will come. Worshiping and glorifying God, Jesus (Emanuel God with us) and the Holy Spirit is what the gospel of the Kingdom of God is all about. Jesus came and, though He was not known for his power or strength, He has influenced the world like no other. He has provided hope and a refuge for all who put their trust in Him. This Parable was a prediction of things to come concerning the spread of the gospel throughout the world. We can choose to see all the prophecies that have come true, Jesus' teaching and miracles, and His influence on history as just a chance happening of good luck. Or we can accept and believe in the inerrant Scriptures and Christ Atonement as a free gift of Grace to sinful man. What is the kingdom of God like? Some people see an inconsequential myth while others see and embrace His promises of redemption and eternal love with a humble and joyful gratitude.

John 4: 21-24

21 Jesus said to her, "Woman, believe me, the hour comes, when neither in this mountain, nor in Jerusalem, will you worship the Father. 22 You worship that which you don't know. We worship that which we know; for salvation is from the Jews. 23 But the hour comes, and now is, when the true worshipers will worship the Father in spirit and truth, for the Father seeks such to be his worshipers. 24 God is spirit, and those who worship him must worship in spirit and truth."

Mark 1: 14-15

14 Now after John was taken into custody, Jesus came into Galilee, preaching the Good News of God's Kingdom, 15 and saying, "The time is fulfilled, and God's Kingdom is at hand! Repent, and believe in the Good News."

Matthew 24: 14

14 This Good News of the Kingdom will be preached in the whole world for a testimony to all the nations, and then the end will come.

Colossians 1: 10-14

10 that you may walk worthily of the Lord, to please him in all respects, bearing fruit in every good work, and increasing in the knowledge of God; 11 strengthened with all power, according to the might of his glory, for all endurance and perseverance with joy; 12 giving thanks to the Father, who made us fit to be partakers of the inheritance of the saints in light; 13 who delivered us out of the power of darkness, and translated us into the Kingdom of the Son of his love; 14 in whom we have our redemption, the forgiveness of our sins.

Matthew 6: 32-33

32 For the Gentiles seek after all these things; for your heavenly Father knows that you need all these things. 33 But seek first God's Kingdom, and his righteousness; and all these things will be given to you as well.

Matthew 13: 41-43

41 The Son of Man will send out his angels, and they will gather out of his Kingdom all things that cause stumbling, and those who do iniquity, 42 and will cast them into the furnace of fire. There will be weeping and the gnashing of teeth. 43 Then the righteous will shine like the sun in the Kingdom of their Father. He who has ears to hear, let him hear.

Mark 4: 10-12

10 When he was alone, those who were around him with the twelve asked him about the parables. 11 He said to them, "To you is given the mystery of God's Kingdom, but to those who are outside, all things are done in parables, 12 that 'seeing they may see, and not perceive; and hearing they may hear, and not understand; lest perhaps they should turn again, and their sins should be forgiven them.'"

John 3: 5-6

5 Jesus answered, "Most certainly I tell you, unless one is born of water and spirit, he can't enter into God's Kingdom. 6 That which is born of the flesh is flesh. That which is born of the Spirit is spirit.

1 Thessalonians 2: 10-13

10 You are witnesses with God, how holy, righteously, and blamelessly we behaved ourselves toward you who believe. 11 As you know, we exhorted, comforted, and implored every one of you, as a father does his own children, 12 to the end that you should walk worthily of God, who calls you into his own Kingdom and glory.
13 For this cause we also thank God without ceasing, that, when you received from us the word of the message of God, you accepted it not as the word of men, but, as it is in truth, the word of God, which also works in you who believe.

Parable of the Rich Man and Lazarus

Luke 16: 19-31

19 "Now there was a certain rich man, and he was clothed in purple and fine linen, living in luxury every day. 20 A certain beggar, named Lazarus, was taken to his gate, full of sores, 21 and desiring to be fed with the crumbs that fell from the rich man's table. Yes, even the dogs came and licked his sores. 22 The beggar died, and he was carried away by the angels to Abraham's bosom. The rich man also died, and was buried. 23 In Hades, he lifted up his eyes, being in torment, and saw Abraham far off, and Lazarus at his bosom. 24 He cried and said, 'Father Abraham, have mercy on me, and send Lazarus, that he may dip the tip of his finger in water, and cool my tongue! For I am in anguish in this flame.' 25 "But Abraham said, 'Son, remember that you, in your lifetime, received your good things, and Lazarus, in the same way, bad things. But here he is now comforted, and you are in anguish. 26 Besides all this, between us and you there is a great gulf fixed, that those who want to pass from here to you are not able, and that no one may cross over from there to us.' 27 "He said, 'I ask you therefore, father, that you would send him to my father's house; 28 for I have five brothers, that he may testify to them, so they won't also come into this place of torment.' 29 "But Abraham said to him, 'They have Moses and the prophets. Let them listen to them.' 30 "He said, 'No, father Abraham, but if one goes to them from the dead, they will repent.' 31 "He said to him, 'If they don't listen to Moses and the prophets, neither will they be persuaded if one rises from the dead.'"

Author's Opinion

The Parable of the Rich Man and Lazarus speaks to man's need for repentance and inevitable accountability. It paints a stark picture of a place that we call Hell, a place of fire and continual torment. The rich man was not in Hell because of his wealth. He was there because he had a lifetime of pride and luxurious living with no regard or fear of God and no compassion for his poor neighbor Lazarus. Lazarus on the other hand had only experienced wretched things during his lifetime, but trusted in God. The rich man recognized Abraham and knew all about Moses and the Prophets. He came to know, after it was too late, that the final destination of Heaven or Hell depended on personal repentance. Unfortunately if people do not regard or listen to God's Word, they will not understand the reality of being held accountable to God. There is no free pass to do what ever we please during our lifetime. This parable is about our need to look diligently to our redeemer for forgiveness as there is no second chance after death. Today is the day of salvation, but only if we repent and embrace God's offer of grace through Jesus Christ.

Hebrews 12: 14-17

> 14 Follow after peace with all men, and the sanctification without which no man will see the Lord, 15 looking carefully lest there be any man who falls short of the grace of God; lest any root of bitterness springing up trouble you, and many be defiled by it; 16 lest there be any sexually immoral person, or profane person, like Esau, who sold his birthright for one meal. 17 For you know that even when he afterward desired to inherit the blessing, he was rejected, for he found no place for a change of mind though he sought it diligently with tears.

Revelation 3: 19

> 19 As many as I love, I reprove and chasten. Be zealous therefore, and repent.

Parable of the Hidden Treasure

Matthew 13: 44

44 "Again, the Kingdom of Heaven is like treasure hidden in the field, which a man found, and hid. In his joy, he goes and sells all that he has, and buys that field.

Author's Opinion

The Parable of the Hidden Treasure is about Jesus the Word of Truth. The mystery in this parable (if you can see it) is that the real treasure is Jesus Christ within the Kingdom of Heaven. The saving knowledge of Christ becomes hidden in his heart. With joy he counts the cost of securing and living a life for Christ, not a life of living for himself only. This treasure may cost him all that the world holds near and dear.

Psalms 119: 10-12 (NASB)

10 With all my heart I have sought You; Do not let me wander from Your commandments. 11 Your word I have treasured in my heart, That I may not sin against You. 12 Blessed are You, O Lord; Teach me Your statutes.

Matthew 11: 28-30

28 "Come to me, all you who labor and are heavily burdened, and I will give you rest. 29 Take my yoke upon you, and learn from me, for I am gentle and humble in heart; and you will find rest for your souls. 30 For my yoke is easy, and my burden is light."

Parable of the Pearl of Great Price

Matthew 13: 45-46

45 "Again, the Kingdom of Heaven is like a man who is a merchant

seeking fine pearls, 46 who having found one pearl of great price, he went and sold all that he had, and bought it.

Author's Opinion

The Parable of the Pearl of Great Price is similar to the Hidden Treasure Parable.

It is about Jesus the Word of Truth. The merchant is a wise man who searches the scriptures and finds Salvation which is the very best a man can hope for in this world. The merchant knew that Christ was the one pearl of great value and gave all that he had to possess the prize. That is why they call it the pearly gate. We all must pass through Jesus Christ before we get to Heaven. One of the hardest Biblical mysteries for man to accept is Jesus' teaching in *Luke 9: 2* *2 For whoever desires to save his life will lose it, but whoever will lose his life for my sake, the same will save it.*

Psalms 1: 1-3 (NASB)

> 1 How blessed is the man who does not walk in the counsel of the wicked, Nor stand in the path of sinners, Nor sit in the seat of scoffers! 2 But his delight is in the law of the Lord, And in His law he meditates day and night. 3 He will be like a tree firmly planted by streams of water, Which yields its fruit in its season And its leaf does not wither; And in whatever he does, he prospers.

1 Corinthians 1: 5-9

> 5 that in everything you were enriched in him, in all speech and all knowledge; 6 even as the testimony of Christ was confirmed in you: 7 so that you come behind in no gift; waiting for the revelation of our Lord Jesus Christ; 8 who will also confirm you until the end, blameless in the day of our Lord Jesus Christ. 9 God is faithful, through whom you were called into the fellowship of his Son, Jesus Christ, our Lord.

Chapter 2

> 16 As also in all *his* epistles, [b] speaking in them of these things; in which are some things hard to be understood, which they that are unlearned and unstable wrest, as *they do* also the other scriptures, unto their own destruction.

Why is the Bible hard to understand?

Proverbs 2: 1-9 (NASB)

> 1 My son, if you will receive my words And treasure my commandments within you, 2 Make your ear attentive to wisdom, Incline your heart to understanding; 3 For if you cry for discernment, Lift your voice for understanding; 4 If you seek her as silver And search for her as for hidden treasures; 5 Then you will discern the fear of the Lord And discover the knowledge of God. 6 For the Lord gives wisdom; From His mouth come knowledge and understanding. 7 He stores up sound wisdom for the upright; He is a shield to those who walk in integrity, 8 Guarding the paths of justice, And He preserves the way of His godly ones. 9 Then you will discern righteousness and justice And equity and every good course.

All Authority

Isaiah 55: 8-9 (NASB)

> 8 "For My thoughts are not your thoughts, Nor are your ways My ways," declares the Lord. 9 "For as the heavens are higher than the earth, So are My ways higher than your ways And My thoughts than your thoughts.

1 Corinthians 1: 20-21

> 20 Where is the wise? Where is the scribe? Where is the lawyer of this world? Hasn't God made foolish the wisdom of this world? 21 For seeing that in the wisdom of God, the world through its wisdom didn't know God, it was God's good pleasure through the foolishness of the preaching to save those who believe.

1 Corinthians 2: 14-16

> 14 Now the natural man doesn't receive the things of God's Spirit, for they are foolishness to him, and he can't know them, because they are spiritually discerned. 15 But he who is spiritual discerns all things, and he himself is judged by no one. 16 "For who has known the mind of the Lord, that he should instruct him?" But we have Christ's mind.

2 Corinthians 4: 1-6

> 1 Therefore seeing we have this ministry, even as we obtained mercy, we don't faint. 2 But we have renounced the hidden things of shame, not walking in craftiness, nor handling the word of God deceitfully; but by the manifestation of the truth commending ourselves to every man's conscience in the sight of God. 3 Even if our Good News is veiled, it is veiled in those who are dying; 4 in whom the god of this world has blinded the minds of the unbelieving, that the light of the Good News of the glory of Christ, who is the image of God, should not dawn on them. 5 For we don't preach ourselves, but Christ Jesus as Lord, and ourselves as your servants for Jesus' sake; 6 seeing it is God who said, "Light will shine out of darkness," who has shone in our hearts, to give the light of the knowledge of the glory of God in the face of Jesus Christ.

1 Chronicles 28: 19-20 (NASB)

19 "All this," said David, "the Lord made me understand in writing by His hand upon me, all the details of this pattern." 20 Then David said to his son Solomon, "Be strong and courageous, and act; do not fear nor be dismayed, for the Lord God, my God, is with you. He will not fail you nor forsake you until all the work for the service of the house of the Lord is finished.

Jeremiah 10: 12-13

12 God has made the earth by his power. He has established the world by his wisdom, and by his understanding has he stretched out the heavens. 13 When he utters his voice, the waters in the heavens roar, and he causes the vapors to ascend from the ends of the earth. He makes lightning for the rain, and brings the wind out of his treasuries.

Jeremiah 17: 9-10 (NASB)

9 "The heart is more deceitful than all else And is desperately sick; Who can understand it? 10 "I, the Lord, search the heart, I test the mind, Even to give to each man according to his ways, According to the results of his deeds.

Luke 24: 44-49

44 He said to them, "This is what I told you, while I was still with you, that all things which are written in the law of Moses, the prophets, and the psalms, concerning me must be fulfilled." 45 Then he opened their minds, that they might understand the Scriptures. 46 He said to them, "Thus it is written, and thus it was necessary for the Christ to suffer and to rise from the dead the third day, 47 and that repentance and remission of sins should be preached in his name to all the nations, beginning at Jerusalem. 48 You are witnesses of these things. 49 Behold, I send out the promise of my Father on you. But wait in the city of Jerusalem until you are clothed with power from on high."

John 8: 42-47

42 Therefore Jesus said to them, "If God were your father, you would love me, for I came out and have come from God. For I haven't come of myself, but he sent me. 43 Why don't you understand my speech? Because you can't hear my word. 44 You are of your father, the devil, and you want to do the desires of your father. He was a murderer from the beginning, and doesn't stand in the truth, because there is no truth in him. When he speaks a lie, he speaks on his own; for he is a liar, and the father of lies. 45 But because I tell the truth, you don't believe me. 46 Which of you convicts me of sin? If I tell the truth, why do you not believe me? 47 He who is of God hears the words of God. For this cause you don't hear, because you are not of God."

Romans 11: 33-36

33 Oh the depth of the riches both of the wisdom and the knowledge of God! How unsearchable are his judgments, and his ways past tracing out! 34 "For who has known the mind of the Lord? Or who has been his counselor?" 35 "Or who has first given to him, and it will be repaid to him again?" 36 For of him, and through him, and to him, are all things. To him be the glory for ever! Amen.

Ephesians 4: 17-19

17 This I say therefore, and testify in the Lord, that you no longer walk as the rest of the Gentiles also walk, in the futility of their mind, 18 being darkened in their understanding, alienated from the life of God, because of the ignorance that is in them, because of the hardening of their hearts; 19 who having become callous gave themselves up to lust, to work all uncleanness with greediness.

James 2: 17-24

17 Even so faith, if it has no works, is dead in itself. 18 Yes, a man will say, "You have faith, and I have works." Show me your faith without works, and I by my works will show you my faith. 19 You believe that God is one. You do well. The demons also believe, and

shudder. 20 But do you want to know, vain man, that faith apart from works is dead? 21 Wasn't Abraham our father justified by works, in that he offered up Isaac his son on the altar? 22 You see that faith worked with his works, and by works faith was perfected; 23 and the Scripture was fulfilled which says, "Abraham believed God, and it was accounted to him as righteousness"; and he was called the friend of God. 24 You see then that by works, a man is justified, and not only by faith.

2 Peter 3: 14-18

14 Therefore, beloved, seeing that you look for these things, be diligent to be found in peace, without defect and blameless in his sight. 15 Regard the patience of our Lord as salvation; even as our beloved brother Paul also, according to the wisdom given to him, wrote to you; 16 as also in all of his letters, speaking in them of these things. In those, there are some things that are hard to understand, which the ignorant and unsettled twist, as they also do to the other Scriptures, to their own destruction. 17 You therefore, beloved, knowing these things beforehand, beware, lest being carried away with the error of the wicked, you fall from your own steadfastness. 18 But grow in the grace and knowledge of our Lord and Savior Jesus Christ. To him be the glory both now and forever. Amen.

Author's Opinion

The question; Why is the Bible hard to understand? Initially, most people read the Bible with today's mindset. *Hoping for a passing grade and a free pass into Heaven without too much commitment to an unseen God.* Then we read and come to understand about our personal sin nature and that He has provided for us a straight and very narrow path to follow, which is specifically a personal relationship with Jesus Christ. 13 *For "whoever will call on the name of the Lord will be saved." Romans 10: 13.* God has and will continue to rule the world with His sense of justice, not ours. Jesus' atonement has provided a place in Heaven for us as honored family members. God created our universe for God's pleasure, not for man. It can be very discouraging if we forget God's Grace and see only the consequences of God's wrath. God destroyed the earth's corrupt population by flood with the exception of Noah and his family. He instructed Israel to destroy, without mercy or exception, a number of idolatrous groups of people. His word tells us that He is a jealous God, visiting the inequity of the fathers on the children to the third and fourth generation. In another instance he tell us to "Believe on the Lord Jesus Christ, and you will be saved, you and your household." The hardest part of all is that He will hold each and every one of us accountable to Him, ignorance and/or the fact that we, do not like the rules, will not excuse us. His Word in *Genesis 6: 3* tells us that there is a limit to God's patience. Either we worship Him and receive peace and joy of Heaven or we will see the wrath of eternal separation from God. God is a consuming fire. He created the world and rules the world. Even though we cannot see Him, we must believe and fear Him! Jesus said to him, 29 *"Because you have seen Me, you have believed. Blessed are those who have not seen and have believed." John 20: 29* Understanding the Bible depends on our need of reconciliation, our repentance and a trusting heart, rather than a rebellious spirit. If a proud and self-righteous individual reads the Bible from a self-centered point of view, it is hard to see the good in the Bible.

Psalm 78: 1-4 (NASB)

> 1 Listen, O my people, to my instruction; Incline your ears to the words of my mouth. 2 I will open my mouth in a parable; I will utter dark sayings of old, 3 Which we have heard and known, And our fathers have told us. 4 We will not conceal them from their children, But tell to the generation to come the praises of the Lord, And His strength and His wondrous works that He has done.

Colossians 3: 15-16

15 And let the peace of God rule in your hearts, to which also you were called in one body; and be thankful. 16 Let the word of Christ dwell in you richly; in all wisdom teaching and admonishing one another with psalms, hymns, and spiritual songs, singing with grace in your heart to the Lord.

Paradoxes to be examined

Creation

Genesis 1: 1-2

1 In the beginning, God created the heavens and the earth. 2 The earth was formless and empty. Darkness was on the surface of the deep and God's Spirit was hovering over the surface of the waters.

Genesis 1: 29-31

29 God said, "Behold, I have given you every herb yielding seed, which is on the surface of all the earth, and every tree, which bears fruit yielding seed. It will be your food. 30 To every animal of the earth, and to every bird of the sky, and to everything that creeps on the earth, in which there is life, I have given every green herb for food;" and it was so. 31 God saw everything that he had made, and, behold, it was very good. There was evening and there was morning, a sixth day.

Psalm 33: 6-9 (NASB)

6 By the word of the Lord the heavens were made, And by the breath of His mouth all their host. 7 He gathers the waters of the sea together as a heap; He lays up the deeps in storehouses. 8 Let all the earth fear the Lord; Let all the inhabitants of the world stand in awe of Him. 9 For He spoke, and it was done; He commanded, and it stood fast.

Isaiah 44: 24-25 (NASB)

24 Thus says the Lord, your Redeemer, and the one who formed you from the womb, "I, the Lord, am the maker of all things, Stretching out the heavens by Myself And spreading out the earth all alone, 25 Causing the omens of boasters to fail, Making fools out of diviners, Causing wise men to draw back And turning their knowledge into foolishness,

Acts 17: 24-28

24 The God who made the world and all things in it, he, being Lord of heaven and earth, doesn't dwell in temples made with hands, 25 neither is he served by men's hands, as though he needed anything, seeing he himself gives to all life and breath, and all things. 26 He made from one blood every nation of men to dwell on all the surface of the earth, having determined appointed seasons, and the boundaries of their dwellings, 27 that they should seek the Lord, if perhaps they might reach out for him and find him, though he is not far from each one of us. 28 'For in him we live, and move, and have our being.' As some of your own poets have said, 'For we are also his offspring.'

Colossians 1: 16

16 For by him all things were created, in the heavens and on the earth, things visible and things invisible, whether thrones or dominions or principalities or powers; all things have been created through him, and for him.

2 Peter 3: 3-7

3 knowing this first, that in the last days mockers will come, walking after their own lusts, 4 and saying, "Where is the promise of his coming? For, from the day that the fathers fell asleep, all things continue as they were from the beginning of the creation." 5 For this they willfully forget, that there were heavens from of old, and an earth formed out of water and amid water, by the word of God; 6 by

which means the world that then was, being overflowed with water, perished. 7 But the heavens that now exist, and the earth, by the same word have been stored up for fire, being reserved against the day of judgment and destruction of ungodly men.

False Teaching

Isaiah 5: 20-21 (NASB)

20 Woe to those who call evil good, and good evil; Who substitute darkness for light and light for darkness; Who substitute bitter for sweet and sweet for bitter! 21 Woe to those who are wise in their own eyes And clever in their own sight!

Matthew 7: 15-20

15 "Beware of false prophets, who come to you in sheep's clothing, but inwardly are ravening wolves. 16 By their fruits you will know them. Do you gather grapes from thorns, or figs from thistles? 17 Even so, every good tree produces good fruit; but the corrupt tree produces evil fruit. 18 A good tree can't produce evil fruit, neither can a corrupt tree produce good fruit. 19 Every tree that doesn't grow good fruit is cut down, and thrown into the fire. 20 Therefore by their fruits you will know them.

Mark 12: 38-40

38 In his teaching he said to them, "Beware of the scribes, who like to walk in long robes, and to get greetings in the marketplaces, 39 and the best seats in the synagogues, and the best places at feasts: 40 those who devour widows' houses, and for a pretense make long prayers. These will receive greater condemnation."

1 Corinthians 4: 18-21

18 Now some are puffed up, as though I were not coming to you. 19 But I will come to you shortly, if the Lord is willing. And I will know,

not the word of those who are puffed up, but the power. 20 For God's Kingdom is not in word, but in power. 21 What do you want? Shall I come to you with a rod, or in love and a spirit of gentleness?

Colossians 2: 8

8 Be careful that you don't let anyone rob you through his philosophy and vain deceit, after the tradition of men, after the elements of the world, and not after Christ.

Ephesians 4: 14

14 that we may no longer be children, tossed back and forth and carried about with every wind of doctrine, by the trickery of men, in craftiness, after the wiles of error;

Hebrews 6: 1-8 (NASB)

1 Therefore leaving the elementary teaching about the Christ, let us press on to maturity, not laying again a foundation of repentance from dead works and of faith toward God, 2 of instruction about washings and laying on of hands, and the resurrection of the dead and eternal judgment. 3 And this we will do, if God permits. 4 For in the case of those who have once been enlightened and have tasted of the heavenly gift and have been made partakers of the Holy Spirit, 5 and have tasted the good word of God and the powers of the age to come, 6 and then have fallen away, it is impossible to renew them again to repentance, since they again crucify to themselves the Son of God and put Him to open shame. 7 For ground that drinks the rain which often falls on it and brings forth vegetation useful to those for whose sake it is also tilled, receives a blessing from God; 8 but if it yields thorns and thistles, it is worthless and close to being cursed, and it ends up being burned.

Titus 1: 9-11

9 holding to the faithful word which is according to the teaching, that he may be able to exhort in the sound doctrine, and to convict those

who contradict him. 10 For there are also many unruly men, vain talkers and deceivers, especially those of the circumcision, 11 whose mouths must be stopped; men who overthrow whole houses, teaching things which they ought not, for dishonest gain's sake.

2 Peter 2: 1-3 (NASB)

1 But false prophets also arose among the people, just as there will also be false teachers among you, who will secretly introduce destructive heresies, even denying the Master who bought them, bringing swift destruction upon themselves. 2 Many will follow their sensuality, and because of them the way of the truth will be maligned; 3 and in their greed they will exploit you with false words; their judgment from long ago is not idle, and their destruction is not asleep.

2 Peter 2: 21-22

21 For it would be better for them not to have known the way of righteousness, than, after knowing it, to turn back from the holy commandment delivered to them. 22 But it has happened to them according to the true proverb, "The dog turns to his own vomit again," and "the sow that has washed to wallowing in the mire."

Stumbling Blocks

1 Peter 2: 7-10

7 For you who believe therefore is the honor, but for those who are disobedient, "The stone which the builders rejected, has become the chief cornerstone," 8 and, "a stone of stumbling, and a rock of offense." For they stumble at the word, being disobedient, to which also they were appointed. 9 But you are a chosen race, a royal priesthood, a holy nation, a people for God's own possession, that you may proclaim the excellence of him who called you out of darkness into his marvelous light: 10 who in time past were no

people, but now are God's people, who had not obtained mercy, but now have obtained mercy.

Romans 9: 30-33

30 What shall we say then? That the Gentiles, who didn't follow after righteousness, attained to righteousness, even the righteousness which is of faith; 31 but Israel, following after a law of righteousness, didn't arrive at the law of righteousness. 32 Why? Because they didn't seek it by faith, but as it were by works of the law. They stumbled over the stumbling stone; 33 even as it is written, "Behold, I lay in Zion a stumbling stone and a rock of offense; and no one who believes in him will be disappointed."

Romans 14: 12-13

12 So then each one of us will give account of himself to God. 13 Therefore let's not judge one another any more, but judge this rather, that no man put a stumbling block in his brother's way, or an occasion for falling.

1 Corinthians 1: 23-25

23 but we preach Christ crucified; a stumbling block to Jews, and foolishness to Greeks, 24 but to those who are called, both Jews and Greeks, Christ is the power of God and the wisdom of God. 25 Because the foolishness of God is wiser than men, and the weakness of God is stronger than men.

Mark 9: 42

42 Whoever will cause one of these little ones who believe in me to stumble, it would be better for him if he were thrown into the sea with a millstone hung around his neck.

Luke 17: 1-2

1 He said to the disciples, "It is impossible that no occasions of stumbling should come, but woe to him through whom they come!

2 It would be better for him if a millstone were hung around his neck, and he were thrown into the sea, rather than that he should cause one of these little ones to stumble.

Matthew 18: 6

6 but whoever causes one of these little ones who believe in me to stumble, it would be better for him that a huge millstone should be hung around his neck, and that he should be sunk in the depths of the sea.

1 John 2: 9-11

9 He who says he is in the light and hates his brother, is in the darkness even until now. 10 He who loves his brother remains in the light, and there is no occasion for stumbling in him. 11 But he who hates his brother is in the darkness, and walks in the darkness, and doesn't know where he is going, because the darkness has blinded his eyes.

James 3: 1-2

1 Let not many of you be teachers, my brothers, knowing that we will receive heavier judgment. 2 For in many things we all stumble. If anyone doesn't stumble in word, the same is a perfect man, able to bridle the whole body also.

Jude 1: 24-25

24 Now to him who is able to keep them from stumbling, and to present you faultless before the presence of his glory in great joy, 25 to God our Savior, who alone is wise, be glory and majesty, dominion and power, both now and forever. Amen.

Scandal (Shame)

1 Samuel 2: 24-25 (NASB)

> 24 No, my sons; for the report is not good which I hear the Lord's people circulating. 25 If one man sins against another, God will mediate for him; but if a man sins against the Lord, who can intercede for him?" But they would not listen to the voice of their father, for the Lord desired to put them to death.

Philippians 3: 18-20

> 18 For many walk, of whom I told you often, and now tell you even weeping, as the enemies of the cross of Christ, 19 whose end is destruction, whose god is the belly, and whose glory is in their shame, who think about earthly things. 20 For our citizenship is in heaven, from where we also wait for a Savior, the Lord Jesus Christ;

Ephesians 5: 1-13

> 1 Be therefore imitators of God, as beloved children. 2 Walk in love, even as Christ also loved you, and gave himself up for us, an offering and a sacrifice to God for a sweet-smelling fragrance. 3 But sexual immorality, and all uncleanness, or covetousness, let it not even be mentioned among you, as becomes saints; 4 nor filthiness, nor foolish talking, nor jesting, which are not appropriate; but rather giving of thanks. 5 Know this for sure, that no sexually immoral person, nor unclean person, nor covetous man, who is an idolater, has any inheritance in the Kingdom of Christ and God. 6 Let no one deceive you with empty words. For because of these things, the wrath of God comes on the children of disobedience. 7 Therefore don't be partakers with them. 8 For you were once darkness, but are now light in the Lord. Walk as children of light, 9 for the fruit of the Spirit is in all goodness and righteousness and truth, 10 proving what is well pleasing to the Lord. 11 Have no fellowship with the unfruitful deeds of darkness, but rather even reprove them. 12 For the things

which are done by them in secret, it is a shame even to speak of. 13 But all things, when they are reproved, are revealed by the light, for everything that reveals is light.

2 Corinthians 4: 1-4

1 Therefore seeing we have this ministry, even as we obtained mercy, we don't faint. 2 But we have renounced the hidden things of shame, not walking in craftiness, nor handling the word of God deceitfully; but by the manifestation of the truth commending ourselves to every man's conscience in the sight of God. 3 Even if our Good News is veiled, it is veiled in those who are dying; 4 in whom the god of this world has blinded the minds of the unbelieving, that the light of the Good News of the glory of Christ, who is the image of God, should not dawn on them.

Colossians 2: 18-23

18 Let no one rob you of your prize by a voluntary humility and worshiping of the angels, dwelling in the things which he has not seen, vainly puffed up by his fleshly mind, 19 and not holding firmly to the Head, from whom all the body, being supplied and knit together through the joints and ligaments, grows with God's growth. 20 If you died with Christ from the elements of the world, why, as though living in the world, do you subject yourselves to ordinances, 21 "Don't handle, nor taste, nor touch" 22 (all of which perish with use), according to the precepts and doctrines of men? 23 Which things indeed appear like wisdom in self-imposed worship, and humility, and severity to the body; but aren't of any value against the indulgence of the flesh.

Hebrews 6: 4-6

4 For concerning those who were once enlightened and tasted of the heavenly gift, and were made partakers of the Holy Spirit, 5 and tasted the good word of God, and the powers of the age to come, 6 and then fell away, it is impossible to renew them again

to repentance; seeing they crucify the Son of God for themselves again, and put him to open shame.

Parables to be grasped

The Parable of the Sower

Matthew 13: 3-23

3 He spoke to them many things in parables, saying, "Behold, a farmer went out to sow. 4 As he sowed, some seeds fell by the roadside, and the birds came and devoured them. 5 Others fell on rocky ground, where they didn't have much soil, and immediately they sprang up, because they had no depth of earth. 6 When the sun had risen, they were scorched. Because they had no root, they withered away. 7 Others fell among thorns. The thorns grew up and choked them. 8 Others fell on good soil, and yielded fruit: some one hundred times as much, some sixty, and some thirty. 9 He who has ears to hear, let him hear." 10 The disciples came, and said to him, "Why do you speak to them in parables?" 11 He answered them, "To you it is given to know the mysteries of the Kingdom of Heaven, but it is not given to them. 12 For whoever has, to him will be given, and he will have abundance, but whoever doesn't have, from him will be taken away even that which he has. 13 Therefore I speak to them in parables, because seeing they don't see, and hearing, they don't hear, neither do they understand. 14 In them the prophecy of Isaiah is fulfilled, which says, By hearing you will hear, and will in no way understand; Seeing you will see, and will in no way perceive: 15 for this people's heart has grown callous, their ears are dull of hearing, they have closed their eyes; or else perhaps they might perceive with their eyes, hear with their ears, understand with their heart, and would turn again; and I would heal them.' 16 "But blessed are your eyes, for they see; and your ears, for they hear. 17 For most certainly

I tell you that many prophets and righteous men desired to see the things which you see, and didn't see them; and to hear the things which you hear, and didn't hear them. 18 "Hear, then, the parable of the farmer. 19 When anyone hears the word of the Kingdom, and doesn't understand it, the evil one comes, and snatches away that which has been sown in his heart. This is what was sown by the roadside. 20 What was sown on the rocky places, this is he who hears the word, and immediately with joy receives it; 21 yet he has no root in himself, but endures for a while. When oppression or persecution arises because of the word, immediately he stumbles. 22 What was sown among the thorns, this is he who hears the word, but the cares of this age and the deceitfulness of riches choke the word, and he becomes unfruitful. 23 What was sown on the good ground, this is he who hears the word, and understands it, who most certainly bears fruit, and produces, some one hundred times as much, some sixty, and some thirty."

Author's Opinion

The Parable of the Sower is about Jesus' Word of Truth dwelling in our hearts. It also teaches why Jesus used parables. 11 He answered them, "To you it is given to know the mysteries of the Kingdom of Heaven, but it is not given to them. 12 For whoever has, to him will be given, and he will have abundance, but whoever doesn't have, from him will be taken away even that which he has." Matthew 13: 11-12

Simply stated God gives the gift of Bible knowledge and wisdom to some people and not to others. Blessed are the eyes that see, and the ears that hear. The first explanation in this parable shows people hearing the Word but not fully understanding. Satan then comes and takes away what little they did have in their heart; Satan is relentless in trying to dissuade us from coming to the Lord. The second example is when people hear the Word with Joy but run away when being doers of the Word becomes difficult. The third example is when people hear and receive the word but care more for deceitful world riches, rather than trusting and worshiping God. There are many in and out of our churches today that hear the gospel and are familiar with the blessing available to them from the scriptures. They hear the clear invitation to glorify God in truth and spirit, but decline for the reasons listed above. But mostly the sin of self-pride prevents their surrender to Christ. There is an invisible spiritual war raging in the hearts and minds of every individual today. Pride and self-interest often choke out the good news of the gospel, hindering our understanding of the Bible. The fourth and final example is when the people hear and understand the Word, believing and faithfully becoming productive doers of the Word. Jesus is the potter and we are the clay. If we let Him, He will make us into honorable vessels useful to the kingdom of God. Some hear the word with joy and proclaim the good news to all that will listen.

Psalms 119: 10-12 (NASB)

> 10 With all my heart I have sought You; Do not let me wander from Your commandments. 11 Your word I have treasured in my heart, That I may not sin against You. 12 Blessed are You, O Lord; Teach me Your statutes.

2 Timothy 2: 20-22

> 20 Now in a large house there are not only vessels of gold and of silver, but also of wood and of clay. Some are for honor, and some for dishonor. 21 If anyone therefore purges himself from these, he will be a vessel for honor, sanctified, and suitable for the master's use, prepared for every good work. 22 Flee from youthful lusts; but pursue righteousness, faith, love, and peace with those who call on the Lord out of a pure heart

The Parable of the Leaven

Matthew 13: 33

Luke 13: 20-21

> 33 He spoke another parable to them. "The Kingdom of Heaven is like yeast, which a woman took, and hid in three measures of meal, until it was all leavened."

Author's Opinion

This *Parable of the Leaven* is about the misuse of Jesus' Word of Truth or doctrine within the church. Leaven was Jesus' way of telling His disciples to beware of the Pharisees and Sadducees bureaucratic hypocrisy. The Meal is the gospel message from God's Word. The woman represents Satan's false teachers of doctrine. The leaven is the false and evil doctrine that can permeate the church or Kingdom of Heaven from within. Leaven is when man trusts in what seems right in their own eyes and not what is written in God's Holy Word. This Leaven is a perversion of the gospel message and it becomes spoiled and rancid. Leven changes the message, making the Bible even more difficult to understand. It can start as a small issue in the beginning when an individual thinks, "That does not seem right." Then their reasoning tries to justify believing only the parts in the Bible that he or she likes. When an individual or church becomes distracted, taking their eyes off Jesus, seeing only the world around them, Satan wins the spiritual battle. It is futile to think we can crash Heaven's narrow gate, when we are burdened down with denominational pride and prejudices or we believe only a portion of God's Word, while rejecting other parts. Repentance means we relinquish any idea of negotiating special terms with God before or after death. God did not intend for his children to pick and choose from His inspired Word and then discredit the other parts of the Bible. This kind of doctrine fosters rebellion that is a self-eliminating stumbling block that prevents a person from believing. Our faith relationship with Jesus is an all or nothing, one-to-one proposition. There will not be any third party originations, individuals or churches pleading our case on judgment day. Trying to justify a smorgasbord approach to believing does not fit the definition of a humble servant.

Matthew 16: 12

> 12 Then they understood that he didn't tell them to beware of the yeast of bread, but of the teaching of the Pharisees and Sadducees.

Matthew 7: 13-15

> 13 "Enter in by the narrow gate; for wide is the gate and broad is the way that leads to destruction, and many are those who enter in by it. 14 How narrow is the gate, and restricted is the way that leads to life! Few are those who find it. 15 "Beware of false prophets, who come to you in sheep's clothing, but inwardly are ravening wolves.

Matthew 7: 21-23

> 21 Not everyone who says to me, 'Lord, Lord,' will enter into the Kingdom of Heaven; but he who does the will of my Father who is in heaven. 22 Many will tell me in that day, 'Lord, Lord, didn't we prophesy in your name, in your name cast out demons, and in your name do many mighty works?' 23 Then I will tell them, 'I never knew you. Depart from me, you who work iniquity.'

2 Corinthians 4: 18

> 18 while we don't look at the things which are seen, but at the things which are not seen. For the things which are seen are temporal, but the things which are not seen are eternal.

The Parable of the Wicked Vinedressers

Matthew 21: 33-45

Mark 12: 1-2

Luke 20: 9-19

33 "Hear another parable. There was a man who was a master of a household, who planted a vineyard, set a hedge about it, dug a wine press in it, built a tower, leased it out to farmers, and went into another country. 34 When the season for the fruit came near, he sent his servants to the farmers, to receive his fruit. 35 The farmers took his servants, beat one, killed another, and stoned another. 36 Again, he sent other servants more than the first: and they treated them the same way. 37 But afterward he sent to them his son, saying, 'They will respect my son.' 38 But the farmers, when they saw the son, said among themselves, 'This is the heir. Come, let's kill him, and seize his inheritance.' 39 So they took him, and threw him out of the vineyard, and killed him. 40 When therefore the lord of the vineyard comes, what will he do to those farmers?" 41 They told him, "He will miserably destroy those miserable men, and will lease out the vineyard to other farmers, who will give him the fruit in its season." 42 Jesus said to them, "Did you never read in the Scriptures, The stone which the builders rejected, the same was made the head of the corner. This was from the Lord. It is marvelous in our eyes?' 43 "Therefore I tell you, God's Kingdom will be taken away from you, and will be given to a nation producing its fruit. 44 He who falls on this stone will be broken to pieces, but on whomever it will fall, it will scatter him as dust." 45 When the chief priests and the Pharisees heard his parables, they perceived that he spoke about them.

Author's Opinion

The Parable of the Wicked Vinedressers is about being accountable for our worship and exposes Israel's disbelief and disobedience. It tells how God's chosen people mistreated His prophets and would eventually kill Christ, the Son of God. Jesus is the Builder's Cornerstone that was and still is being rejected by the Jewish people. 3 *Even if our Good News is veiled, it is veiled in those who are dying;* 4 *in whom the god of this world has blinded the minds of the unbelieving, that the light of the Good News of the glory of Christ, who is the image of God, should not dawn on them. 2 Corinthians 4: 3-4.* It is hard to understand that God's wrath has, for a time, created a stumbling block that blinds His chosen Jewish people from seeing their promised Messiah. *John 8: 31-32* is telling the Jews to overcome this stumbling block and believe in Him. 31 *Jesus therefore said to those Jews who had believed him, "If you remain in my word, then you are truly my disciples.* 32 *You will know the truth, and the truth will make you free."* There will come a time when this stumbling block will be removed from his chosen people. The future days are coming when the new covenant will restore Israel and Judah. 33 *"But this is the covenant which I will make with the house of Israel after those days," declares the Lord, "I will put My law within them and on their heart I will write it; and I will be their God, and they shall be My people." Jeremiah 31: 33*

     But at present, Jesus has become offensive to them. When Jesus said, *"Therefore I tell you, God's Kingdom will be taken away from you, and will be given to a nation producing its fruit."* He was predicting that God would give to the gentile people, the Good News Gospel to embrace and proclaim to anyone that will listen. These new tenants (the gentiles) have glorified the name of Jesus, producing the crop of worshippers for the coming harvest. Anyone that falls on this cornerstone is rejecting Jesus as Lord and Savior. They will be broken in this life and will be crushed and put to shame for all eternity on judgment day. This Gospel message has and will continue producing fruit for the coming harvest in every corner of the world. Everyone at some point will encounter spiritual stumbling blocks, but these issues can and should be surrendered to the Lord completely, without any reservation. Jesus, our Messiah, is calling both the Jew and Gentile today to believe and worship Him. *Romans 10: 12 tells us* 12 *"For there is no distinction between Jew and Greek; for the same Lord is Lord of all, and is rich to all who call on him."*

Ezekiel 33: 11 (NASB)

> 11 Say to them, 'As I live!' declares the Lord God, 'I take no pleasure in the death of the wicked, but rather that the wicked turn from his way and live. Turn back, turn back from your evil ways! Why then will you die, O house of Israel?'

Romans 1: 17-21

> 17 For in it is revealed God's righteousness from faith to faith. As it is written, "But the righteous shall live by faith." 18 For the wrath of God is revealed from heaven against all ungodliness and unrighteousness of men, who suppress the truth in unrighteousness, 19 because that which is known of God is revealed in them, for God revealed it to them. 20 For the invisible things of him since the creation of the world are clearly seen, being perceived through the things that are made, even his everlasting power and divinity; that they may be without excuse. 21 Because, knowing God, they didn't glorify him as God, neither gave thanks, but became vain in their reasoning, and their senseless heart was darkened.

Romans 9: 30

> 30 What shall we say then? That the Gentiles, who didn't follow after righteousness, attained to righteousness, even the righteousness which is of faith;

Romans 10: 21

> 21 But as to Israel he says, "All day long I stretched out my hands to a disobedient and contrary people."

The Parable of the Great Supper

Luke 14: 16-24

16 But he said to him, "A certain man made a great supper, and he invited many people. 17 He sent out his servant at supper time to tell those who were invited, 'Come, for everything is ready now.' 18 They all as one began to make excuses. "The first said to him, 'I have bought a field, and I must go and see it. Please have me excused.' 19 "Another said, 'I have bought five yoke of oxen, and I must go try them out. Please have me excused.' 20 "Another said, 'I have married a wife, and therefore I can't come.' 21 "That servant came, and told his lord these things. Then the master of the house, being angry, said to his servant, 'Go out quickly into the streets and lanes of the city, and bring in the poor, maimed, blind, and lame.' 22 "The servant said, 'Lord, it is done as you commanded, and there is still room.' 23 "The lord said to the servant, 'Go out into the highways and hedges, and compel them to come in, that my house may be filled. 24 For I tell you that none of those men who were invited will taste of my supper.'

Author's Opinion

The Parable of the Great Supper is about the Jewish people rejecting Jesus as their Messiah and accountability. They, the Jewish people, are His chosen people and were intended to be the invited guest. The wrath of God is like a consuming fire and greatly to be feared. (For I tell you that none of those men who were invited will taste of my supper.) Because His beloved chosen people refused to accept His invitation, a stumbling block has for now been placed to prevent them from entering his Great supper. The master, being angry, extended his invitation to the poor and downtrodden of the world (including the Gentile people, who were previously excluded from His kingdom) to come and fill the House of the

Lord. This parable is telling us *there is still room* in Heaven for any that will come.

Isaiah 1: 2-4 (NASB)

2 Listen, O heavens, and hear, O earth; For the Lord speaks, "Sons I have reared and brought up, But they have revolted against Me. 3 "An ox knows its owner, And a donkey its master's manger, But Israel does not know, My people do not understand." 4 Alas, sinful nation, People weighed down with iniquity, Offspring of evildoers, Sons who act corruptly! They have abandoned the Lord, They have despised the Holy One of Israel, They have turned away from Him.

Luke 2: 28-32

28 then he received him into his arms, and blessed God, and said, 29 "Now you are releasing your servant, Master, according to your word, in peace; 30 for my eyes have seen your salvation, 31 which you have prepared before the face of all peoples; 32 a light for revelation to the nations, and the glory of your people Israel."

Romans 3: 28-31

28 We maintain therefore that a man is justified by faith apart from the works of the law. 29 Or is God the God of Jews only? Isn't he the God of Gentiles also? Yes, of Gentiles also, 30 since indeed there is one God who will justify the circumcised by faith, and the uncircumcised through faith. 31 Do we then nullify the law through faith? May it never be! No, we establish the law.

The Parable of the Barren Fig Tree

Luke 13: 6-9

6 He spoke this parable. "A certain man had a fig tree planted in his vineyard, and he came seeking fruit on it, and found none. 7 He said to the vine dresser, 'Behold, these three years I have come looking

for fruit on this fig tree, and found none. Cut it down. Why does it waste the soil?' 8 He answered, 'Lord, leave it alone this year also, until I dig around it, and fertilize it. 9 If it bears fruit, fine; but if not, after that, you can cut it down.'"

Author's Opinion

The Parable of the Barren Fig Tree is about people seeing and hearing Jesus' words of truth but due to the hardening of their hearts, they are not bearing fruit for the Kingdom of God or glorifying God. Then comes the judgment part of the parable, which is their eventual accountability for rejecting God's Grace. The barren fig tree was cared for by the vine keeper and was a valued part of God's vineyard. The fig tree represents all nonbelievers, not just Jewish nonbelievers. There is no partiality with God. 15 *"for this people's heart has grown callous, their ears are dull of hearing, they have closed their eyes; or else perhaps they might perceive with their eyes, hear with their ears, understand with their heart, and would turn again; and I would heal them." Matthew 13: 15.*

We have only one lifetime to bear fruit for the kingdom of Heaven. We personally and the church corporately are not to be casual or complacent concerning our commitment to Jesus. When congregations lose sight of the purpose and vision of glorifying God, they turn into social clubs.

The pride of building bigger churches, expecting the sheep to wander in, feels good and safe and comfortable. But leaving the gospel message to the church leaders is not the same as encouraging believers to go after the lost sheep. A humble personal testimony to a stranger may mean far more, than an invitation to hear a minister's eloquent sermon. Religious bureaucrats with their focus on the social aspects are the ones that make a big show of being concerned with procedural correctness (like the Scribes and Pharisees) at the spiritual expense of other people. Real people, both respectable and unholy notorious sinners, have the same need to hear the gospel, a gospel that can change lives and turn people from their evil ways. Soup kitchens without sermons and personal testimonies are like clouds without rain; they fall short of what Christ had in mind. The complacent business model of good works that disregards our duty to evangelizing faithfully misses the point and does not bring glory to God.

We know all believers are given visible attributes from God. They are called the Fruit of the Spirit and we are expected to use them, to the glory of God. Both the believer and the church have the responsibility to be diligent in presenting Christ to the world. *(I have come looking for fruit on this fig tree, and found none.)* God did not intend for Christendom to grow cold and unproductive. Christ's Great Commission to the church was to go and preach repentance and remission of sin, as stated in *Luke 24: 46-48.* It will not go unnoticed if we take up space or occupy the ground that other people could use more productively for the Master's use. We are given many chances to be productive, bearing fruit for the kingdom of Heaven. God will not contend with us forever. The accountability part of this Parable is when it becomes evident that no production from this fruit tree is forthcoming, the vineyard keeper is instructed to cut it down.

Matthew 5: 13

13 "You are the salt of the earth, but if the salt has lost its flavor, with what will it be salted? It is then good for nothing, but to be cast out and trodden under the feet of men.

Luke 11: 46-52

46 He said, "Woe to you lawyers also! For you load men with burdens that are difficult to carry, and you yourselves won't even lift one

finger to help carry those burdens. 47 Woe to you! For you build the tombs of the prophets, and your fathers killed them. 48 So you testify and consent to the works of your fathers. For they killed them, and you build their tombs. 49 Therefore also the wisdom of God said, 'I will send to them prophets and apostles; and some of them they will kill and persecute, 50 that the blood of all the prophets, which was shed from the foundation of the world, may be required of this generation; 51 from the blood of Abel to the blood of Zachariah, who perished between the altar and the sanctuary.' Yes, I tell you, it will be required of this generation. 52 Woe to you lawyers! For you took away the key of knowledge. You didn't enter in yourselves, and those who were entering in, you hindered."

Chapter 3

> 17 I love those who love me,
>   and those who seek me diligently
>   find me.
> 18 Riches and honor are with me,
>   enduring wealth and prosperity.
> 19 My fruit is better than gold, even
>   fine gold,
>   and my yield than choice silver.
> 20 I walk in the way of righteousness,
>   in the paths of justice,

Why did God create man?

Deuteronomy 5: 7-10

> 7 'You shall have no other gods before Me. 8 'You shall not make for yourself a carved image—any likeness of anything that is in heaven above, or that is in the earth beneath, or that is in the water under the earth; 9 you shall not bow down to them nor serve them. For I, the Lord your God, am a jealous God, visiting the iniquity of the fathers upon the children to the third and fourth generations of those who hate Me, 10 but showing mercy to thousands, to those who love Me and keep My commandments.

Isaiah 43: 7

> 7 everyone who is called by my name, and whom I have created for my glory, whom I have formed, yes, whom I have made.'"

Matthew. 5: 16

16 Even so, let your light shine before men; that they may see your good works, and glorify your Father who is in heaven.

Ephesians 1: 11-12

11 in whom also we were assigned an inheritance, having been foreordained according to the purpose of him who does all things after the counsel of his will; 12 to the end that we should be to the praise of his glory, we who had before hoped in Christ.

Ephesians 2: 1-10

1 You were made alive when you were dead in transgressions and sins, 2 in which you once walked according to the course of this world, according to the prince of the power of the air, the spirit who now works in the children of disobedience; 3 among whom we also all once lived in the lusts of our flesh, doing the desires of the flesh and of the mind, and were by nature children of wrath, even as the rest. 4 But God, being rich in mercy, for his great love with which he loved us, 5 even when we were dead through our trespasses, made us alive together with Christ (by grace you have been saved), 6 and raised us up with him, and made us to sit with him in the heavenly places in Christ Jesus, 7 that in the ages to come he might show the exceeding riches of his grace in kindness toward us in Christ Jesus; 8 for by grace you have been saved through faith, and that not of yourselves; it is the gift of God, 9 not of works, that no one would boast. 10 For we are his workmanship, created in Christ Jesus for good works, which God prepared before that we would walk in them.

Romans 9: 22-23

22 What if God, willing to show his wrath, and to make his power known, endured with much patience vessels of wrath prepared for destruction, 23 and that he might make known the riches of his glory on vessels of mercy, which he prepared beforehand for glory,

Romans 11: 33-36

33 Oh, the depth of the riches both of the wisdom and knowledge of God! How unsearchable are His judgments and His ways past finding out! 34 "For who has known the mind of the Lord? Or who has become His counselor?" 35 "Or who has first given to Him And it shall be repaid to him?" 36 For of Him and through Him and to Him are all things, to whom be glory forever. Amen.

1 Corinthians 10: 31

31 Whether therefore you eat, or drink, or whatever you do, do all to the glory of God.

Philippians 2: 9-11

9 Therefore God also highly exalted him, and gave to him the name which is above every name; 10 that at the name of Jesus every knee should bow, of those in heaven, those on earth, and those under the earth, 11 and that every tongue should confess that Jesus Christ is Lord, to the glory of God the Father.

Revelation 5: 13-14

13 I heard every created thing which is in heaven, on the earth, under the earth, on the sea, and everything in them, saying, "To him who sits on the throne, and to the Lamb be the blessing, the honor, the glory, and the dominion, forever and ever! Amen!" 14 The four living creatures said, "Amen!" Then the elders fell down and worshiped.

Author's Opinion

Why did God create man? This is a question every man, woman and child should be confronted with and seek to discover the answer. This kind of issue is not talked about much, if at all, unless someone is in great despair. It is unfortunate that churches are not making this a prominent issue in their worship service messages today. The reason why we have churches is very much tied to "why God created man." Man and the church were created from the beginning for one purpose only, and that is to glorify God. We are to worship Him in truth and spirit. God's Word makes it clear regarding man's purpose and our proper relationship with Him. Throughout all the ages, peace, mercy and blessings are given to the people who honor and fear Him from generation to generation. History shows us that man can be prone to egocentric thinking. Without God in the picture, man naturally thinks the world revolves around him and everything else is secondary. Just as in the intellectual community (including the church) it was originally thought the earth and not the sun was the center of our planetary system. Few men understood that there was a larger being to be considered. This egocentric thinking has and still limits our perspective. Mary the mother of Jesus found favor with God, making her forever blessed among women, because of her humble devotion and submission to God's will. God created man, to worship and glorify Himself. Mary showed us the proper response to God, for His love and mercy to us. 49 *For he who is mighty has done great things for me. Holy is his name.* 50 *His mercy is for generations of generations on those who fear him. Luke 1: 49-50*

Psalm 96: 1-4 (NASB)

> 1 Sing to the Lord a new song; Sing to the Lord, all the earth. 2 Sing to the Lord, bless His name; Proclaim good tidings of His salvation from day to day. 3 Tell of His glory among the nations, His wonderful deeds among all the peoples. 4 For great is the Lord and greatly to be praised; He is to be feared above all gods.

John 15: 7-11

> 7 If you remain in me, and my words remain in you, you will ask

whatever you desire, and it will be done for you. 8 "In this is my Father glorified, that you bear much fruit; and so you will be my disciples. 9 Even as the Father has loved me, I also have loved you. Remain in my love. 10 If you keep my commandments, you will remain in my love; even as I have kept my Father's commandments, and remain in his love. 11 I have spoken these things to you, that my joy may remain in you, and that your joy may be made full.

2 Corinthians 4: 13-15

13 But having the same spirit of faith, according to that which is written, "I believed, and therefore I spoke." We also believe, and therefore also we speak; 14 knowing that he who raised the Lord Jesus will raise us also with Jesus, and will present us with you. 15 For all things are for your sakes, that the grace, being multiplied through the many, may cause the thanksgiving to abound to the glory of God.

Paradoxes to be examined

Worship

Exodus 7: 16 (NASB)

16 You shall say to him, 'The Lord, the God of the Hebrews, sent me to you, saying, "Let My people go, that they may serve Me in the wilderness. But behold, you have not listened until now."

Exodus 20: 5 (NASB)

5 You shall not worship them or serve them; for I, the Lord your God, am a jealous God, visiting the iniquity of the fathers on the children, on the third and the fourth generations of those who hate Me,

Psalms 119: 105

105 Thy word is a lamp unto my feet, and a light unto my path.

Acts 20: 26-27

26 Therefore I testify to you today that I am clean from the blood of all men, 27 for I didn't shrink from declaring to you the whole counsel of God.

Romans 12: 1-2

1 Therefore I urge you, brothers, by the mercies of God, to present your bodies a living sacrifice, holy, acceptable to God, which is your spiritual service. 2 Don't be conformed to this world, but be transformed by the renewing of your mind, so that you may prove what is the good, well-pleasing, and perfect will of God.

Colossians 3: 16

16 Let the word of Christ dwell in you richly; in all wisdom teaching and admonishing one another with psalms, hymns, and spiritual songs, singing with grace in your heart to the Lord.

Ephesians 1: 12-14

12 to the end that we should be to the praise of his glory, we who had before hoped in Christ. 13 In him you also, having heard the word of the truth, the Good News of your salvation—in whom, having also believed, you were sealed with the promised Holy Spirit, 14 who is a pledge of our inheritance, to the redemption of God's own possession, to the praise of his glory.

Ephesians 3: 9

9 and to make all men see what is the administration of the mystery which for ages has been hidden in God, who created all things through Jesus Christ;

Hebrews 12: 28-29

28 Therefore, receiving a Kingdom that can't be shaken, let us have grace, through which we serve God acceptably, with reverence and awe, 29 for our God is a consuming fire.

James 4: 8

8 Draw near to God, and he will draw near to you. Cleanse your hands, you sinners; and purify your hearts, you double-minded.

1 Peter 2: 1-3

1 Putting away therefore all wickedness, all deceit, hypocrisies, envies, and all evil speaking, 2 as newborn babies, long for the pure milk of the Word, that with it you may grow, 3 if indeed you have tasted that the Lord is gracious:

1 Peter 4: 11

11 If anyone speaks, let it be as it were the very words of God. If anyone serves, let it be as of the strength which God supplies, that in all things God may be glorified through Jesus Christ, to whom belong the glory and the dominion forever and ever. Amen.

1 John 5: 3

3 For this is loving God, that we keep his commandments. His commandments are not grievous.

1 John 4: 19

19 We love him, because he first loved us.

Revelation 4: 11

11 "Worthy are you, our Lord and God, the Holy One, to receive the glory, the honor, and the power, for you created all things, and because of your desire they existed, and were created!"

Revelation 5: 12

12 saying with a loud voice, "Worthy is the Lamb who has been killed to receive the power, wealth, wisdom, strength, honor, glory, and blessing!"

Predestination

Acts 13: 48

48 As the Gentiles heard this, they were glad, and glorified the word of God. As many as were appointed to eternal life believed.

Romans 8: 28-30

28 We know that all things work together for good for those who love God, to those who are called according to his purpose. 29 For whom he foreknew, he also predestined to be conformed to the image of his Son, that he might be the firstborn among many brothers. 30 Whom he predestined, those he also called. Whom he called, those he also justified. Whom he justified, those he also glorified.

Romans 9: 6-21

6 But it is not as though the word of God has come to nothing. For they are not all Israel, that are of Israel. 7 Neither, because they are Abraham's offspring, are they all children. But, "your offspring will be accounted as from Isaac." 8 That is, it is not the children of the flesh who are children of God, but the children of the promise are counted as heirs. 9 For this is a word of promise, "At the appointed time I will come, and Sarah will have a son." 10 Not only so, but Rebekah also conceived by one, by our father Isaac. 11 For being not yet born, neither having done anything good or bad, that the purpose of God according to election might stand, not of works, but of him who calls, 12 it was said to her, "The elder will serve the younger." 13 Even as it is written, "Jacob I loved, but Esau I hated." 14 What shall we say then? Is there unrighteousness with God? May it never be! 15 For

he said to Moses, "I will have mercy on whom I have mercy, and I will have compassion on whom I have compassion." 16 So then it is not of him who wills, nor of him who runs, but of God who has mercy. 17 For the Scripture says to Pharaoh, "For this very purpose I caused you to be raised up, that I might show in you my power, and that my name might be proclaimed in all the earth." 18 So then, he has mercy on whom he desires, and he hardens whom he desires. 19 You will say then to me, "Why does he still find fault? For who withstands his will?" 20 But indeed, O man, who are you to reply against God? Will the thing formed ask him who formed it, "Why did you make me like this?" 21 Or hasn't the potter a right over the clay, from the same lump to make one part a vessel for honor, and another for dishonor?

1 Thessalonians 1: 4-5

4 For we know, brothers and sisters loved by God, that he has chosen you, 5 because our gospel came to you not simply with words but also with power, with the Holy Spirit and deep conviction. You know how we lived among you for your sake.

Ephesians 1: 4-6

4 We know, brothers loved by God, that you are chosen, 5 and that our Good News came to you not in word only, but also in power, and in the Holy Spirit, and with much assurance. You know what kind of men we showed ourselves to be among you for your sake. 6 You became imitators of us, and of the Lord, having received the word in much affliction, with joy of the Holy Spirit,

2 Thessalonians 2: 13

13 But we are bound to always give thanks to God for you, brothers loved by the Lord, because God chose you from the beginning for salvation through sanctification of the Spirit and belief in the truth;

2 Timothy 1: 8-10

8 Therefore don't be ashamed of the testimony of our Lord, nor of me his prisoner; but endure hardship for the Good News according to the power of God, 9 who saved us and called us with a holy calling, not according to our works, but according to his own purpose and grace, which was given to us in Christ Jesus before times eternal, 10 but has now been revealed by the appearing of our Savior, Christ Jesus, who abolished death, and brought life and immortality to light through the Good News.

1 Peter 2: 3-10

3 if indeed you have tasted that the Lord is gracious: 4 coming to him, a living stone, rejected indeed by men, but chosen by God, precious. 5 You also, as living stones, are built up as a spiritual house, to be a holy priesthood, to offer up spiritual sacrifices, acceptable to God through Jesus Christ. 6 Because it is contained in Scripture, "Behold, I lay in Zion a chief cornerstone, chosen, and precious: He who believes in him will not be disappointed." 7 For you who believe therefore is the honor, but for those who are disobedient, "The stone which the builders rejected, has become the chief cornerstone," 8 and, "a stone of stumbling, and a rock of offense." For they stumble at the word, being disobedient, to which also they were appointed. 9 But you are a chosen race, a royal priesthood, a holy nation, a people for God's own possession, that you may proclaim the excellence of him who called you out of darkness into his marvelous light: 10 who in time past were no people, but now are God's people, who had not obtained mercy, but now have obtained mercy.

Faith

Acts 26: 15-18

15 "I said, 'Who are you, Lord?' "He said, 'I am Jesus, whom you are

persecuting. 16 But arise, and stand on your feet, for I have appeared to you for this purpose: to appoint you a servant and a witness both of the things which you have seen, and of the things which I will reveal to you; 17 delivering you from the people, and from the Gentiles, to whom I send you, 18 to open their eyes, that they may turn from darkness to light and from the power of Satan to God, that they may receive remission of sins and an inheritance among those who are sanctified by faith in me.'

Romans 1: 16-17

16 For I am not ashamed of the Good News of Christ, because it is the power of God for salvation for everyone who believes; for the Jew first, and also for the Greek. 17 For in it is revealed God's righteousness from faith to faith. As it is written, "But the righteous shall live by faith."

Romans 3: 20-22

20 Because by the works of the law, no flesh will be justified in his sight. For through the law comes the knowledge of sin. 21 But now apart from the law, a righteousness of God has been revealed, being testified by the law and the prophets; 22 even the righteousness of God through faith in Jesus Christ to all and on all those who believe. For there is no distinction,

Romans 3: 28

28 We maintain therefore that a man is justified by faith apart from the works of the law.

Romans 4: 1-5

1 What then will we say that Abraham, our forefather, has found according to the flesh? 2 For if Abraham was justified by works, he has something to boast about, but not toward God. 3 For what does the Scripture say? "Abraham believed God, and it was accounted to him for righteousness." 4 Now to him who works, the reward is

not counted as grace, but as something owed. 5 But to him who doesn't work, but believes in him who justifies the ungodly, his faith is accounted for righteousness.

Romans 11: 20

20 True; by their unbelief they were broken off, and you stand by your faith. Don't be conceited, but fear;

2 Corinthians 5: 7

7 for we walk by faith, not by sight.

Ephesians 2: 8

8 for by grace you have been saved through faith, and that not of yourselves; it is the gift of God,

Hebrews 11: 1

1 Now faith is assurance of things hoped for, proof of things not seen.

James 1: 2-4

2 Count it all joy, my brothers, when you fall into various temptations, 3 knowing that the testing of your faith produces endurance. 4 Let endurance have its perfect work, that you may be perfect and complete, lacking in nothing.

Soul

Job 12: 10

10 In whose hand is the life of every living thing, and the breath of all mankind?

Job 32: 8

8 But there is a spirit in man, and the breath of the Almighty gives them understanding.

Psalm 49: 15 (NASB)

15 But God will redeem my soul from the power of Sheol, for He will receive me.

Matthew 10: 28 (NASB)

28 Do not fear those who kill the body but are unable to kill the soul; but rather fear Him who is able to destroy both soul and body in hell.

Matthew 16: 26 (NASB)

26 For what will it profit a man if he gains the whole world and forfeits his soul? Or what will a man give in exchange for his soul?

Mark 8: 35-37

35 For whoever wants to save his life will lose it; and whoever will lose his life for my sake and the sake of the Good News will save it. 36 For what does it profit a man, to gain the whole world, and forfeit his life? 37 For what will a man give in exchange for his life?

John 8: 51

51 Most certainly, I tell you, if a person keeps my word, he will never see death."

1 Corinthians 15: 53-54

53 For this perishable body must become imperishable, and this mortal must put on immortality. 54 But when this perishable body will have become imperishable, and this mortal will have put on immortality, then what is written will happen: "Death is swallowed up in victory."

Parables to be grasped

The Parable of the Lamp and Salt

Matthew 5: 13- 16

> 13 "You are the salt of the earth, but if the salt has lost its flavor, with what will it be salted? It is then good for nothing, but to be cast out and trodden under the feet of men. 14 You are the light of the world. A city located on a hill can't be hidden. 15 Neither do you light a lamp, and put it under a measuring basket, but on a stand; and it shines to all who are in the house. 16 Even so, let your light shine before men; that they may see your good works, and glorify your Father who is in heaven.

Author's opinion

The Parable of the Lamp and Salt is about being a faithful servant witnessing in word and deed to God's Grace. Man is to be salt and light to the world. Man was created to shine His light to others around us, for God's glory *(let your light shine before men; that they may see your good works, and glorify your Father who is in Heaven).* This light must not be hidden but exposed, put up on a pedestal. The light and salt is for all to see and be a blessing for all who come near. If the salt has no flavor and the light is hidden, then that man has lost his usefulness, just to be discarded and forgotten (but to be cast out and trodden under the feet of men.) His servants are to witness to others, the Word's of Jesus and His mercy. Though many people like to do good works they also like to bask in the glory for themselves and not give glory to the Father in Heaven.

Psalm 40: 10

10 I have not hidden your righteousness within my heart. I have declared your faithfulness and your salvation. I have not concealed your loving kindness and your truth from the great assembly.

John 8: 12

12 Again, therefore, Jesus spoke to them, saying, "I am the light of the world. He who follows me will not walk in the darkness, but will have the light of life."

Matthew 28: 18-20

18 Jesus came to them and spoke to them, saying, "All authority has been given to me in heaven and on earth. 19 Go and make disciples of all nations, baptizing them in the name of the Father and of the Son and of the Holy Spirit, 20 teaching them to observe all things that I commanded you. Behold, I am with you always, even to the end of the age." Amen.

The Parable of the Lost Sheep

Luke 15: 3-7

Matthew 18: 12-14

3 He told them this parable. 4 "Which of you men, if you had one hundred sheep, and lost one of them, wouldn't leave the ninety-nine in the wilderness, and go after the one that was lost, until he found it? 5 When he has found it, he carries it on his shoulders, rejoicing. 6 When he comes home, he calls together his friends and his neighbors, saying to them, 'Rejoice with me, for I have found my sheep which was lost!' 7 I tell you that even so there will be more joy in heaven over one sinner who repents, than over ninety-nine righteous people who need no repentance.

Author's opinion

The Parable of the Lost Sheep is about going out preaching, witnessing to the lost, and being very clear about man's need for repentance. It was Jesus' response to the criticism from the Scribes and Pharisees that He and the disciples were associating with seemingly unholy and notorious sinners. Jesus tells this parable about the joy of Heaven at the repentance and return of one lost (sheep) sinner. Most believers also find great peace and joy in the thought of the Great Shepherd holding them in His arms and taking then home to be with Him. This was to contrast the hypocrisy of the 99 self-righteous unrepentant, who were outwardly claiming to be religious. Religious bureaucrats are the ones that have lost sight of Christ's love and mercy only to make a big show of being concerned with procedural correctness at the expense of other peoples' spiritual and physical needs. Christ said *"Doesn't he leave the ninety-nine in the wilderness, and go after the one that was lost, until he found it?* We cannot be arrogant and complacent before the Lord and expect to receive forgiveness. The Great Shepherd finds no joy in the *ninety-nine righteous persons who need no repentance.* This means preaching repentance as a requirement before we can receive forgiveness of sin. Repentance is not a mechanical thing that requires an equal and opposite declaration every time we sin. A rebellious attitude describes a person's governing motivation as to how we conduct our lives. True repentance replaces rebellion with an attitude of gratitude in the believer, one that is humble before the Lord, and is remorseful and regrets our personal sin nature.

How we start out in life (rebellious and self-righteous) is not as important as how we finish (repentant and humble) in our relationship with Jesus Christ our redeemer and Lord. Man was created to glorify God in a humble and meaningful way. But the arrogant criticism by the Scribes and Pharisees exposed the bureaucratic hypocrisy of their religious traditions. There is no Grace for the self-righteous people who does not feel the need to repent.

Ezekiel 33: 10-11 (NASB)

10 "Now as for you, son of man, say to the house of Israel, 'Thus you have spoken, saying, "Surely our transgressions and our sins are upon us, and we are rotting away in them; how then can we survive?"' 11 Say to them, 'As I live!' declares the Lord God, 'I take no pleasure in the death of the wicked, but rather that the wicked turn from his way and live. Turn back, turn back from your evil ways! Why then will you die, O house of Israel?'

Matthew 4: 4

4 But he answered, "It is written, 'Man shall not live by bread alone, but by every word that proceeds out of the mouth of God.

Matthew 5: 19-20

19 Whoever, therefore, shall break one of these least commandments, and teach others to do so, shall be called least in the Kingdom of Heaven; but whoever shall do and teach them shall be called great in the Kingdom of Heaven. 20 For I tell you that unless your righteousness exceeds that of the scribes and Pharisees, there is no way you will enter into the Kingdom of Heaven.

Luke 24: 47

47 and that repentance and remission of sins should be preached in his name to all the nations, beginning at Jerusalem.

2 Corinthians 7: 10

10 For godly sorrow produces repentance to salvation, which brings no regret. But the sorrow of the world produces death.

The Parable of the Good Samaritan

Luke 10: 25-37

25 Behold, a certain lawyer stood up and tested him, saying, "Teacher, what shall I do to inherit eternal life?" 26 He said to him, "What is written in the law? How do you read it?" 27 He answered, "You shall love the Lord your God with all your heart, with all your soul, with all your strength, and with all your mind; and your neighbor as yourself." 28 He said to him, "You have answered correctly. Do this, and you will live." 29 But he, desiring to justify himself, asked Jesus, "Who is my neighbor?" 30 Jesus answered, "A certain man was going down from Jerusalem to Jericho, and he fell among robbers, who both stripped him and beat him, and departed, leaving him half dead. 31 By chance a certain priest was going down that way. When he saw him, he passed by on the other side. 32 In the same way a Levite also, when he came to the place, and saw him, passed by on the other side. 33 But a certain Samaritan, as he traveled, came where he was. When he saw him, he was moved with compassion, 34 came to him, and bound up his wounds, pouring on oil and wine. He set him on his own animal, and brought him to an inn, and took care of him. 35 On the next day, when he departed, he took out two denarii, and gave them to the host, and said to him, 'Take care of him. Whatever you spend beyond that, I will repay you when I return.' 36 Now which of these three do you think seemed to be a neighbor to him who fell among the robbers?" 37 He said, "He who showed mercy on him."

Author's Opinion

The Parable of the Good Samaritan is about being accountable to love your neighbor, not in word only, but also in deed. It tells us that loving the Lord your God with all your heart, soul, strength and mind are things that should happen on the inside and the outside of a person so that our good works may be visible for the world to see that brings glory to God. What can we give back to God, the creator of all things? Loving our neighbor is how the world sees the love of God that is in us. It is letting the light shine, so that the world may see our good works and give glory to our Father who is in Heaven. This lawyer knew this law very well, but tried to justify himself by asking the question; *"Who is my neighbor?"* Jesus was talking to a Jewish religious teacher with prejudices and hatred of the Samaritan people. Jesus is praising the compassion and love of the hated Samaritan and exposing the hypocrisy of their religious leaders. The Good Samaritan did not say to himself " What's in it for me? Or this is not my problem" and proceed to walk on the other side of the road as the Jewish religious leaders had done. The Child of God believes that God has shown mercy on us and we are accountable to God, to show love and mercy to our neighbors. The love we show to others are credited by God, as though we are showing love to God. The correct answer has always been that man was created to bring glory to God by loving Christ and believing, demonstrating Christ's love for us to others.

The Parable of the Expedient Servant

Luke 12: 35-48 (NASB)

> 35 "Be dressed in readiness, and keep your lamps lit. 36 Be like men who are waiting for their master when he returns from the wedding feast, so that they may immediately open the door to him when he comes and knocks. 37 Blessed are those slaves whom the master will find on the alert when he comes; truly I say to you, that he will gird himself to serve, and have them recline at the table, and will come up and wait on them. 38 Whether he comes in the second watch,

or even in the third, and finds them so, blessed are those slaves. 39 "But be sure of this, that if the head of the house had known at what hour the thief was coming, he would not have allowed his house to be broken into. 40 You too, be ready; for the Son of Man is coming at an hour that you do not expect." 41 Peter said, "Lord, are You addressing this parable to us, or to everyone else as well?" 42 And the Lord said, "Who then is the faithful and sensible steward, whom his master will put in charge of his servants, to give them their rations at the proper time? 43 Blessed is that slave whom his master finds so doing when he comes. 44 Truly I tell you, that he will set him over all that he has. 45 But if that servant says in his heart, 'My lord delays his coming,' and begins to beat the menservants and the maidservants, and to eat and drink, and to be drunken, 46 then the lord of that servant will come in a day when he isn't expecting him, and in an hour that he doesn't know, and will cut him in two, and place his portion with the unfaithful. 47 That servant, who knew his lord's will, and didn't prepare, nor do what he wanted, will be beaten with many stripes, 48 but he who didn't know, and did things worthy of stripes, will be beaten with few stripes. To whomever much is given, of him will much be required; and to whom much was entrusted, of him more will be asked.

Author's Opinion

The Parable of the Expedient Servant is about being diligent, not complacent, in our devotion to Christ. *37 Blessed are those servants, whom the lord will find watching when he comes.* It is a warning to believers, not to become inattentive or unconcerned regarding their devotion to Christ. *To whom much was entrusted, of him more will be asked.* This means believers and especially church leaders must be faithful, not deviating, from Jesus words of truth, diligently feeding His sheep their rations at the proper time. For almost 2000 years Christians have said, "The end time is near." The tension of not knowing when Jesus will return is a good thing. *"Therefore be ready also, for the Son of Man is coming in an hour that you don't expect him."* Blessed are those servants whom the master finds have remained faithful to the end. But *That servant, who knew his lord's will and didn't prepare, nor do what he wanted, will be beaten with many stripes.* If a person has a right relationship with the Lord, the thought of His coming brings a sense of urgency and joy to the heart, not complacency. Jesus is telling us to be diligent and keep the faith always. *Amen! Yes, come Lord Jesus.* We were created to worship and bring glory to God. If a person does not have this saving relationship with the Lord, the thought of the end time will bring dread to the heart.

John 21: 17

> 17 He said to him the third time, "Simon, son of Jonah, do you have affection for me?" Peter was grieved because he asked him the third time, "Do you have affection for me?" He said to him, "Lord, you know everything. You know that I have affection for you." Jesus said to him, "Feed my sheep.

Revelation 22: 20-21

> 20 He who testifies these things says, "Yes, I come quickly." Amen! Yes, come, Lord Jesus. 21 The grace of the Lord Jesus Christ be with all the saints. Amen.

The Parable of the Marriage Feast

Matthew 22: 2-14

> 2 "The Kingdom of Heaven is like a certain king, who made a marriage feast for his son, 3 and sent out his servants to call those who were invited to the marriage feast, but they would not come. 4 Again he sent out other servants, saying, 'Tell those who are

invited, "Behold, I have prepared my dinner. My cattle and my fatlings are killed, and all things are ready. Come to the marriage feast!"' 5 But they made light of it, and went their ways, one to his own farm, another to his merchandise, 6 and the rest grabbed his servants, and treated them shamefully, and killed them. 7 When the king heard that, he was angry, and sent his armies, destroyed those murderers, and burned their city. 8 "Then he said to his servants, 'The wedding is ready, but those who were invited weren't worthy. 9 Go therefore to the intersections of the highways, and as many as you may find, invite to the marriage feast.' 10 Those servants went out into the highways, and gathered together as many as they found, both bad and good. The wedding was filled with guests. 11 But when the king came in to see the guests, he saw there a man who didn't have on wedding clothing, 12 and he said to him, 'Friend, how did you come in here not wearing wedding clothing?' He was speechless. 13 Then the king said to the servants, 'Bind him hand and foot, take him away, and throw him into the outer darkness. That is where the weeping and grinding of teeth will be.' 14 For many are called, but few chosen."

Author's Opinion

The Parable of the Marriage Feast is about the Word of Truth, (God's Good News Gospel) and is saying as many as you may find, invite to the marriage feast, to come and worship the Son, Jesus Christ. It is a very short version of God's offer of redemption for mankind, from the beginning to the end. The whole purpose of the Kingdom of Heaven, as reveled in the scriptures, was God's plan to create man to glorify and worship God. Early on, God declared that He was a jealous God. *(Exodus 20: 5)* The story begins with the King (God) arranging a celebration to Glorify His Son in the form of a wedding feast. God sent out his servants (the prophets) to invite His chosen (Hebrews) people to the wedding feast, but

The Parable of the Marriage Feast

they were not willing to come. The King repeatedly sent out His invitations, but only to His chosen people. His servants described the heavenly arrangements prepared for them to live with the King. There only the invited guest may come to honor and be honored by the King, as adopted children of the King. But some of these special invited people did not take the invitation seriously, giving lame excuses for not attending. Others on the guest list abused and killed His servants. The King's wrath showed no mercy for the guilty; as a result they were totally annihilated. The King said "These blessings were prepared for them *The wedding is ready, but those who were invited weren't worthy.* Go and find whoever will come to my heavenly wedding celebration (Christ's wedding to his Church). Invite all to come, *as many as they found, both bad and good.* The King came to see who came to the wedding feast. It was then that the King noticed and declared, "This man is unworthy, an imposter, he is not dressed in the righteousness of Christ. He has disguised himself in his own self-righteousness." The unrepentant impostor had nothing to say, because he knew there was nothing to justify his disbelief in the eyes of the King. *Many are called, but few chosen.* Satan's lies can deceive us into thinking of ourselves as righteous and not needing repentance or the other extreme that our past sins are too grievous to be chosen as one of His guests. But that is not the case with God's love and mercy, which includes the bad people as well as the good, if we humble ourselves and believe in Him. Many people hear the Gospel invitation, but only a few respond appropriately by diligently seeking Him. We all should be repentant and pray that we are amongst the few that are chosen to be on His guest list.

1 John 1: 8-9

8 If we say that we have no sin, we deceive ourselves, and the truth is not in us. 9 If we confess our sins, he is faithful and righteous to forgive us the sins and to cleanse us from all unrighteousness.

Revelation 3: 20-22 (NASB)

20 Behold, I stand at the door and knock; if anyone hears My voice and opens the door, I will come in to him and will dine with him, and he with Me. 21 He who overcomes, I will grant to him to sit down with Me on My throne, as I also overcame and sat down with My Father on His throne. 22 He who has an ear, let him hear what the Spirit says to the churches.'"

Chapter 4

What does a Child of God believe?

Genesis 15: 4-7 (NASB)

> 4 Then behold, the word of the Lord came to him, saying, "This man will not be your heir; but one who will come forth from your own body, he shall be your heir." 5 And He took him outside and said, "Now look toward the heavens, and count the stars, if you are able to count them." And He said to him, "So shall your descendants be." 6 Then he believed in the Lord; and He reckoned it to him as righteousness. 7 And He said to him, "I am the Lord who brought you out of Ur of the Chaldeans, to give you this land to possess it."

Isaiah 53: 1-6 (NASB)

> 1 Who has believed our message? And to whom has the arm of the Lord been revealed? 2 For He grew up before Him like a tender

shoot, And like a root out of parched ground; He has no stately form or majesty That we should look upon Him, Nor appearance that we should be attracted to Him. 3 He was despised and forsaken of men, A man of sorrows and acquainted with grief; And like one from whom men hide their face He was despised, and we did not esteem Him. 4 Surely our grief He Himself bore, And our sorrows He carried; Yet we ourselves esteemed Him stricken, Smitten of God, and afflicted. 5 But He was pierced through for our transgressions, He was crushed for our iniquities; The chastening for our well-being fell upon Him, And by His scourging we are healed. 6 All of us like sheep have gone astray, Each of us has turned to his own way; But the Lord has caused the iniquity of us all To fall on Him.

John 1: 9-13

9 The true light that enlightens everyone was coming into the world. 10 He was in the world, and the world was made through him, and the world didn't recognize him. 11 He came to his own, and those who were his own didn't receive him. 12 But as many as received him, to them he gave the right to become God's children, to those who believe in his name: 13 who were born not of blood, nor of the will of the flesh, nor of the will of man, but of God.

John 14: 1-4

1 Don't let your heart be troubled. Believe in God. Believe also in me. 2 In my Father's house are many homes. If it weren't so, I would have told you. I am going to prepare a place for you. 3 If I go and prepare a place for you, I will come again, and will receive you to myself; that where I am, you may be there also. 4 Where I go, you know, and you know the way.

Romans 10: 8-13

8 But what does it say? "The word is near you, in your mouth, and in your heart"; that is, the word of faith, which we preach: 9 that if you will confess with your mouth that Jesus is Lord, and believe in

your heart that God raised him from the dead, you will be saved. 10 For with the heart, one believes unto righteousness; and with the mouth confession is made unto salvation. 11 For the Scripture says, "Whoever believes in him will not be disappointed." 12 For there is no distinction between Jew and Greek; for the same Lord is Lord of all, and is rich to all who call on him. 13 For, "Whoever will call on the name of the Lord will be saved."

Hebrews 11: 6

6 Without faith it is impossible to be well pleasing to him, for he who comes to God must believe that he exists, and that he is a rewarder of those who seek him.

Author's Opinion

A Child of God believes in God's Grace through Jesus Christ's atonement. His life and death on the cross pay the required blood price for our sin and redeems us, His Children. Grace is the free gift of salvation if we repent and believe in Jesus. We must know that our salvation does not depend upon our knowing every detail or getting every doctrinal issue right.

6 Jesus said to him, "I am the way, the truth, and the life. No one comes to the Father, except through me. John 14: 6 The brevity, clarity and most of all, the exclusiveness of this statement, can only come from God Himself. In God's eyes, it is considered disbelief if we find fault with scriptures, or repudiate the scriptures. *1 John 5: 9-11* tells us *9 If we receive the witness of men, the witness of God is greater; for this is God's testimony which he has testified concerning his Son. 10 He who believes in the Son of God has the testimony in himself. He who doesn't believe God has made him a liar, because he has not believed in the testimony that God has given concerning his Son. 11 The testimony is this, that God gave to us eternal life, and this life is in his Son.* We cannot claim to be a believer and disclaim Jesus' words of truth. Jesus is the author and finisher of our faith.

Hebrews 4: 12

> 12 For the word of God is living, and active, and sharper than any two-edged sword, and piercing even to the dividing of soul and spirit, of both joints and marrow, and is able to discern the thoughts and intentions of the heart.

When a person first believes in Jesus as Lord and Savior, it will be the beginning of a journey that will see God triumphant over Satan. *Hebrews 13: 5* tell us *5 Be free from the love of money, content with such things as you have, for he has said, "I will in no way leave you, neither will I in any way forsake you."* We will not be alone on this lifelong journey of faith in Jesus. There is the promise to believers that the power and presence of the Holy Spirit will come to them. The Holy Spirit will endow His divine nature of diligence, virtue, knowledge, self-control, perseverance, godliness, brotherly kindness, and love. Jeremiah 23: 23-24 (NASB) *23 "Am I a God who is near," declares the Lord," And not a God far off? 24 "Can a man hide himself in hiding places So I do not see him?" declares the Lord. "Do I not fill the heavens and the earth?" declares the Lord.* God is Spirit. We are not alone. He is ours and we are His children when we are in the family of God.

1 John 5: 10-11

> 10 He who believes in the Son of God has the testimony in himself. He who doesn't believe God has made him a liar, because he has not believed in the testimony that God has given concerning his Son. 11 The testimony is this, that God gave to us eternal life, and this life is in his Son.

2 Peter 1: 2-11

> 2 Grace to you and peace be multiplied in the knowledge of God and

of Jesus our Lord, 3 seeing that his divine power has granted to us all things that pertain to life and godliness, through the knowledge of him who called us by his own glory and virtue; 4 by which he has granted to us his precious and exceedingly great promises; that through these you may become partakers of the divine nature, having escaped from the corruption that is in the world by lust. 5 Yes, and for this very cause adding on your part all diligence, in your faith supply moral excellence; and in moral excellence, knowledge; 6 and in knowledge, self-control; and in self-control perseverance; and in perseverance godliness; 7 and in godliness brotherly affection; and in brotherly affection, love. 8 For if these things are yours and abound, they make you to be not idle or unfruitful in the knowledge of our Lord Jesus Christ. 9 For he who lacks these things is blind, seeing only what is near, having forgotten the cleansing from his old sins. 10 Therefore, brothers, be more diligent to make your calling and election sure. For if you do these things, you will never stumble. 11 For thus you will be richly supplied with the entrance into the eternal Kingdom of our Lord and Savior, Jesus Christ.

Biblical knowledge, not man's reason, is the way to please God. Understanding His plan for us will come in time by reading the scriptures and with much prayer. Our faith will become more and more significant in our lives as we grow in the knowledge of Jesus Christ. Our saving faith must be in Jesus not our denominational doctrine beliefs. There will be believers in Heaven from different churches and different doctrines, not because they figured out God's perfect doctrine, but because he or she simply committed their life in faith to Jesus. The pride of denominational theology by church leaders, teachers and individuals is both shameful and destructive if it encourages contempt for brothers and sisters of the faith because they are from a different theological persuasion.

Today this is a very common form of self-righteous

arrogance that is being flaunted before God and man very similar to what Jesus saw happening by the Pharisees and Sadducees. If two people read the same Bible verse, each person will have a slightly different description of what is being said. (Example; after the trial, it was the criminal's decided opinion that the judge had been entirely too legalistic.) This difference of perception is because we see other people and issues through the prism of our own soul. Subsequently, over time different denominational theologies have developed. Please know Biblical doctrine (what we believe) is very important; it shapes who we are. God's wisdom from the Bible comes to us when we fear Him, not through arrogance and self pride. God recognizes the subtle difference of faith in "who" we believe as apposed to having faith in "what" we believe.

Romans 14: 1-4

> 1 Now accept one who is weak in faith, but not for disputes over opinions. 2 One man has faith to eat all things, but he who is weak eats only vegetables. 3 Don't let him who eats despise him who doesn't eat. Don't let him who doesn't eat judge him who eats, for God has accepted him. 4 Who are you who judge another's servant? To his own lord he stands or falls. Yes, he will be made to stand, for God has power to make him stand.

James 3: 1-2

> 1 Let not many of you be teachers, my brothers, knowing that we will receive heavier judgment. 2 For in many things we all stumble. If anyone doesn't stumble in word, the same is a perfect man, able to bridle the whole body also.

Salvation (our personal relation to Christ) is a divine gift. Here in lies the mystery; we must want forgiveness of our sin or repentance before we can receive Jesus Christ's salvation, but forgiveness is not our right, it is an undeserved gift. Belief and trust in the truth of Scripture is our grateful response to our reconciliation with God and the only trustworthy light that guides our path to Heaven's narrow gate. In the Bible, and especially the parables, there are examples that are repeated over and over, telling us of His gift of grace, for all that will come to Him. The Satanic confusion about doctrine comes when we trust man's reasoning that deviates from God's word. Consequently there is a wide spectrum of doctrinal belief in Christian churches today. The visible things of religion (our churches, denominations, doctrines, the clergy, and our congregations) can be deceptive if we forget that God is spirit. The kingdom of God rules in our hearts, by His unseen spirit of grace, not by the visible things of this world. The disciples asked Jesus, "Who can be saved?" His reply was recorded in Matthew 19: 26. *"...With man this is impossible, but with God all things are possible."*

Ephesians 2: 8-9

> 8 for by grace you have been saved through faith, and that not of yourselves; it is the gift of God, 9 not of works, that no one would boast.

As an illustration, if a person jumped out of a burning building into a firemen's net to be saved from certain death, that person could not say that he or she had saved their own life. It was the fireman's net that prevented hitting the pavement and subsequent loss of life. No matter how righteous a person may think of himself, we do not have the power to save our self. To be saved, we can only make the giant leap of repentance and faith in Jesus Christ. Falling into the heavenly arms of the Great Shepherd (our safety net) was made possible by Christ's atonement on the cross for our sins. Salvation is the gift of God; Jesus Christ alone is our (saving) net.

There are two other unsatisfactory outcomes to our burning building example. One is of people ignoring that God is a consuming fire and choosing not to jump. By ignoring God's Grace they are by default accepting their fate, of an unrepentant lifestyle. Another example is of the indiscriminately religious person who believes one religion or cult is as good as another putting trust in a mortal person or organization that does not exalt Jesus. There is no saving grace for a sincere religious person who jumps off our burning building in the wrong direction, misses the safety net. Salvation will not come simply through righteousness or membership in any religious group. God has made possible our salvation, only through our repentance and believing in Jesus. Jesus said: *20 Behold, I stand at the door and knock. If anyone hears my voice and opens the door, then I will come in to him, and will dine with him, and he with me. Revelations 3: 20*

It could not be simpler – if we repent and put our trust in Jesus. Christ's atonement (His death on the cross) redeemed us; He paid the price for our sins and blotted out all record of our past and future sin. Christ is our mediator and advocate for us with the Father. With true faith we pass from death to life as His children in the family of God.

John 4: 24

24 God is spirit, and those who worship him must worship in spirit and truth."

John 4: 47

47 Most certainly, I tell you, he who believes in me has eternal life.

Acts 16: 31

31 They said, "Believe in the Lord Jesus Christ, and you will be saved, you and your household."

1 Timothy 4: 6-10

6 If you instruct the brothers of these things, you will be a good servant of Christ Jesus, nourished in the words of the faith, and of the good doctrine which you have followed. 7 But refuse profane and old wives' fables. Exercise yourself toward godliness. 8 For bodily exercise has some value, but godliness has value in all things, having the promise of the life which is now, and of that which is to come. 9 This saying is faithful and worthy of all acceptance. 10 For to this end we both labor and suffer reproach, because we have set our trust in the living God, who is the Savior of all men, especially of those who believe.

Titus 1: 5-16

5 I left you in Crete for this reason, that you would set in order the things that were lacking, and appoint elders in every city, as I directed you; 6 if anyone is blameless, the husband of one wife, having children who believe, who are not accused of loose or unruly behavior. 7 For the overseer must be blameless, as God's steward; not self-pleasing, not easily angered, not given to wine, not violent, not greedy for dishonest gain; 8 but given to hospitality, a lover of good, sober minded, fair, holy, self-controlled; 9 holding to the faithful word which is according to the teaching, that he may be able to exhort in the sound doctrine, and to convict those who contradict him. 10 For there are also many unruly men, vain talkers and deceivers, especially those of the circumcision, 11 whose mouths must be stopped; men who overthrow whole houses, teaching things which they ought not, for dishonest gain's sake. 12 One of them, a prophet of their own, said, "Cretans are always liars, evil beasts, and idle gluttons." 13 This testimony is true. For this cause, reprove them sharply, that they may be sound in the faith, 14 not paying attention to Jewish fables and commandments of men who turn away from the truth. 15 To the pure, all things are pure; but to those who are defiled and unbelieving, nothing is pure; but both

their mind and their conscience are defiled. 16 They profess that they know God, but by their deeds they deny him, being abominable, disobedient, and unfit for any good work.

Revelations 22: 18-19

18 I testify to everyone who hears the words of the prophecy of this book, if anyone adds to them, may God add to him the plagues which are written in this book. 19 If anyone takes away from the words of the book of this prophecy, may God take away his part from the tree of life, and out of the holy city, which are written in this book.

The Short Answer

Exactly what is it that Christians believe? The stories of the thief on the cross and the woman at the well might be the best and shortest answer to this question. Both repented and trusted Jesus as their messiah. They were people who did not know a lot about religious doctrine, but came to know and trust Jesus personally. Today we would say to be a believer requires a personal faith relationship with Jesus. The scriptures encourage baptism, membership in a Bible-believing church (fellowship), a good understanding of the Bible and a lifetime of showing love for neighbors, to the glory of God. While these are all good things and should be pursued, they are not required before a person becomes a believer.

The thief on the cross

Luke 23: 39-43

39 One of the criminals who was hanged insulted him, saying, "If you are the Christ, save yourself and us!" 40 But the other answered, and

rebuking him said, "Don't you even fear God, seeing you are under the same condemnation? 41 And we indeed justly, for we receive the due reward for our deeds, but this man has done nothing wrong." 42 He said to Jesus, "Lord, remember me when you come into your Kingdom." 43 Jesus said to him, "Assuredly I tell you, today you will be with me in Paradise."

The woman at the well

John 4: 21-26

21 Jesus said to her, "Woman, believe me, the hour comes, when neither in this mountain, nor in Jerusalem, will you worship the Father. 22 You worship that which you don't know. We worship that which we know; for salvation is from the Jews. 23 But the hour comes, and now is, when the true worshipers will worship the Father in spirit and truth, for the Father seeks such to be his worshipers. 24 God is spirit, and those who worship him must worship in spirit and truth." 25 The woman said to him, "I know that Messiah comes, he who is called Christ. When he has come, he will declare to us all things." 26 Jesus said to her, "I am he, the one who speaks to you."

The Long Answer

The long answer as to what a child of God believes is varied and includes a wide spectrum of teachings. There are two main camps or schools of thought concerning church doctrine. These divisions can be described as *orthodox* and *unorthodox*. The distinction between these two camps is that the orthodox beliefs include only belief's that do not deviate from the original doctrine and comes exclusively from the scriptures. Unorthodox or liberal doctrine continues to look for meaning beyond the scriptures. It is important to understand and not question that both of these camps have believing worshipers in them.

An example of what the church historically taught and believed (before the divisions of orthodox and unorthodox churches occurred) might be the third century Apostles' Creed. It should be noted that the Apostles' Creed uses the term "catholic church." In the third century this term was used to describe the orthodox undivided universal Christian church as a whole. Today the use of the term may also be understood to mean Christian Church universal (the body of Christ), or some may choose to understand it to be exclusively the Roman Catholic Church, excluding protestant churches.

Matthew 16: 18 (NASB)

> 18 I also say to you that you are Peter, and upon this rock I will build My church; and the gates of Hades will not overpower it.

Ephesians 1: 19-23 (NASB)

> 19 and what is the surpassing greatness of His power toward us who believe. These are in accordance with the working of the strength of His might 20 which He brought about in Christ, when He raised Him from the dead and seated Him at His right hand in the heavenly places, 21 far above all rule and authority and power and dominion, and every name that is named, not only in this age but also in the one to come. 22 And He put all things in subjection under His feet, and gave Him as head over all things to the church, 23 which is His body, the fullness of Him who fills all in all.

Apostles' Creed

1. I believe in God the Father, Almighty, Maker of heaven and earth;
2. And in Jesus Christ, his only begotten Son, our Lord;
3. Who was conceived by the Holy Ghost, born of the Virgin Mary;
4. Suffered under Pontius Pilate; was crucified, dead and buried;

5. The third day he rose again from the dead;
6. He ascended into heaven, and sits at the right hand of God the Father Almighty;
7. From thence He shall come to judge the quick and the dead;
8. I believe in the Holy Ghost;
9. I believe in the holy catholic church: the communion of saints;
10. The forgiveness of sins;
11. The resurrection of the body;
12. And the life everlasting. Amen.

Also there are two significant issues not included in the Apostles' Creed that the Bible teaches, (they may have been understood but were not listed).

Number 1. The inerrancy of scripture (God did not give us a lie).

Number 2. The fall or depravity of man (Every one needs forgiveness).

Hebrews 6: 17-20 (NASB)

> 17 In the same way God, desiring even more to show to the heirs of the promise the unchangeableness of His purpose, interposed with an oath, 18 so that by two unchangeable things in which it is impossible for God to lie, we who have taken refuge would have strong encouragement to take hold of the hope set before us. 19 This hope we have as an anchor of the soul, a hope both sure and steadfast and one which enters within the veil, 20 where Jesus has entered as a forerunner for us, having become a high priest forever according to the order of Melchizedek.

The Distinction between Orthodox and Unorthodox Beliefs

Today there is a line of thought that differs from the original doctrine, known as the unorthodox or *liberal* view. Mr. Maurice Wiles is the author of the 16th chapter titled, *What Christianity Believes* (pg. 553-571) in the book, Oxford Illustrated History of Christianity / edited by John McManners (Oxford University Press, New York, 1990). Mr. Wiles has elaborated in great detail on the liberal perspective and what he thinks Christians should believe, given today's age of enlightenment. He espouses the belief that the nature of Christian belief is both a personal matter and a communal matter. The foundation of Mr. Wiles' theology or communal belief (by virtue of man's reason) teaches that because God is good, i.e., God's creation (man) is also good, and cannot be intrinsically evil. Please note: this concept is in opposition to God's words of truth. *Jeremiah 17: 9* Is very specific. ₉*The heart is deceitful above all things and it is exceedingly corrupt. Who can know it?* Mr. Wiles describes and advocates liberal theology by telling us that man's sociological awareness of historical knowledge and scientific knowledge are incompatible with (orthodox) past traditions. Their "enlightened" understanding has affected the way Christians understand the Bible and God's actions in the world. He sites the changing human attitudes on feminism, as self-evident and justifies the need for further change in Christian belief. Mr. Wiles calls into doubt the adequacy of Scripture and implies that to the moral sensitivity of Christians, the doctrine of Atonement is not a precise enough description for them, and it is this imperfection has led to stress between believers.

Luke 17: 20-21

₂₀Being asked by the Pharisees when God's Kingdom would come, he answered them, "God's Kingdom doesn't come with observation; 21 neither will they say, 'Look, here!' or, 'Look, there!' for behold, God's Kingdom is within you."

Hebrews 2: 17-18

> 17 Therefore he was obligated in all things to be made like his brothers, that he might become a merciful and faithful high priest in things pertaining to God, to make atonement for the sins of the people. 18 For in that he himself has suffered being tempted, he is able to help those who are tempted.

Mr. Wiles' statement about stress between orthodox and liberal believers is unfortunately true and he has accurately described the liberal line of thought that divides the church today.

James 4: 4

> 4 You adulterers and adulteresses, don't you know that friendship with the world is hostility toward God? Whoever therefore wants to be a friend of the world makes himself an enemy of God.

I have included the above brief paraphrase of Mr. Wiles' description of unorthodox or liberal theology to show a few of the stark contrasts between orthodox and unorthodox beliefs. The disaccord or lack of unity between orthodox and unorthodox doctrine is significant and painful to acknowledge because it can have the appetence of being judgmental (one side pointing fingers at the other) – which is why these issues are not often freely discussed. My intention is not to judge or offend anyone, but to show the marked differences between these two belief systems. Exposing the differences in religious thinking is vital. We must go far enough to recognize our contrasting ways of approaching God, but stop short of judging our neighbor. Mr. Wiles and the people who embrace his liberal view have made their choice, they are sincere and feel secure in their beliefs.

Romans 14: 10-12

> 10 But you, why do you judge your brother? Or you again, why do you despise your brother? For we will all stand before the judgment seat of Christ. 11 For it is written, "'As I live,' says the Lord, 'to me every knee will bow. Every tongue will confess to God.'" 12 So then each one of us will give account of himself to God.

It is my hope that the Scriptures will ring true and speak to us concerning these diverging doctrinal beliefs. In his writings Mr. Wiles has described and attempted to justify as "self-evident" his liberal theology that contrasts with what he calls, the too old-old fashioned and too static alternative, for the awareness of todays more sensitive Western Christian believers. As God gives each person the right to choose, for them-selves, how to worship and believe in God it is my belief that we should be patient and be mindful to other people's personal choice, even when we disagree.

2 Timothy 2: 24-26

> 24 The Lord's servant must not quarrel, but be gentle towards all, able to teach, patient, 25 in gentleness correcting those who oppose him: perhaps God may give them repentance leading to a full knowledge of the truth, 26 and they may recover themselves out of the devil's snare, having been taken captive by him to his will.

The unorthodox or liberal view of what it means to believe is often considered to be new and enlightened. New and enlightened ("sociological awareness of historical knowledge and scientific knowledge") relies on trusting only the visible and temporal things of this world over the 'hard-to-understand" spiritual aspects of the Scriptures. Demanding hard evidence before belief devalues hope and faith. If man by nature is good and righteous, as Mr. Wiles' doctrinal belief seems to be saying, it discredits our need for repentance. Without repentance and faith, man remains' arrogant and self-righteous before God. White-washing or denying man's sin nature is wrong in the eyes of God who will forgive the repentant person, but will not tolerate rebellion. I do not believe that theology that elevates man and promotes human rules and reason over God's Word is new or enlightened. Satan's first lie to Eve in the garden followed the same path. (See Genesis 3: 1-13.)

Romans 9: 20-21 (NASB)

> 20 On the contrary, who are you, O man, who answers back to God? The thing molded will not say to the molder, "Why did you make me like this," will it? 21 Or does not the potter have a right over the clay, to make from the same lump one vessel for honorable use and another for common use?

Hebrews 3: 12-14 (NASB)

> 12 Take care, brethren, that there not be in any one of you an evil, unbelieving heart that falls away from the living God. 13 But encourage one another day after day, as long as it is still called "Today," so that none of you will be hardened by the deceitfulness of sin. 14 For we have become partakers of Christ, if we hold fast the beginning of our assurance firm until the end,

Mr. Wiles' ways of thinking are significant because they show that critical attitudes toward the Word of truth can influence how people develop their belief systems, especially when they are not studying the Scriptures for themselves. All Christians have unanswered questions, and some questions may never be answered in this life. If a person does not understand a difficult passage in the Bible, that fact alone does not justify disparaging the Scriptures. Changing doctrine to accommodate man's comfort zone is Satan's way of subverting our belief system. Religion without faith is a hollow sham, a social club with religious banners. "What you see, is all you get" is not the definition of hope or faith. Child-like faith, not intellectual understanding, is man's responsibility in his reconciliation with God

Romans 8: 24

> 24 For we were saved in hope, but hope that is seen is not hope. For who hopes for that which he sees?

Hebrews 11: 1

> 1 Now faith is assurance of things hoped for, proof of things not seen.

Mr. Wiles makes reference to feminism, which is a significant stumbling block for many in today's society. These "stumbling blocks" prevent us from moving forward in our beliefs. Most stumbling blocks (including feminism) can be seen as self-interest spiritual issues that threaten our relationship with our redeemer. We need to relinquish any stumbling block that is in opposition to Jesus' Word of Truth. This should not be a problem if professing Christians are willing to humble themselves as servants, worshiping and trusting Jesus as their master. Either we believe God's Word to be right and true or we let these stumbling blocks (difficult issues that challenge our beliefs) impede our progress and defeat us. *(... They stumble, being disobedient to the word... 1 Peter 2: 7)* Any school of thought that opposes Scripture (even if it seems self-evident to man's reason) will not prevail. God's Word cannot and will not be invalidated by man's perception of a changing world or by man's pride.

Romans 8: 5-6

> 5 For those who live according to the flesh set their minds on the things of the flesh, but those who live according to the Spirit, the things of the Spirit. 6 For the mind of the flesh is death, but the mind of the Spirit is life and peace;

1 John 4: 4-6

> 4 You are of God, little children, and have overcome them; because greater is he who is in you than he who is in the world. 5 They are of the world. Therefore they speak of the world, and the world hears them. 6 We are of God. He who knows God listens to us. He who is not of God doesn't listen to us. By this we know the spirit of truth, and the spirit of error.

It will be for the reader to decide if Mr. Wiles' writings are extreme and believed by an isolated few or if he has exposed the prevailing church politics that motivates the majority of mainline liberal denominations. Does Mr. Wiles' liberal or unorthodox views advocate an ongoing and relentless attempt to make God serve man?

Matthew 16: 23

> 23 But he turned, and said to Peter, "Get behind me, Satan! You are a stumbling block to me, for you are not setting your mind on the things of God, but on the things of men."

Unfortunately many churches teach, and people believe, that the mainstream of their human understanding of the world and/or their enlightened intellect justifies sociological changes in church doctrine.

Job 40: 1-2 (NASB)

> 1 Then the Lord said to Job, 2 "Will the faultfinder contend with the Almighty? Let him who reproves God answer it."

Mark 7: 6-9

> 6 He answered them, "Well did Isaiah prophesy of you hypocrites, as it is written, 'This people honors me with their lips, but their heart is far from me. 7 But they worship me in vain, teaching as doctrines the commandments of men.' 8 "For you set aside the commandment of God, and hold tightly to the tradition of men—the washing of pitchers and cups, and you do many other such things." 9 He said

to them, "Full well do you reject the commandment of God, that you may keep your tradition.

Hebrews 13: 7-9

7 Remember your leaders, men who spoke to you the word of God, and considering the results of their conduct, imitate their faith.
8 Jesus Christ is the same yesterday, today, and forever. 9 Don't be carried away by various and strange teachings, for it is good that the heart be established by grace, not by food, through which those who were so occupied were not benefited.

The Child of God believes in the unseen spiritual effects of God. It means keeping the faith when others trust only the things that can be seen, felt and/or physically embraced. Believing is a personal issue with the Child of God, not a corporate issue. Believing in Christ will lift the burden of sin from our hearts and change us from a self-seeking to a self-giving, grateful personality.

The visible Church should be seen as the coming together of individuals to worship and praise Jesus. Hebrews 12: 22-23 Describes the true Church. 22 *But you have come to Mount Zion, and to the city of the living God, the heavenly Jerusalem, and to innumerable multitudes of angels,* 23 *to the festal gathering and assembly of the firstborn who are enrolled in heaven, to God the Judge of all, to the spirits of just men made perfect.* Worshiping and glorifying Jesus Christ in truth and spirit is the thing that defines the true Church. Revelation 5: 12 Shows us how to worship 12 *Saying with a loud voice, "Worthy is the Lamb who has been killed to receive the power, wealth, wisdom, strength, honor, glory, and blessing!"* That is why the church is called "the bride of Christ." Without Christ there is no Church. Jesus prayed to the Father in behalf of His believers in His Church as recorded in John 17: 9-11. 9 *I pray for them. I don't pray for the world, but for those whom you have given me, for they are yours. 10 All things that are mine are yours, and yours are mine, and I am glorified in them. 11 I am no more in the world, but these are in the world, and I am coming to you. Holy Father, keep them through your name which you have given me, that they may be one, even as we are.* It is the corruption of self-interest that causes confusion and division within the visible Church. Ideally we would like the visible church to be united, without divisions, pure, consistent and without wrinkle or blemish. But experience and His Word's of truth reveal to us that good and evil exist in every person and in every church. We must love Christ with heart, soul and mind and let God be the judge of all these other issues.

Matthew 5: 18-19 (NASB)

> 18 For truly I say to you, until heaven and earth pass away, not the smallest letter or stroke shall pass from the Law until all is accomplished. 19 Whoever then annuls one of the least of these commandments, and teaches others to do the same, shall be called least in the kingdom of heaven; but whoever keeps and teaches them, he shall be called great in the kingdom of heaven.

2 Peter 3: 1-3

> 1 This is now, beloved, the second letter that I have written to you; and in both of them I stir up your sincere mind by reminding you; 2 that you should remember the words which were spoken before by the holy prophets, and the commandment of us, the apostles of the Lord and Savior: 3 knowing this first, that in the last days mockers will come, walking after their own lusts,

The believer is undoubtedly influenced by the religious system or the church he or she attends. God knows who is repentant and worships Jesus in a manner that is pleasing to Him. We must not judge others or be arrogant or proud before God. *20 True; by their unbelief they were broken off, and you stand by your faith. Don't be conceited, but fear;* 21 *for if God didn't spare the natural branches, neither will he spare you. Romans 11: 20-21.* The Bible tells us that the Child of God should fear and believe in the Holiness and Righteousness of God. God is faithful and true to his word, without exception. Christians believe that Christ's atonement redeemed us, making possible our reconciliation with God. Denying God's gift of Grace may seem insignificant to the unrepentant person who does not fear God. But Christ's atonement is very significant; it makes possible the difference between our eternal joy in Heaven or the agony of eternal separation from God. When the stakes are so high, how often does a person get to choose which side to be on after the contest has already been decided? God's Grace will prevail over Satan's self-serving destructive worldview. For God's believers, the true Church (the bride of Christ) will be called to the heavenly marriage feast of the Lamb. But Satan and his captives have already lost the battle. *Revelations 20: 15* tell us that anyone not found written in the Book of Life will be put to eternal shame.

Jude 1: 20-23

> 20 But you, beloved, keep building up yourselves on your most holy faith, praying in the Holy Spirit. 21 Keep yourselves in God's love, looking for the mercy of our Lord Jesus Christ to eternal life. 22 On some have compassion, making a distinction, 23 and some save, snatching them out of the fire with fear, hating even the clothing stained by the flesh.

Revelation 12: 10-12

> 10 I heard a loud voice in heaven, saying, "Now the salvation, the power, and the Kingdom of our God, and the authority of his Christ has come; for the accuser of our brothers has been thrown down, who accuses them before our God day and night. 11 They overcame him because of the Lamb's blood, and because of the word of their

testimony. They didn't love their life, even to death. 12 Therefore rejoice, heavens, and you who dwell in them. Woe to the earth and to the sea, because the devil has gone down to you, having great wrath, knowing that he has but a short time."

After examining the long and the short of our question, *What does a child of God believe?* The answer: The Child of God must be repentant and have a child-like faith in Jesus. This faith means submitting in reverent fear, to God's will and becoming a servant. First and foremost, we faithfully believe in Jesus and then we look to the scriptures for His written guidance, all the days of our life.

Proverbs 3: 5-6 (NASB)

> 5 Trust in the Lord with all your heart And do not lean on your own understanding. 6 In all your ways acknowledge Him, And He will make your paths straight.

Matthew 18: 4

> 4 Whoever therefore humbles himself as this little child, the same is the greatest in the Kingdom of Heaven.

Paradoxes to be examined

Divisions

Luke 12: 51-53

> 51 Do you think that I have come to give peace in the earth? I tell you, no, but rather division. 52 For from now on, there will be five in one house divided, three against two, and two against three. 53 They will be divided, father against son, and son against father; mother against daughter, and daughter against her mother; mother-in-law against her daughter-in-law, and daughter-in-law against her mother-in-law."

Romans 16: 17-18

17 Now I beg you, brothers, look out for those who are causing the divisions and occasions of stumbling, contrary to the doctrine which you learned, and turn away from them. 18 For those who are such don't serve our Lord, Jesus Christ, but their own belly; and by their smooth and flattering speech, they deceive the hearts of the innocent.

1 Corinthians 1: 6-10

6 even as the testimony of Christ was confirmed in you: 7 so that you come behind in no gift; waiting for the revelation of our Lord Jesus Christ; 8 who will also confirm you until the end, blameless in the day of our Lord Jesus Christ. 9 God is faithful, through whom you were called into the fellowship of his Son, Jesus Christ, our Lord. 10 Now I beg you, brothers, through the name of our Lord, Jesus Christ, that you all speak the same thing, and that there be no divisions among you, but that you be perfected together in the same mind and in the same judgment.

1 Corinthians 3: 1-5 (NASB)

1 And I, brethren, could not speak to you as to spiritual men, but as to men of flesh, as to infants in Christ. 2 I gave you milk to drink, not solid food; for you were not yet able to receive it. Indeed, even now you are not yet able, 3 for you are still fleshly. For since there is jealousy and strife among you, are you not fleshly, and are you not walking like mere men? 4 For when one says, "I am of Paul," and another, "I am of Apollos," are you not mere men? 5 What then is Apollos? And what is Paul? Servants through whom you believed, even as the Lord gave opportunity to each one.

Titus 1: 15-16

15 To the pure, all things are pure; but to those who are defiled and unbelieving, nothing is pure; but both their mind and their conscience are defiled. 16 They profess that they know God, but by

their deeds they deny him, being abominable, disobedient, and unfit for any good work.

Jude 1: 4

1 Jude a servant of Jesus Christ, and brother of James, to those who are called, sanctified by God the Father, and kept for Jesus Christ: 2 Mercy to you and peace and love be multiplied. 3 Beloved, while I was very eager to write to you about our common salvation, I was constrained to write to you exhorting you to contend earnestly for the faith which was once for all delivered to the saints. 4 For there are certain men who crept in secretly, even those who were long ago written about for this condemnation: ungodly men, turning the grace of our God into indecency, and denying our only Master, God, and Lord, Jesus Christ

The fall or depravity of man

Genesis 3: 22-24 (NASB)

22 Then the Lord God said, "Behold, the man has become like one of us, knowing good and evil; and now, he might stretch out his hand, and take also from the tree of life, and eat, and live forever" — 23 therefore the Lord God sent him out from the garden of Eden, to cultivate the ground from which he was taken. 24 So He drove the man out; and at the east of the garden of Eden He stationed the cherubim and the flaming sword which turned every direction to guard the way to the tree of life.

Romans 1: 28-30 (NASB)

28 And just as they did not see fit to acknowledge God any longer, God gave them over to a depraved mind, to do those things which are not proper, 29 being filled with all unrighteousness, wickedness, greed, evil; full of envy, murder, strife, deceit, malice; they are gossips, 30 slanderers, haters of God, insolent, arrogant, boastful, inventors of evil, disobedient to parents,

Romans 3: 21-26

21 But now apart from the law, a righteousness of God has been revealed, being testified by the law and the prophets; 22 even the righteousness of God through faith in Jesus Christ to all and on all those who believe. For there is no distinction, 23 for all have sinned, and fall short of the glory of God; 24 being justified freely by his grace through the redemption that is in Christ Jesus; 25 whom God sent to be an atoning sacrifice, through faith in his blood, for a demonstration of his righteousness through the passing over of prior sins, in God's forbearance; 26 to demonstrate his righteousness at this present time; that he might himself be just, and the justifier of him who has faith in Jesus.

2 Timothy 3: 1-7

1 But know this, that in the last days, grievous times will come. 2 For men will be lovers of self, lovers of money, boastful, arrogant, blasphemers, disobedient to parents, unthankful, unholy, 3 without natural affection, unforgiving, slanderers, without self-control, fierce, not lovers of good, 4 traitors, headstrong, conceited, lovers of pleasure rather than lovers of God; 5 holding a form of godliness, but having denied its power. Turn away from these, also. 6 For some of these are people who creep into houses, and take captive gullible women loaded down with sins, led away by various lusts, 7 always learning, and never able to come to the knowledge of the truth.

Man's sin nature

Genesis 8: 21 (NASB)

21 The Lord smelled the soothing aroma; and the Lord said to Himself, "I will never again curse the ground on account of man, for the intent of man's heart is evil from his youth; and I will never again destroy every living thing, as I have done.

Jeremiah 9: 3-6 (NASB)

> 3 "They bend their tongue like their bow; Lies and not truth prevail in the land; For they proceed from evil to evil, And they do not know Me," declares the Lord. 4 "Let everyone be on guard against his neighbor, And do not trust any brother; Because every brother deals craftily, And every neighbor goes about as a slanderer. 5 "Everyone deceives his neighbor And does not speak the truth, They have taught their tongue to speak lies; They weary themselves committing iniquity. 6 "Your dwelling is in the midst of deceit;
> Through deceit they refuse to know Me," declares the Lord.

Ezekiel 33: 11 (NASB)

> 11 Say to them, 'As I live!' declares the Lord God, 'I take no pleasure in the death of the wicked, but rather that the wicked turn from his way and live. Turn back, turn back from your evil ways! Why then will you die, O house of Israel?'

Proverbs 5: 12-13

> 12 and say, "How I have hated instruction, and my heart despised reproof; 13 neither have I obeyed the voice of my teachers, nor turned my ear to those who instructed me!

Proverbs 5: 21-23 (NASB)

> 21 For the ways of a man are before the eyes of the Lord, And He watches all his paths. 22 His own iniquities will capture the wicked, And he will be held with the cords of his sin. 23 He will die for lack of instruction, And in the greatness of his folly he will go astray.

Matthew 15: 18-19

> 18 But the things which proceed out of the mouth come out of the heart, and they defile the man. 19 For out of the heart come evil thoughts, murders, adulteries, sexual sins, thefts, false testimony, and blasphemies.

Romans 1: 21

21 Because, knowing God, they didn't glorify him as God, neither gave thanks, but became vain in their reasoning, and their senseless heart was darkened.

Romans 3: 23

23 for all have sinned, and fall short of the glory of God;

Romans 5: 13-19

13 For until the law, sin was in the world; but sin is not charged when there is no law. 14 Nevertheless death reigned from Adam until Moses, even over those whose sins weren't like Adam's disobedience, who is a foreshadowing of him who was to come. 15 But the free gift isn't like the trespass. For if by the trespass of the one the many died, much more did the grace of God, and the gift by the grace of the one man, Jesus Christ, abound to the many. 16 The gift is not as through one who sinned: for the judgment came by one to condemnation, but the free gift came of many trespasses to justification. 17 For if by the trespass of the one, death reigned through the one; so much more will those who receive the abundance of grace and of the gift of righteousness reign in life through the one, Jesus Christ. 18 So then as through one trespass, all men were condemned; even so through one act of righteousness, all men were justified to life. 19 For as through the one man's disobedience many were made sinners, even so through the obedience of the one, many will be made righteous.

Ephesians 2: 1-10

1 You were made alive when you were dead in transgressions and sins, 2 in which you once walked according to the course of this world, according to the prince of the power of the air, the spirit who now works in the children of disobedience; 3 among whom we also all once lived in the lusts of our flesh, doing the desires of the flesh and of the mind, and were by nature children of wrath, even as the

rest. 4 But God, being rich in mercy, for his great love with which he loved us, 5 even when we were dead through our trespasses, made us alive together with Christ (by grace you have been saved), 6 and raised us up with him, and made us to sit with him in the heavenly places in Christ Jesus, 7 that in the ages to come he might show the exceeding riches of his grace in kindness toward us in Christ Jesus; 8 for by grace you have been saved through faith, and that not of yourselves; it is the gift of God, 9 not of works, that no one would boast. 10 For we are his workmanship, created in Christ Jesus for good works, which God prepared before that we would walk in them.

Romans 5: 8

8 But God commends his own love toward us, in that while we were yet sinners, Christ died for us.

Galatians 3: 22

22 But the Scriptures imprisoned all things under sin, that the promise by faith in Jesus Christ might be given to those who believe.

James 1: 14-15

14 But each one is tempted when he is drawn away by his own lust, and enticed. 15 Then the lust, when it has conceived, bears sin; and the sin, when it is full grown, produces death.

1 John 1: 8-10

8 If we say that we have no sin, we deceive ourselves, and the truth is not in us. 9 If we confess our sins, he is faithful and righteous to forgive us the sins, and to cleanse us from all unrighteousness. 10 If we say that we haven't sinned, we make him a liar, and his word is not in us.

1 John 3: 8

8 He who sins is of the devil, for the devil has been sinning from the beginning. To this end the Son of God was revealed: that he might destroy the works of the devil.

Parables to be grasped

The Parable of the Pharisee and the Tax Collector

Luke 18: 9-14 (NASB)

9 And He also told this parable to some people who trusted in themselves that they were righteous, and viewed others with contempt: 10 "Two men went up into the temple to pray, one a Pharisee and the other a tax collector. 11 The Pharisee stood and was praying this to himself: 'God, I thank You that I am not like other people: swindlers, unjust, adulterers, or even like this tax collector. 12 I fast twice a week; I pay tithes of all that I get.' 13 But the tax collector, standing some distance away, was even unwilling to lift up his eyes to heaven, but was beating his breast, saying, 'God, be merciful to me, the sinner!' 14 I tell you, this man went to his house justified rather than the other; for everyone who exalts himself will be humbled, but he who humbles himself will be exalted."

Author's Opinion

This *Parable of the Pharisee and the Tax Collector* is about repentance and humility. There were two men, one was self-righteous and the other was humble. Both men were in the same religious system, praying in the temple. The Pharisee seemed to be very self-assured, (righteous in his own eyes) when he prayed to God with a prideful arrogance. He thought he had nothing to worry about. He had a poor opinion of the tax collector because of his lower social standing in the community. The tax collector had the same opinion of himself as the Pharisee, one of remorse and self-contempt. Please note; the tax collector was repentant and prayed to God in reverent fear and humility. Please *"God, be merciful to me, the sinner!"* The story ends with the repentant tax collector being forgiven and included in the family of God. Sadly, the self-righteous Pharisee went on his way, happily not knowing that he was in jeopardy. Also, the people within the religious community had no understanding as to how God viewed the two men. God's perspective is much different than man's perspective. God shows mercy on those that fear Him. True repentance, reverent fear and humility are attributes that please God. Today we see a church divided because of denominational pride and arrogance that encourages contempt for other denominations that differs from their understanding.

Luke 15: 7

> 7 I tell you that even so there will be more joy in heaven over one sinner who repents, than over ninety-nine righteous people who need no repentance.

Acts 2: 38

> 38 Peter said to them, "Repent, and be baptized, every one of you, in the name of Jesus Christ for the forgiveness of sins, and you will receive the gift of the Holy Spirit.

1 Peter 5: 5

> 5 Likewise, you younger ones, be subject to the elder. Yes, all of you clothe yourselves with humility, to subject yourselves to one another; for "God resists the proud, but gives grace to the humble."

The Parable of the Wheat and Tares

Matthew 13: 24-30 (NASB)

24 Jesus presented another parable to them, saying, "The kingdom of heaven may be compared to a man who sowed good seed in his field. 25 But while his men were sleeping, his enemy came and sowed tares among the wheat, and went away. 26 But when the wheat sprouted and bore grain, then the tares became evident also. 27 The slaves of the landowner came and said to him, 'Sir, did you not sow good seed in your field? How then does it have tares?' 28 And he said to them, 'An enemy has done this!' The slaves *said to him, 'Do you want us, then, to go and gather them up?' 29 But he *said, 'No; for while you are gathering up the tares, you may uproot the wheat with them. 30 Allow both to grow together until the harvest; and in the time of the harvest I will say to the reapers, "First gather up the tares and bind them in bundles to burn them up; but gather the wheat into my barn.

Matthew 13: 37-43 (NASB)

37 And He said, "The one who sows the good seed is the Son of Man, 38 and the field is the world; and as for the good seed, these are the sons of the kingdom; and the tares are the sons of the evil one; 39 and the enemy who sowed them is the devil, and the harvest is the end of the age; and the reapers are angels. 40 So just as the tares are gathered up and burned with fire, so shall it be at the end of the age. 41 The Son of Man will send forth His angels, and they will gather out of His kingdom all stumbling blocks, and those who commit lawlessness, 42 and will throw them into the furnace of fire; in that place there will be weeping and gnashing of teeth. 43 Then the righteous will shine forth as the sun in the kingdom of their Father. He who has ears, let him hear.

Author's Opinion

The *Parable of the Wheat and Tares* is about God's gift of Grace to His believers and warns us not to exceed our authority as servants by trying to uproot unbelievers from within the church or the world. The servants (God's servants) asked the owner (God) if He had planted good seed (believers) in the fields (the world). We (God's servants) are told not to separate the tare (unbelievers) from the wheat (believers). The enemy is Satan. Within the kingdom of Heaven here on Earth (within the world and the Church) there are both good and evil spirits at work. God sees the heart and knows who belongs to Him. Judgment is to be left up to God. The tares (the unrepentant) will be gathered up by His angels and burned at the same time the wheat is being gathered up into Heaven's glory. We see the anxiety of servants when identifying the tares that Satan (the enemy) has been planting amongst believers, but the servants are told not to uproot them. By uprooting the tares, some of the wheat may also be uprooted from His kingdom. Christ Jesus is the sower of the good seed (the Word, God's plan of salvation) and the field is the world. The wheat represents God's chosen believers and the tares or weeds are the unsaved sons and daughters of Satan.

When things seem not as they should be, do not loose heart. The Child of God believes with blind faith that God is in control and that all good things come from God even if we cannot see them. Jesus clearly said; "If we lose faith and deny Christ in this world He will deny us before the Father in the age to come." There will be no excuses or exceptions for any of us. There is within every church organization or society both good and the not so good. Jesus was not pleased with the leaders in the temple when He pointed out the widow putting all she had into the temple treasury *(Luke 21: 1-4)*. She was worshiping God in the most meaningful way she could. It is wrong to paint everyone in an organization with the same paintbrush or show contempt for them. We should not judge or label any one of a different tradition or doctrine as unacceptable to God. Clearly it is not for us to say. Separating the wheat from the tares goes too far and may do untold damage in places that were never intended. So we know the spirit of the wicked one is sowing the hypocrisy of denying the validity of scripture, while claiming to be religious. This is a real problem within our churches today. Satan, the enemy, will always be with us and his influence, and resultant lack of unity both inside and outside the church, has caused great stress and confusion for believers. The question that Christians have been asking for centuries is, "How far is too far? How hard do we push back and what are the limits? How do we deal with this inconsistency within the church and glorify Christ to the world around us?"

    The church's inconsistent teachings are not without wrinkle and not without controversy. Both the Orthodox and Unorthodox camps are often blind to their own errors because of pride. Problems or criticisms found in one camp can also be found in the other camp. That is because both sides of this church division are made up of fallible people. We all fall short of the glory of God. When the church does not practice what it preaches, unbelievers see and are quick to point out our hypocrisy, foolishness and sham.

    This we do know from *2 Timothy 3: 16-17* [16]*Every Scripture is God-breathed and profitable for teaching, for reproof, for correction, and for instruction in righteousness,* [17]*that the man of God may be complete, thoroughly equipped for every good work.* So the differences between orthodox and unorthodox should be recognized. Orthodoxy holds exclusively to the Scriptures; non-orthodox doctrine does not limit itself to belief in Scripture exclusively, and the nonbelieving world around us holds very little value in the Scriptures at all.

1 John 5: 9-11

9 If we receive the witness of men, the witness of God is greater; for this is God's testimony which he has testified concerning his Son. 10 He who believes in the Son of God has the testimony in himself. He who doesn't believe God has made him a liar, because he has not believed in the testimony that God has given concerning his Son. 11 The testimony is this, that God gave to us eternal life, and this life is in his Son.

Titus 1: 7-11

7 For the overseer must be blameless, as God's steward; not self-pleasing, not easily angered, not given to wine, not violent, not greedy for dishonest gain; 8 but given to hospitality, a lover of good, sober minded, fair, holy, self-controlled; 9 holding to the faithful word which is according to the teaching, that he may be able to exhort in the sound doctrine, and to convict those who contradict him. 10 For there are also many unruly men, vain talkers and deceivers, especially those of the circumcision, 11 whose mouths must be stopped; men who overthrow whole houses, teaching things which they ought not, for dishonest gain's sake

If we are to adhere to a straight and narrow path, we are limited to a disciplined civil discussion. We should witness tenderly and humbly, handling accurately, God's word of truth. If we do this, we cannot go wrong in the sight of God. We are to be bold in God's Spirit and meek in our own spirit. Doing this in a loving manner brings glory to the Lord. We are to be faithful witnesses to both believers and nonbelievers inside or outside the church. Saying nothing at all or going to the other extreme and extending professional courtesy that lends legitimacy to individuals who oppose the scriptures seems a wrong approach. Our contrasting witness that supports orthodox belief in the truth of Scripture is our way of fulfilling the Great Commission. We should continue in making disciples, teaching them to observe Jesus' commandments. It will be enough for others to see clearly and judge for themselves the gravity of the issues being discussed. Our part is to be a faithful witness. The Holy Spirit will convict and bring the saving knowledge of Jesus to whomever He chooses. The power is in Jesus' words of truth. Appearing judgmental will offend people, making them defensive. We must know and honor that God has given man a free choice to either harden their heart to his word, or not. Often unbeknownst to themselves or anyone else, a person's personal choice can separate them from God's salvation plan. They simply cannot muster the ability to believe. We can and should be diligent to witness accurately to the Scriptures. But we are prohibited from publicly uprooting or discrediting an individual or group of people inside or outside the church, as shown in the Parable of the Wheat and the Tares.

Luke 21: 1-4

> 1 He looked up, and saw the rich people who were putting their gifts into the treasury. 2 He saw a certain poor widow casting in two small brass coins. 3 He said, "Truly I tell you, this poor widow put in more than all of them, 4 for all these put in gifts for God from their abundance, but she, out of her poverty, put in all that she had to live on."

John 12: 37-43

> 37 But though he had done so many signs before them, yet they didn't believe in him, 38 that the word of Isaiah the prophet might be fulfilled, which he spoke, "Lord, who has believed our report? To whom has the arm of the Lord been revealed?" 39 For this cause they couldn't believe, for Isaiah said again, 40 "He has blinded their eyes and he hardened their heart, lest they should see with their eyes, and perceive with their heart, and would turn, and I would heal them." 41 Isaiah said these things when he saw his glory, and spoke of him.

42 Nevertheless even of the rulers many believed in him, but because of the Pharisees they didn't confess it, so that they wouldn't be put out of the synagogue, 43 for they loved men's praise more than God's praise.

Isaiah 28; 16-17 (NASB)

16 Therefore thus says the Lord God, "Behold, I am laying in Zion a stone, a tested stone, A costly cornerstone for the foundation, firmly placed. He who believes in it will not be disturbed. 17 "I will make justice the measuring line And righteousness the level; Then hail will sweep away the refuge of lies And the waters will overflow the secret place.

Hebrews 4: 1-3

1 Let us fear therefore, lest perhaps anyone of you should seem to have come short of a promise of entering into his rest. 2 For indeed we have had good news preached to us, even as they also did, but the word they heard didn't profit them, because it wasn't mixed with faith by those who heard. 3 For we who have believed do enter into that rest, even as he has said, "As I swore in my wrath, they will not enter into my rest"; although the works were finished from the foundation of the world.

Matthew 7: 21-23

21 Not everyone who says to me, 'Lord, Lord,' will enter into the Kingdom of Heaven; but he who does the will of my Father who is in heaven. 22 Many will tell me in that day, 'Lord, Lord, didn't we prophesy in your name, in your name cast out demons, and in your name do many mighty works?' 23 Then I will tell them, 'I never knew you. Depart from me, you who work iniquity.'

Matthew 10: 33

33 But whoever denies me before men, him I will also deny before my Father who is in heaven.

Isaiah 55: 11

11 so is my word that goes out of my mouth: it will not return to me void, but it will accomplish that which I please, and it will prosper in the thing I sent it to do.

John 14: 23-24

23 Jesus answered him, "If a man loves me, he will keep my word. My Father will love him, and we will come to him, and make our home with him. 24 He who doesn't love me doesn't keep my words. The word which you hear isn't mine, but the Father's who sent me

John 17: 15-17

15 I pray not that you would take them from the world, but that you would keep them from the evil one. 16 They are not of the world even as I am not of the world. 17 Sanctify them in your truth. Your word is truth.

Philippians 2: 14-16

14 Do all things without murmurings and disputes, 15 that you may become blameless and harmless, children of God without defect in the middle of a crooked and perverse generation, among whom you are seen as lights in the world, 16 holding up the word of life; that I may have something to boast in the day of Christ, that I didn't run in vain nor labor in vain.

1 Peter 1: 22-23

22 Seeing you have purified your souls in your obedience to the truth through the Spirit in sincere brotherly affection, love one another from the heart fervently: 23 having been born again, not of corruptible seed, but of incorruptible, through the word of God, which lives and remains forever.

1 John 3: 18-21

18 My little children, let's not love in word only, or with the tongue

only, but in deed and truth. 19 And by this we know that we are of the truth, and persuade our hearts before him, 20 because if our heart condemns us, God is greater than our heart, and knows all things. 21 Beloved, if our hearts don't condemn us, we have boldness toward God;

Luke 6: 46-49

46 "But why do you call Me 'Lord, Lord,' and not do the things which I say? 47 Whoever comes to Me, and hears My sayings and does them, I will show you whom he is like: 48 He is like a man building a house, who dug deep and laid the foundation on the rock. And when the flood arose, the stream beat vehemently against that house, and could not shake it, for it was founded on the rock. 49 But he who heard and did nothing is like a man who built a house on the earth without a foundation, against which the stream beat vehemently; and immediately it fell. And the ruin of that house was great."

James 1: 22-25

22 But be doers of the word, and not hearers only, deceiving yourselves. 23 For if anyone is a hearer of the word and not a doer, he is like a man observing his natural face in a mirror; 24 for he observes himself, goes away, and immediately forgets what kind of man he was. 25 But he who looks into the perfect law of liberty and continues in it, and is not a forgetful hearer but a doer of the work, this one will be blessed in what he does.

The Parable of the Faithful Servant

Luke 12: 42-48

42 The Lord said, "Who then is the faithful and wise steward, whom his lord will set over his household, to give them their portion of food at the right times? 43 Blessed is that servant whom his lord will find doing so when he comes. 44 Truly I tell you, that he will set

him over all that he has. 45 But if that servant says in his heart, 'My lord delays his coming,' and begins to beat the menservants and the maidservants, and to eat and drink, and to be drunken, 46 then the lord of that servant will come in a day when he isn't expecting him, and in an hour that he doesn't know, and will cut him in two, and place his portion with the unfaithful. 47 That servant, who knew his lord's will, and didn't prepare, nor do what he wanted, will be beaten with many stripes, 48 but he who didn't know, and did things worthy of stripes, will be beaten with few stripes. To whomever much is given, of him will much be required; and to whom much was entrusted, of him more will be asked.

Author's Opinion

The *Parable of the Faithful Servants* is about our accountability. We all, but especially leaders, are to be faithful Christians.

Some churches have grown large and impersonal, forgetting their purpose, which is to make disciples for Christ. Today too many image sensitive leaders are avoiding messages and Bible passages that have a convicting tone. Alter calls seem to be a thing of the past and are considered old fashioned. Sincere and talented professional clergy are delivering fine intellectual sermons. Congregations are always learning, but are not being asked to come to a point of commitment. In every church there are individuals that are hurting for different reasons. It may be a personal need, health issue, unhealthy addiction and/or animosity that needs to be surrendered to the Lord. Churches sometimes lose their vision by closing the sermon with a prayer and asking then to come back next week, for business as usual. Both the pillars of the church and the lost sheep, that happens to wander in, need to hear the message and come to the threshold when Jesus is knocking at their door. They often pray that the Holy Spirit will speak to peoples' hearts but seldom given the people a time when they can reflect or respond to the message. Jesus saves and rejuvenates when we humble ourselves and plead for mercy. The time of silent prayer when heads are bowed and eyes are closed is the congregation's time of reflection, a time of personal soul searching circumspection between the individual and the Lord. Our relationship with the Lord is personal, a one to one relationship. Old and new believers need the cleansing intimacy of confessing their sins, submitting every day in reverent fear to His authority in our life.

Psalms 4: 5 (NASB)

> 5 Offer the sacrifices of righteousness, And trust in the Lord.

1 John 3: 16

> 16 By this we know love, because he laid down his life for us. And we ought to lay down our lives for the brothers.

God is Spirit. Servants who are put in charge of feeding the flock must believe and trust the indwelling power of the Holy Spirit for strength and guidance to adhere faithfully to the Master's instruction.

Romans 8: 9-11

> 9 But you are not in the flesh but in the Spirit, if it is so that the Spirit of God dwells in you. But if any man doesn't have the Spirit of Christ, he is not his. 10 If Christ is in you, the body is dead because of sin, but the spirit is alive because of righteousness. 11 But if the Spirit of him who raised up Jesus from the dead dwells in you, he who raised up Christ Jesus from the dead will also give life to your mortal bodies through his Spirit who dwells in you.

The faithful servants (Clergy, elders, deacons, Sunday school teachers and believers) must not modify the old and new treasure of wisdom (the Bible) that comes out of the kingdom storehouse. If and when the Master comes back unexpectedly and finds the servants complacent and unproductive about their duties and/or is found feeding His sheep theological garbage, the servant will be excluded from the household and receive severe punishment. The degree of severity of punishment speaks to the Master's fairness of executing judgment. See Matthew 5: 19-20. If the Master finds the servant has performed his duties faithfully, the servant's reward will be great. The greater the responsibility given to the servant will necessitate a greater requirement for the servant to meet and exceed expectations.

1 Timothy 6: 12

> 12 Fight the good fight of faith. Take hold of the eternal life to which you were called, and you confessed the good confession in the sight of many witnesses.

2 Timothy 2: 14-16

> 14 Remind them of these things, charging them in the sight of the Lord, that they don't argue about words, to no profit, to the subverting of those who hear. 15 Give diligence to present yourself approved by God, a workman who doesn't need to be ashamed, properly handling the Word of Truth. 16 But shun empty chatter, for it will go further in ungodliness,

Romans 13: 8-10

> 8 Owe no one anything, except to love one another; for he who loves his neighbor has fulfilled the law. 9 For the commandments, "You shall not commit adultery," "You shall not murder," "You shall not steal," "You shall not covet," and whatever other commandments there are, are all summed up in this saying, namely, "You shall love your neighbor as yourself." 10 Love doesn't harm a neighbor. Love therefore is the fulfillment of the law.

Colossians 3: 12-15

12 Put on therefore, as God's chosen ones, holy and beloved, a heart of compassion, kindness, lowliness, humility, and perseverance; 13 bearing with one another, and forgiving each other, if any man has a complaint against any; even as Christ forgave you, so you also do. 14 Above all these things, walk in love, which is the bond of perfection. 15 And let the peace of God rule in your hearts, to which also you were called in one body; and be thankful.

The parable of the Ten Virgins

Matthew 25: 1-13

1 "Then the Kingdom of Heaven will be like ten virgins, who took their lamps, and went out to meet the bridegroom. 2 Five of them were foolish, and five were wise. 3 Those who were foolish, when they took their lamps, took no oil with them, 4 but the wise took oil in their vessels with their lamps. 5 Now while the bridegroom delayed, they all slumbered and slept. 6 But at midnight there was a cry, 'Behold! The bridegroom is coming! Come out to meet him!' 7 Then all those virgins arose, and trimmed their lamps. 8 The foolish said to the wise, 'Give us some of your oil, for our lamps are going out.' 9 But the wise answered, saying, 'What if there isn't enough for us and you? You go rather to those who sell, and buy for yourselves.' 10 While they went away to buy, the bridegroom came, and those who were ready went in with him to the marriage feast, and the door was shut. 11 Afterward the other virgins also came, saying, 'Lord, Lord, open to us.' 12 But he answered, 'Most certainly I tell you, I don't know you.' 13 Watch therefore, for you don't know the day nor the hour in which the Son of Man is coming.

Author's Opinion

The *Parable of the Ten Virgins* refers to what will become of believing and unbelieving church members. Some people within the church are imposters who will not be permitted to pass into the heavenly wedding banquet. This is a description of ten people that claimed to be believers and belonged to the same (church) religious system. The outward signs of belief are represented by their possession of lamps. Five virgins had oil in their lamps. This oil represents the indwelling Holy Spirit of true believers. The five without oil were not true believers. The coming of the bridegroom represents Christ taking the true believers to be with Him in His glory. This Parable tells us that the coming of the bridegroom will take a long time. The wise virgins were true and diligent in their worship, without being self-righteous and unrepentant. The remaining foolish virgins came to realize after it was too late they would not be admitted because of their disbelief. This message is telling us to seek first a right relationship with the Lord today, for no one knows when it will be too late to repent and be included in His eternal wedding party. This also speaks to the fact that there is nothing hidden from God and to His fairness of judgment. God is Spirit; therefore, having the Holy Spirit in us is what makes us believers, faithful to Him all the days of our life.

Matthew 7: 21-23

> 21 Not everyone who says to me, 'Lord, Lord,' will enter into the Kingdom of Heaven; but he who does the will of my Father who is in heaven. 22 Many will tell me in that day, 'Lord, Lord, didn't we prophesy in your name, in your name cast out demons, and in your name do many mighty works?' 23 Then I will tell them, 'I never knew you. Depart from me, you who work iniquity.'

Hebrews 12: 28-29

28 Therefore, receiving a Kingdom that can't be shaken, let us have grace, through which we serve God acceptably, with reverence and awe, 29 for our God is a consuming fire.

Matthew 24: 36-44

36 But no one knows of that day and hour, not even the angels of heaven but my Father only. 37 "As the days of Noah were, so will be the coming of the Son of Man. 38 For as in those days which were before the flood they were eating and drinking, marrying and giving in marriage, until the day that Noah entered into the ship, 39 and they didn't know until the flood came, and took them all away, so will be the coming of the Son of Man. 40 Then two men will be in the field: one will be taken and one will be left. 41 Two women will be grinding at the mill: one will be taken and one will be left. 42 Watch therefore, for you don't know in what hour your Lord comes. 43 But know this, that if the master of the house had known in what watch of the night the thief was coming, he would have watched, and would not have allowed his house to be broken into. 44 Therefore also be ready, for in an hour that you don't expect, the Son of Man will come.

Chapter 5

> judgment; and I will be a swift witness against the sorcerers, and against the adulterers, ¹and against false swearers, and against those that ‖oppress the hireling in *his* wages, the widow, and the fatherless, and that turn aside the stranger *from his right*, and fear not me, saith the LORD of hosts.
>
> 6 For I *am* the LORD, ᵐI change not; ⁿtherefore ye sons of Jacob are not consumed.

Does God's Word need to change with the times?

Deuteronomy 32: 4

> 4 The Rock, his work is perfect, for all his ways are just. A God of faithfulness who does no wrong, just and right is he.

Isaiah 45: 19 (NASB)

> 19 "I have not spoken in secret, In some dark land; I did not say to the offspring of Jacob, 'Seek Me in a waste place'; I, the Lord, speak righteousness, Declaring things that are upright.

Isaiah 66: 5 (NASB)

> 5 Hear the word of the Lord, you who tremble at His word: "Your brothers who hate you, who exclude you for My name's sake, Have

said, 'Let the Lord be glorified, that we may see your joy.' But they will be put to shame.

Psalm 19: 7 (NASB)

7 The law of the Lord is perfect, restoring the soul;
The testimony of the Lord is sure, making wise the simple.

Psalm 12: 6 (NASB)

6 The words of the Lord are pure words;
As silver tried in a furnace on the earth, refined seven times.

Psalm 40: 4 (NASB)

4 How blessed is the man who has made the Lord his trust, And has not turned to the proud, nor to those who lapse into falsehood.

John 1: 1-5

1 In the beginning was the Word, and the Word was with God, and the Word was God. 2 The same was in the beginning with God. 3 All things were made through him. Without him was not anything made that has been made. 4 In him was life, and the life was the light of men. 5 The light shines in the darkness, and the darkness hasn't overcome it.

Hebrews 13: 7-9

7 Remember your leaders, men who spoke to you the word of God, and considering the results of their conduct, imitate their faith. 8 Jesus Christ is the same yesterday, today, and forever. 9 Don't be carried away by various and strange teachings, for it is good that the heart be established by grace, not by food, through which those who were so occupied were not benefited.

2 Timothy 2: 15

15 Give diligence to present yourself approved by God, a workman who doesn't need to be ashamed, properly handling the Word of Truth.

1 Peter 1: 25

25 but the Lord's word endures forever." This is the word of Good News which was preached to you.

1 John 2: 15-17

15 Don't love the world or the things that are in the world. If anyone loves the world, the Father's love isn't in him. 16 For all that is in the world, the lust of the flesh, the lust of the eyes, and the pride of life, isn't the Father's, but is the world's. 17 The world is passing away with its lusts, but he who does God's will remains forever.

Matthew 5: 18-19

18 For most certainly, I tell you, until heaven and earth pass away, not even one smallest letter or one tiny pen stroke shall in any way pass away from the law, until all things are accomplished. 19 Whoever, therefore, shall break one of these least commandments, and teach others to do so, shall be called least in the Kingdom of Heaven; but whoever shall do and teach them shall be called great in the Kingdom of Heaven.

Jude 1: 17-19

17 But you, beloved, remember the words which have been spoken before by the apostles of our Lord Jesus Christ. 18 They said to you that "In the last time there will be mockers, walking after their own ungodly lusts." 19 These are they who cause divisions, and are sensual, not having the Spirit.

Acts 20: 26-28

26 Therefore I testify to you today that I am clean from the blood of all men, 27 for I didn't shrink from declaring to you the whole counsel of God. 28 Take heed, therefore, to yourselves, and to all the flock, in which the Holy Spirit has made you overseers, to shepherd the assembly of the Lord and God which he purchased with his own blood.

Revelation 22: 18-19

> 18 I testify to everyone who hears the words of the prophecy of this book, if anyone adds to them, may God add to him the plagues which are written in this book. 19 If anyone takes away from the words of the book of this prophecy, may God take away his part from the tree of life, and out of the holy city, which are written in this book.

Author's Opinion

God's Word is timeless. God has no beginning and no end. God has no equal. He has no limits. Expecting God to change to accommodate man is short-sighted and foolish and reveals a kind of self-centered contempt for God. How much respect would man have for any god that was not light years more intelligent and powerful than man? Even the mysteries of God give us hope, whereas history shows us that man's self-centered, ever-changing reasoning is small and pathetic in comparison to the wisdom of God's Holy Word.

Job 32: 8

> 8 But there is a spirit in man, and the breath of the Almighty gives them understanding.

If one takes the time to read the Scriptures, it becomes evident that all the issues that concerned man when the Bible was written are still relevant today. I know of no other book that you can say that about. Man's narrow-minded reasoning tries to discredit the Scriptures, to justify their unbelief.

Romans 8: 7

> 7 because the mind of the flesh is hostile towards God; for it is not subject to God's law, neither indeed can it be.

While God's perspective is all-inclusive. Man's perspective is limited by time, space and personal interest. God is in control. Man's intellect or reason cannot change anything that God has created or set in motion.

Isaiah 9: 6-7

> 6 For a child will be born to us, a son will be given to us; And the government will rest on His shoulders; And His name will be called Wonderful Counselor, Mighty God, Eternal Father, Prince of Peace. 7 There will be no end to the increase of *His* government or of peace, On the throne of David and over his kingdom, To establish it and to uphold it with justice and righteousness From then on and forevermore. The zeal of the Lord of hosts will accomplish this.

The empowerment of the individual is so engrained into us that we forget that Christianity is not a Democracy or Representative type of Government. It is a Theocracy. God's authority in our lives is like God himself; there are no limits if we let him into our hearts. Jesus humbled himself on the cross, for man's sin debt and our reconciliation to our Holy Father in Heaven. The question, "Will God's Word change to suit man?" is foolish; the question should be: "Will man submit to God's authority and glorify Jesus during our limited time on earth?"

Jeremiah 9: 23 (NASB)

> 23 Thus says the Lord, "Let not a wise man boast of his wisdom, and let not the mighty man boast of his might, let not a rich man boast of his riches;

Hebrews 4: 12-13

> 12 For the word of God is living and active, and sharper than any two-edged sword, piercing even to the dividing of soul and spirit, of both joints and marrow, and is able to discern the thoughts and intentions of the heart. 13 There is no creature that is hidden from his sight, but all things are naked and laid open before the eyes of him to whom we must give an account.

1 Corinthians 1: 27-31

27 but God chose the foolish things of the world that he might put to shame those who are wise. God chose the weak things of the world, that he might put to shame the things that are strong; 28 and God chose the lowly things of the world, and the things that are despised, and the things that are not, that he might bring to nothing the things that are: 29 that no flesh should boast before God. 30 Because of him, you are in Christ Jesus, who was made to us wisdom from God, and righteousness and sanctification, and redemption: 31 that, according as it is written, "He who boasts, let him boast in the Lord."

2 Peter 3: 1-7

1 This is now, beloved, the second letter that I have written to you; and in both of them I stir up your sincere mind by reminding you; 2 that you should remember the words which were spoken before by the holy prophets, and the commandment of us, the apostles of the Lord and Savior: 3 knowing this first, that in the last days mockers will come, walking after their own lusts, 4 and saying, "Where is the promise of his coming? For, from the day that the fathers fell asleep, all things continue as they were from the beginning of the creation." 5 For this they willfully forget, that there were heavens from of old, and an earth formed out of water and amid water, by the word of God; 6 by which means the world that then was, being overflowed with water, perished. 7 But the heavens that now exist, and the earth, by the same word have been stored up for fire, being reserved against the day of judgment and destruction of ungodly men.

Paradoxes to be examined

Eternal Life

Mark 10: 29-30

29 Jesus said, "Most certainly I tell you, there is no one who has left house, or brothers, or sisters, or father, or mother, or wife, or children, or land, for my sake, and for the sake of the Good News, 30 but he will receive one hundred times more now in this time, houses, brothers, sisters, mothers, children, and land, with persecutions; and in the age to come eternal life

John 10: 27-30

27 My sheep hear my voice, and I know them, and they follow me. 28 I give eternal life to them. They will never perish, and no one will snatch them out of my hand. 29 My Father, who has given them to me, is greater than all. No one is able to snatch them out of my Father's hand. 30 I and the Father are one."

John 17: 1-3

1 Jesus said these things, and lifting up his eyes to heaven, he said, "Father, the time has come. Glorify your Son, that your Son may also glorify you; 2 even as you gave him authority over all flesh, so he will give eternal life to all whom you have given him. 3 This is eternal life, that they should know you, the only true God, and him whom you sent, Jesus Christ.

2 Corinthians 4: 18

18 while we don't look at the things which are seen, but at the things which are not seen. For the things which are seen are temporal, but the things which are not seen are eternal.

Titus 1: 1-3

1 Paul, a servant of God, and an apostle of Jesus Christ, according to the faith of God's chosen ones, and the knowledge of the truth which is according to godliness, 2 in hope of eternal life, which God, who can't lie, promised before time began; 3 but in his own time revealed his word in the message with which I was entrusted according to the commandment of God our Savior;

1 John 5: 11-13

11 The testimony is this, that God gave to us eternal life, and this life is in his Son. 12 He who has the Son has the life. He who doesn't have God's Son doesn't have the life. 13 These things I have written to you who believe in the name of the Son of God, that you may know that you have eternal life, and that you may continue to believe in the name of the Son of God.

1 John 5: 20

20 We know that the Son of God has come, and has given us an understanding, that we know him who is true, and we are in him who is true, in his Son Jesus Christ. This is the true God, and eternal life.

Jude 1: 20-21

20 But you, beloved, keep building up yourselves on your most holy faith, praying in the Holy Spirit. 21 Keep yourselves in God's love, looking for the mercy of our Lord Jesus Christ to eternal life.

Fairness of God's Law

Ezekiel 33: 12-20

12 "You, son of man, tell the children of your people, 'The righteousness of the righteous will not deliver him in the day of his disobedience. And as for the wickedness of the wicked, he will not fall thereby in the day that he turns from his wickedness; neither will he who is righteous be able to live by it in the day that he sins. 13 When I tell the righteous that he will surely live; if he trusts in his righteousness, and commits iniquity, none of his righteous deeds will be remembered; but he will die in his iniquity that he has committed. 14 Again, when I say to the wicked, "You will surely die;" if he turns from his sin, and does that which is lawful and right; 15 if the wicked restore the pledge, give again that which he had taken by robbery, walk in the statutes of life, committing no iniquity; he will surely live.

He will not die. 16 None of his sins that he has committed will be remembered against him. He has done that which is lawful and right. He will surely live. 17 "'Yet the children of your people say, "The way of the Lord is not fair;" but as for them, their way is not fair. 18 When the righteous turns from his righteousness, and commits iniquity, he will even die therein. 19 When the wicked turns from his wickedness, and does that which is lawful and right, he will live thereby. 20 Yet you say, "The way of the Lord is not fair." House of Israel, I will judge every one of you after his ways.'"

Romans 3: 9-24

9 What then? Are we better than they? No, in no way. For we previously warned both Jews and Greeks, that they are all under sin. 10 As it is written, "There is no one righteous; no, not one. 11 There is no one who understands. There is no one who seeks after God. 12 They have all turned away. They have together become unprofitable. There is no one who does good, no, not so much as one." 13 "Their throat is an open tomb. With their tongues they have used deceit." "The poison of vipers is under their lips"; 14 "whose mouth is full of cursing and bitterness." 15 "Their feet are swift to shed blood. 16 Destruction and misery are in their ways. 17 The way of peace, they haven't known." 18 "There is no fear of God before their eyes." 19 Now we know that whatever things the law says, it speaks to those who are under the law, that every mouth may be closed, and all the world may be brought under the judgment of God. 20 Because by the works of the law, no flesh will be justified in his sight. For through the law comes the knowledge of sin. 21 But now apart from the law, a righteousness of God has been revealed, being testified by the law and the prophets; 22 even the righteousness of God through faith in Jesus Christ to all and on all those who believe. For there is no distinction, 23 for all have sinned, and fall short of the glory of God; 24 being justified freely by his grace through the redemption that is in Christ Jesus;

Romans 7: 7-12

7 What shall we say then? Is the law sin? May it never be! However, I wouldn't have known sin, except through the law. For I wouldn't have known coveting, unless the law had said, "You shall not covet." 8 But sin, finding occasion through the commandment, produced in me all kinds of coveting. For apart from the law, sin is dead. 9 I was alive apart from the law once, but when the commandment came, sin revived, and I died. 10 The commandment, which was for life, this I found to be for death; 11 for sin, finding occasion through the commandment, deceived me, and through it killed me. 12 Therefore the law indeed is holy, and the commandment holy, and righteous, and good.

Galatians 3: 10-14

10 For as many as are of the works of the law are under a curse. For it is written, "Cursed is everyone who doesn't continue in all things that are written in the book of the law, to do them." 11 Now that no man is justified by the law before God is evident, for, "The righteous will live by faith." 12 The law is not of faith, but, "The man who does them will live by them." 13 Christ redeemed us from the curse of the law, having become a curse for us. For it is written, "Cursed is everyone who hangs on a tree," 14 that the blessing of Abraham might come on the Gentiles through Christ Jesus; that we might receive the promise of the Spirit through faith.

Galatians 3: 23-24

23 But before faith came, we were kept in custody under the law, confined for the faith which should afterwards be revealed. 24 So that the law has become our tutor to bring us to Christ, that we might be justified by faith.

Resurrection

Psalm 16: 9-11

9 Therefore my heart is glad, and my tongue rejoices. My body shall also dwell in safety. 10 For you will not leave my soul in Sheol, neither will you allow your holy one to see corruption. 11 You will show me the path of life. In your presence is fullness of joy. In your right hand there are pleasures forever more.

Matthew 20: 18-19

18 "Behold, we are going up to Jerusalem, and the Son of Man will be delivered to the chief priests and scribes, and they will condemn him to death, 19 and will hand him over to the Gentiles to mock, to scourge, and to crucify; and the third day he will be raised up."

Matthew 28: 1-20

1 Now after the Sabbath, as it began to dawn on the first day of the week, Mary Magdalene and the other Mary came to see the tomb. 2 Behold, there was a great earthquake, for an angel of the Lord descended from the sky, and came and rolled away the stone from the door, and sat on it. 3 His appearance was like lightning, and his clothing white as snow. 4 For fear of him, the guards shook, and became like dead men. 5 The angel answered the women, "Don't be afraid, for I know that you seek Jesus, who has been crucified. 6 He is not here, for he has risen, just like he said. Come, see the place where the Lord was lying. 7 Go quickly and tell his disciples, 'He has risen from the dead, and behold, he goes before you into Galilee; there you will see him.' Behold, I have told you." 8 They departed quickly from the tomb with fear and great joy, and ran to bring his disciples word. 9 As they went to tell his disciples, behold, Jesus met them, saying, "Rejoice!" They came and took hold of his feet, and worshiped him. 10 Then Jesus said to them, "Don't be afraid. Go tell my brothers that they should go into Galilee, and

there they will see me." 11 Now while they were going, behold, some of the guards came into the city, and told the chief priests all the things that had happened. 12 When they were assembled with the elders, and had taken counsel, they gave a large amount of silver to the soldiers, 13 saying, "Say that his disciples came by night, and stole him away while we slept. 14 If this comes to the governor's ears, we will persuade him and make you free of worry." 15 So they took the money and did as they were told. This saying was spread abroad among the Jews, and continues until today. 16 But the eleven disciples went into Galilee, to the mountain where Jesus had sent them. 17 When they saw him, they bowed down to him, but some doubted. 18 Jesus came to them and spoke to them, saying, "All authority has been given to me in heaven and on earth. 19 Go and make disciples of all nations, baptizing them in the name of the Father and of the Son and of the Holy Spirit, 20 teaching them to observe all things that I commanded you. Behold, I am with you always, even to the end of the age." Amen.

John 5: 28-29

28 Don't marvel at this, for the hour comes, in which all that are in the tombs will hear his voice, 29 and will come out; those who have done good, to the resurrection of life; and those who have done evil, to the resurrection of judgment.

John 12: 25-26

25 He who loves his life will lose it. He who hates his life in this world will keep it to eternal life. 26 If anyone serves me, let him follow me. Where I am, there will my servant also be. If anyone serves me, the Father will honor him.

Luke 24: 5-6

5 They said to them, "Why do you seek the living among the dead? 6 He isn't here, but is risen. Remember what he told you when he was still in Galilee,

Acts 1: 2-4

> 2 until the day in which he was received up, after he had given commandment through the Holy Spirit to the apostles whom he had chosen. 3 To these he also showed himself alive after he suffered, by many proofs, appearing to them over a period of forty days, and speaking about God's Kingdom. 4 Being assembled together with them, he commanded them, "Don't depart from Jerusalem, but wait for the promise of the Father, which you heard from me.

Romans 6: 3-5

> 3 Or don't you know that all we who were baptized into Christ Jesus were baptized into his death? 4 We were buried therefore with him through baptism into death, that just as Christ was raised from the dead through the glory of the Father, so we also might walk in newness of life. 5 For if we have become united with him in the likeness of his death, we will also be part of his resurrection;

1 Peter 1: 19-21

> 19 but with precious blood, as of a lamb without blemish or spot, the blood of Christ; 20 who was foreknown indeed before the foundation of the world, but was revealed in this last age for your sake, 21 who through him are believers in God, who raised him from the dead, and gave him glory; so that your faith and hope might be in God.

Parables to be grasped

The Parable of the householder

Matthew 13: 51- 52

> 51 Jesus said to them, "Have you understood all these things?" They answered him, "Yes, Lord." 52 He said to them, "Therefore every scribe who has been made a disciple in the Kingdom of Heaven is like a man who is a householder, who brings out of his treasure new and old things."

Author's Opinion

The *Parable of the Householder* is about teaching and witnessing from the Bible, God's timeless and unchanging wisdom to others. Believers that are knowledgeable about Scriptures are to speak out and witness to neighbors concerning the New and Old Testament of the Bible.

1 Peter 3: 15

> 15 But sanctify the Lord God in your hearts; and always be ready to give an answer to everyone who asks you a reason concerning the hope that is in you, with humility and fear:

There are many unseen mysteries in the Scriptures that people need to recognize. The more we know about God's Love and Grace, the greater responsibility we have to witness to others. That is what is meant by letting our light shine for the glory of our Father in Heaven.

1 Corinthians 2: 6-8

> 6 We speak wisdom, however, among those who are full grown; yet a wisdom not of this world, nor of the rulers of this world, who are coming to nothing. 7 But we speak God's wisdom in a mystery, the wisdom that has been hidden, which God foreordained before the worlds for our glory, 8 which none of the rulers of this world has known. For had they known it, they wouldn't have crucified the Lord of glory.

Matthew 24: 14

> 14 And this gospel of the kingdom will be preached in the whole world as a testimony to all nations, and then the end will come.

Parable of the foolish man who builds his house on the sand

Matthew 7: 24-27

> 24 "Everyone therefore who hears these words of mine, and does them, I will liken him to a wise man, who built his house on a rock. 25 The rain came down, the floods came, and the winds blew, and beat on that house; and it didn't fall, for it was founded on the rock. 26 Everyone who hears these words of mine, and doesn't do them will be like a foolish man, who built his house on the sand. 27 The rain came down, the floods came, and the winds blew, and beat on that house; and it fell—and great was its fall."

Author's Opinion

The *Parable of the Foolish Man who Builds his House on the Sand* is about making choices and the eventual accountability that comes with bad choices. When a man hears the Gospel and does not strive to please God by obeying His commandments, there are consequences. It is likened to a man building a house the fast and easy way on sand. They are disregarding the precepts from Jesus' words of truth. These foolish and bad choices will eventually lead to the wrath of Hell, a dreadful place of no return. This is describing foolish people who are building their hopes on getting to Heaven by relying on their own reason and righteousness. People who build their lives on the stability of the rock are safe, holding fast to the Rock of our salvation. Jesus is the rock.

Proverbs 10: 25 (NASB)

> 25 When the whirlwind passes, the wicked is no more, but the righteous has an everlasting foundation.

Matthew 7: 13-14

13 "Enter in by the narrow gate; for wide is the gate and broad is the way that leads to destruction, and many are those who enter in by it. 14 How narrow is the gate, and restricted is the way that leads to life! Few are those who find it.

Proverbs 14: 12

12 There is a way which seems right to a man, but in the end it leads to death.

Psalm 62: 7

7 With God is my salvation and my honor. The rock of my strength, and my refuge, is in God.

Psalm 18: 2 (NASB)

2 The Lord is my rock and my fortress and my deliverer, My God, my rock, in whom I take refuge; My shield and the horn of my salvation, my stronghold.

Proverbs 3: 5-6 (NASB)

5 Trust in the Lord with all your heart And do not lean on your own understanding. 6 In all your ways acknowledge Him, And He will make your paths straight.

John 6: 35-40

35 Jesus said to them, "I am the bread of life. He who comes to me will not be hungry, and he who believes in me will never be thirsty. 36 But I told you that you have seen me, and yet you don't believe. 37 All those whom the Father gives me will come to me. He who comes to me I will in no way throw out. 38 For I have come down from heaven, not to do my own will, but the will of him who sent me. 39 This is the will of my Father who sent me, that of all he has given to me I should lose nothing, but should raise him up at the last day. 40 This is the will of the one who sent me, that everyone who sees

the Son, and believes in him, should have eternal life; and I will raise him up at the last day."

1 Corinthians 1: 18-28

18 For the word of the cross is foolishness to those who are dying, but to us who are saved it is the power of God. 19 For it is written, "I will destroy the wisdom of the wise, I will bring the discernment of the discerning to nothing." 20 Where is the wise? Where is the scribe? Where is the lawyer of this world? Hasn't God made foolish the wisdom of this world? 21 For seeing that in the wisdom of God, the world through its wisdom didn't know God, it was God's good pleasure through the foolishness of the preaching to save those who believe. 22 For Jews ask for signs, Greeks seek after wisdom, 23 but we preach Christ crucified; a stumbling block to Jews, and foolishness to Greeks, 24 but to those who are called, both Jews and Greeks, Christ is the power of God and the wisdom of God. 25 Because the foolishness of God is wiser than men, and the weakness of God is stronger than men. 26 For you see your calling, brothers, that not many are wise according to the flesh, not many mighty, and not many noble; 27 but God chose the foolish things of the world that he might put to shame those who are wise. God chose the weak things of the world, that he might put to shame the things that are strong; 28 and God chose the lowly things of the world, and the things that are despised, and the things that are not, that he might bring to nothing the things that are:

Galatians 3: 22 (NASB)

22 But the Scripture has shut up]everyone under sin, so that the promise by faith in Jesus Christ might be given to those who believe.

Hebrews 11: 1-3

1 Now faith is assurance of things hoped for, proof of things not seen. 2 For by this, the elders obtained testimony. 3 By faith, we understand that the universe has been framed by the word of God, so that what is seen has not been made out of things which are visible.

The Parable of the fig tree

Matthew 24: 32-35

> 32 "Now from the fig tree learn this parable. When its branch has now become tender, and produces its leaves, you know that the summer is near. 33 Even so you also, when you see all these things, know that it is near, even at the doors. 34 Most certainly I tell you, this generation will not pass away, until all these things are accomplished. 35 Heaven and earth will pass away, but my words will not pass away.

Author's Opinion

The Parable of the Fig Tree is about recognizing the signs of the times, and knowing that Jesus will fulfill everything as predicted in God's Word, the Bible. We are being put on notice that God's word is sure (unchangeable) and when all Biblical prophesies have taken place, the end of this world, as we know it is near. The thought of the end and judgment day is a fearful thing. *Matthew 12: 36 36 I tell you that every idle word that men speak, they will give account of it in the day of judgment.* With every day that passes, the scroll of time comes closer to the end of this age. *Heaven and earth will pass away, but my words will not pass away. When all these things are accomplished* we must know that it is near. All of us will come before God on the day of accountability. This is a fearful thought for both believers and nonbelievers. God's word tells us in *Isaiah 45:23-24* (NASB) *23 "I have sworn by Myself, The word has gone forth from My mouth in righteousness and will not turn back, That to Me every knee will bow, every tongue will swear allegiance. 24 "They will say of Me, 'Only in the LORD are righteousness and strength.' Men will come to Him, And all who were angry at Him will be put to shame.* We should not be angry but grateful that God's words are unchangeable and makes possible our redemption through the Covenant of Faith as recorded in Genesis. The Covenant of Faith allows us to *swear allegiance* to Him during our lifetime, here on Earth before the grave. Nonbelievers that swear this allegiance only after death are destined to suffer the curse of everlasting separation from God.

Covenants are oath-bound conditional promises of blessings, providing that the party being blessed upholds their part of the covenant. The Old Covenant of Works was made with man in the Garden of Eden see *Genesis 2: 16-17*. The law that guides and convicts us was established with the Mosaic Covenant *(Exodus 19: 5-8)*. Man could not and cannot uphold their part of the Old Covenant of works and/or the Law because of our sin nature. The New Covenant of Faith was made with Abraham for the benefit of all people and all nations *(Genesis 12: 1-3)*. Faith in Jesus (the sacrificial Lamb of God) is the only way to cancel out the penalty of the law. We are all guilty under the law, but believers are redeemed because of Jesus' Atonement on the cross. Jesus paid the required blood price for our sins. There is also a part of the New Covenant provision for the Jewish people that is yet to come in the future *(Jeremiah 31:31-34)*. This generation may scoff at God's Grace and the thought of Jesus' coming to rapture His church. But like it or not, Jesus' words will by no means pass away until all these events take place. Jesus is telling us to take the scriptures seriously. He has made it crystal clear in other passages that by His Word He created the heavens and earth. Through this Parable, He is telling us that His Word will last longer than either of these creations. He is steadfast and His words will stand forever. We must be diligent in our faith and know that what Christ has set in motion will happen just as predicted.

Daniel 6: 26

26 "I make a decree that in all the dominion of my kingdom men tremble and fear before the God of Daniel; "for he is the living God, and steadfast forever. His kingdom is that which will not be destroyed. His dominion will be even to the end.

Zechariah 2: 11

11 "Many nations will join themselves to the Lord in that day and will become My people. Then I will dwell in your midst, and you will know that the Lord of hosts has sent Me to you.

Matthew 24: 7-14

7 For nation will rise against nation, and kingdom against kingdom; and there will be famines, plagues, and earthquakes in various places. 8 But all these things are the beginning of birth pains. 9 Then they will deliver you up to oppression, and will kill you. You will be hated by all of the nations for my name's sake. 10 Then many will stumble, and will deliver up one another, and will hate one another. 11 Many false prophets will arise, and will lead many astray. 12 Because iniquity will be multiplied, the love of many will grow cold. 13 But he who endures to the end, the same will be saved. 14 This Good News of the Kingdom will be preached in the whole world for a testimony to all the nations, and then the end will come.

Luke 21: 20

20 "But when you see Jerusalem surrounded by armies, then know that its desolation is at hand.

1 Corinthians 1: 7-9 (NASB)

7 so that you are not lacking in any gift, awaiting eagerly the revelation of our Lord Jesus Christ, 8 who will also confirm you to the end, blameless in the day of our Lord Jesus Christ. 9 God is faithful, through whom you were called into fellowship with His Son, Jesus Christ our Lord.

The Parable of the absent householder

Mark 13: 33-37

> 33 Watch, keep alert, and pray; for you don't know when the time is. 34 "It is like a man, traveling to another country, having left his house, and given authority to his servants, and to each one his work, and also commanded the doorkeeper to keep watch. 35 Watch therefore, for you don't know when the lord of the house is coming, whether at evening, or at midnight, or when the rooster crows, or in the morning; 36 lest coming suddenly he might find you sleeping. 37 What I tell you, I tell all: Watch."

Author's Opinion

The *Parable of the absent householder* is about being spiritually diligent and proclaiming God's word of truth. All believers are given spiritual gifts and are responsible to use then and do our assigned tasks. We are told not to become complacent. Delegating our Christian witness to the local church and religious leaders is very much like being AWOL (absent without leave). No one knows when Christ will return to rapture His Church. We are to stay active and continually striving to stay faithful in a way that pleases our Father in Heaven. It pleases God to have the Church and individuals proclaim the Gospel that can change peoples' lives. The power of Jesus' Words of Truth will reach whomever He chooses with our preaching and witnessing of His timeless Gospel message.

John 17: 16-20

> 16 They are not of the world even as I am not of the world. 17 Sanctify them in your truth. Your word is truth. 18 As you sent me into the world, even so I have sent them into the world. 19 For their sakes I sanctify myself, that they themselves also may be sanctified in truth.

20 Not for these only do I pray, but for those also who will believe in me through their word,

1 John 2: 28-29

28 Now, little children, remain in him, that when he appears, we may have boldness, and not be ashamed before him at his coming.
29 If you know that he is righteous, you know that everyone who practices righteousness has been born of him.

Chapter 6

How are we to approach God?

Exodus 20: 1-7 (NASB)

> 1 Then God spoke all these words, saying, 2 "I am the Lord your God, who brought you out of the land of Egypt, out of the house of]slavery. 3 "You shall have no other gods before Me. 4 "You shall not make for yourself an idol, or any likeness of what is in heaven above or on the earth beneath or in the water under the earth. 5 You shall not worship them or serve them; for I, the Lord your God, am a jealous God, visiting the iniquity of the fathers on the children, on the third and the fourth generations of those who hate Me, 6 but showing lovingkindness to thousands, to those who love Me and keep My commandments. 7 "You shall not take the name of the Lord your God in vain, for the Lord will not leave him unpunished who takes His name in vain.

Job 40: 1-9 (NASB)

1 Then the Lord said to Job, 2 "Will the faultfinder contend with the Almighty? Let him who reproves God answer it." 3 Then Job answered the Lord and said, 4 "Behold, I am insignificant; what can I reply to You? I lay my hand on my mouth. 5 "Once I have spoken, and I will not answer; Even twice, and I will add nothing more." 6 Then the Lord answered Job out of the storm and said, 7 "Now gird up your loins like a man; I will ask you, and you instruct Me. 8 "Will you really annul My judgment? Will you condemn Me that you may be justified? 9 "Or do you have an arm like God, And can you thunder with a voice like His?

Proverbs 1: 7

7 The fear of the Lord is the beginning of knowledge; Fools despise wisdom and instruction.

Proverbs 9: 10 (NASB)

10 The fear of the Lord is the beginning of wisdom, And the knowledge of the Holy One is understanding.

Psalm 40: 4-5 (NASB)

4 How blessed is the man who has made the Lord his trust, And has not turned to the proud, nor to those who lapse into falsehood. 5 Many, O Lord my God, are the wonders which You have done, And Your thoughts toward us; There is none to compare with You. If I would declare and speak of them, They would be too numerous to count.

Psalm 111: 10 (NASB)

10 The fear of the Lord is the beginning of wisdom; A good understanding have all those who do His commandments; His praise endures forever.

Psalms 119: 110-120 (NASB)

110 The wicked have laid a snare for me, Yet I have not gone astray from Your precepts. 111 I have inherited Your testimonies forever, For they are the joy of my heart. 112 I have inclined my heart to perform Your statutes Forever, even to the end. 113 I hate those who are double-minded, But I love Your law. 114 You are my hiding place and my shield; I wait for Your word. 115 Depart from me, evildoers, That I may observe the commandments of my God. 116 Sustain me according to Your word, that I may live; And do not let me be ashamed of my hope. 117 Uphold me that I may be safe, That I may have regard for Your statutes continually. 118 You have rejected all those who wander from Your statutes, For their deceitfulness is useless. 119 You have removed all the wicked of the earth like dross; Therefore I love Your testimonies. 120 My flesh trembles for fear of You, And I am afraid of Your judgments.

Psalm 1: 1-6 (NASB)

1 How blessed is the man who does not walk in the counsel of the wicked, Nor stand in the path of sinners, Nor sit in the seat of scoffers! 2 But his delight is in the law of the Lord, And in His law he meditates day and night. 3 He will be like a tree firmly planted by streams of water, Which yields its fruit in its season And its leaf does not wither; And in whatever he does, he prospers. 4 The wicked are not so, But they are like chaff which the wind drives away. 5 Therefore the wicked will not stand in the judgment, Nor sinners in the assembly of the righteous. 6 For the Lord knows the way of the righteous, But the way of the wicked will perish.

1 Samuel 12: 20-25 (NASB)

20 Samuel said to the people, "Do not fear. You have committed all this evil, yet do not turn aside from following the Lord, but serve the Lord with all your heart. 21 You must not turn aside, for then you would go after futile things which can not profit or deliver, because they are futile. 22 For the Lord will not abandon His people on account of His great name, because the Lord has been pleased to

make you a people for Himself. 23 Moreover, as for me, far be it from me that I should sin against the Lord by ceasing to pray for you; but I will instruct you in the good and right way. 24 Only fear the Lord and serve Him in truth with all your heart; for consider what great things He has done for you. 25 But if you still do wickedly, both you and your king will be swept away."

Matthew 6: 6-15

6 But you, when you pray, enter into your inner room, and having shut your door, pray to your Father who is in secret, and your Father who sees in secret will reward you openly. 7 In praying, don't use vain repetitions, as the Gentiles do; for they think that they will be heard for their much speaking. 8 Therefore don't be like them, for your Father knows what things you need, before you ask him. 9 Pray like this: 'Our Father in heaven, may your name be kept holy. 10 Let your Kingdom come. Let your will be done, as in heaven, so on earth. 11 Give us today our daily bread. 12 Forgive us our debts, as we also forgive our debtors. 13 Bring us not into temptation, but deliver us from the evil one. For yours is the Kingdom, the power, and the glory forever. Amen.' 14 "For if you forgive men their trespasses, your heavenly Father will also forgive you. 15 But if you don't forgive men their trespasses, neither will your Father forgive your trespasses.

Matthew 10: 32-33

32 Everyone therefore who confesses me before men, him I will also confess before my Father who is in heaven. 33 But whoever denies me before men, him I will also deny before my Father who is in heaven.

Romans 8: 24-27

24 For we were saved in hope, but hope that is seen is not hope. For who hopes for that which he sees? 25 But if we hope for that which we don't see, we wait for it with patience. 26 In the same way, the Spirit also helps our weaknesses, for we don't know how to pray

as we ought. But the Spirit himself makes intercession for us with groanings which can't be uttered. 27 He who searches the hearts knows what is on the Spirit's mind, because he makes intercession for the saints according to God.

Revelations 5: 7-9

7 Then he came, and he took it out of the right hand of him who sat on the throne. 8 Now when he had taken the book, the four living creatures and the twenty-four elders fell down before the Lamb, each one having a harp, and golden bowls full of incense, which are the prayers of the saints. 9 They sang a new song, saying, "You are worthy to take the book, and to open its seals: for you were killed, and bought us for God with your blood, out of every tribe, language, people, and nation,

Author's Opinion

Only in fear and trembling can we approach the mercy seat of God through Jesus Christ, our High Priest and Mediator. We are to be grateful and approach God in adoration and fear. 19 *However God's firm foundation stands, having this seal, "The Lord knows those who are his," and, "Let every one who names the name of the Lord depart from unrighteousness." 2 Timothy 2: 19* Christ is our mediator. He is both man and God. He understands and knows our weakness better than we do. We are to love God, keep His commandments, and treat others as we would like to be treated.

Isaiah 6: 5-8 (NASB)

5 Then I said, "Woe is me, for I am ruined! Because I am a man of unclean lips, And I live among a people of unclean lips; For my eyes have seen the King, the Lord of hosts." 6 Then one of the seraphim flew to me with a burning coal in his hand, which he had taken from the altar with tongs. 7 He touched my mouth with it and said,

"Behold, this has touched your lips; and your iniquity is taken away and your sin is forgiven." 8 Then I heard the voice of the Lord, saying, "Whom shall I send, and who will go for Us?" Then I said, "Here am I. Send me!"

Isaiah 66: 1-2 (NASB)

1 Thus says the Lord, "Heaven is My throne and the earth is My footstool. Where then is a house you could build for Me? And where is a place that I may rest? 2 "For My hand made all these things, Thus all these things came into being," declares the Lord. "But to this one I will look, To him who is humble and contrite of spirit, and who trembles at My word.

1 Timothy 2: 1-6

1 I exhort therefore, first of all, that petitions, prayers, intercessions, and givings of thanks, be made for all men: 2 for kings and all who are in high places; that we may lead a tranquil and quiet life in all godliness and reverence. 3 For this is good and acceptable in the sight of God our Savior; 4 who desires all people to be saved and come to full knowledge of the truth. 5 For there is one God, and one mediator between God and men, the man Christ Jesus, 6 who gave himself as a ransom for all; the testimony in its own times;

Paradoxes to be examined

Repentance

Job 42: 1-6 (NASB)

1 Then Job answered the Lord and said, 2 "I know that You can do all things, And that no purpose of Yours can be thwarted. 3 'Who is this that hides counsel without knowledge?' Therefore I have declared that which I did not understand, Things too wonderful for me, which

I did not know." 4 'Hear, now, and I will speak; I will ask You, and You instruct me.' 5 "I have heard of You by the hearing of the ear; But now my eye sees You; 6 Therefore I retract, And I repent in dust and ashes."

Joel 2: 12 (NASB)

12 "Yet even now," declares the Lord, "Return to Me with all your heart, And with fasting, weeping and mourning;

Matthew 3: 1-3

1 In those days, John the Baptizer came, preaching in the wilderness of Judea, saying, 2 "Repent, for the Kingdom of Heaven is at hand!" 3 For this is he who was spoken of by Isaiah the prophet, saying, "The voice of one crying in the wilderness, make ready the way of the Lord. Make his paths straight."

Matthew 3: 11

11 I indeed baptize you in water for repentance, but he who comes after me is mightier than I, whose shoes I am not worthy to carry. He will baptize you in the Holy Spirit.

Acts 2: 38-39

38 Peter said to them, "Repent, and be baptized, every one of you, in the name of Jesus Christ for the forgiveness of sins, and you will receive the gift of the Holy Spirit. 39 For the promise is to you, and to your children, and to all who are far off, even as many as the Lord our God will call to himself."

Acts 17: 30-31

30 The times of ignorance therefore God overlooked. But now he commands that all people everywhere should repent, 31 because he has appointed a day in which he will judge the world in righteousness by the man whom he has ordained; of which he has given assurance to all men, in that he has raised him from the dead."

Mark 1: 1-5

₁ The beginning of the Good News of Jesus Christ, the Son of God. ₂ As it is written in the prophets, "Behold, I send my messenger before your face, who will prepare your way before you: ₃ the voice of one crying in the wilderness, 'Make ready the way of the Lord! Make his paths straight!'" ₄ John came baptizing in the wilderness and preaching the baptism of repentance for forgiveness of sins. ₅ All the country of Judea and all those of Jerusalem went out to him. They were baptized by him in the Jordan river, confessing their sins.

Luke 15: 7

₇ I tell you that even so there will be more joy in heaven over one sinner who repents, than over ninety-nine righteous people who need no repentance.

2 Corinthians 7: 8-12

₈ For though I made you sorry with my letter, I do not regret it, though I did regret it. For I see that my letter made you sorry, though just for a while. ₉ I now rejoice, not that you were made sorry, but that you were made sorry to repentance. For you were made sorry in a godly way, that you might suffer loss by us in nothing. ₁₀ For godly sorrow produces repentance to salvation, which brings no regret. But the sorrow of the world produces death. ₁₁ For behold, this same thing, that you were made sorry in a godly way, what earnest care it worked in you. Yes, what defense, indignation, fear, longing, zeal, and vengeance! In everything you demonstrated yourselves to be pure in the matter. ₁₂ So although I wrote to you, I wrote not for his cause that did the wrong, nor for his cause that suffered the wrong, but that your earnest care for us might be revealed in you in the sight of God.

2 Timothy 2: 24-26

₂₄ The Lord's servant must not quarrel, but be gentle towards all, able to teach, patient, ₂₅ in gentleness correcting those who oppose him: perhaps God may give them repentance leading to a full knowledge of the truth, 26 and they may recover themselves out of the devil's snare, having been taken captive by him to his will.

Hebrews 6: 4-8

4 For concerning those who were once enlightened and tasted of the heavenly gift, and were made partakers of the Holy Spirit, 5 and tasted the good word of God, and the powers of the age to come, 6 and then fell away, it is impossible to renew them again to repentance; seeing they crucify the Son of God for themselves again, and put him to open shame. 7 For the land which has drunk the rain that comes often on it, and produces a crop suitable for them for whose sake it is also tilled, receives blessing from God; 8 but if it bears thorns and thistles, it is rejected and near being cursed, whose end is to be burned.

2 Peter 3: 9-10

9 The Lord is not slow concerning his promise, as some count slowness; but is patient with us, not wishing that any should perish, but that all should come to repentance. 10 But the day of the Lord will come as a thief in the night; in which the heavens will pass away with a great noise, and the elements will be dissolved with fervent heat, and the earth and the works that are in it will be burned up.

Revelation 3: 18-21

18 I counsel you to buy from me gold refined by fire, that you may become rich; and white garments, that you may clothe yourself, and that the shame of your nakedness may not be revealed; and eye salve to anoint your eyes, that you may see. 19 As many as I love, I reprove and chasten. Be zealous therefore, and repent. 20 Behold, I stand at the door and knock. If anyone hears my voice and opens the door, then I will come in to him, and will dine with him, and he with me. 21 He who overcomes, I will give to him to sit down with me on my throne, as I also overcame, and sat down with my Father on his throne.

Hope

Job 13: 15 (NASB)

15 "Though He slay me, I will hope in Him. Nevertheless I will argue my ways before Him.

Job 19: 25

25 But as for me, I know that my Redeemer lives. In the end, he will stand upon the earth.

Psalm 31: 23-24 (NASB)

23 O love the Lord, all you His godly ones! The Lord preserves the faithful And fully recompenses the proud doer. 24 Be strong and let your heart take courage, All you who hope in the Lord.

Matthew 24: 44

44 Therefore also be ready, for in an hour that you don't expect, the Son of Man will come.

Romans 4: 17-18

17 As it is written, "I have made you a father of many nations." This is in the presence of him whom he believed: God, who gives life to the dead, and calls the things that are not, as though they were. 18 Besides hope, Abraham in hope believed, to the end that he might become a father of many nations, according to that which had been spoken, "So will your offspring be."

2 Thessalonians 2: 16-17

16 Now our Lord Jesus Christ himself, and God our Father, who loved us and gave us eternal comfort and good hope through grace, 17 comfort your hearts and establish you in every good work and word.

Titus 2: 11-14

11 For the grace of God has appeared, bringing salvation to all men, 12 instructing us to the intent that, denying ungodliness and worldly lusts, we would live soberly, righteously, and godly in this present age; 13 looking for the blessed hope and appearing of the glory of our great God and Savior, Jesus Christ; 14 who gave himself for us, that he might redeem us from all iniquity, and purify for himself a people for his own possession, zealous for good works.

Titus 3: 3-7

3 For we were also once foolish, disobedient, deceived, serving various lusts and pleasures, living in malice and envy, hateful, and hating one another. 4 But when the kindness of God our Savior and his love toward mankind appeared, 5 not by works of righteousness which we did ourselves, but according to his mercy, he saved us through the washing of regeneration and renewing by the Holy Spirit, 6 whom he poured out on us richly, through Jesus Christ our Savior; 7 that being justified by his grace, we might be made heirs according to the hope of eternal life.

Hebrews 6: 19

19 This hope we have as an anchor of the soul, a hope both sure and steadfast and entering into that which is within the veil;

1 Peter 1: 3

3 Blessed be the God and Father of our Lord Jesus Christ, who according to his great mercy caused us to be born again to a living hope through the resurrection of Jesus Christ from the dead,

1 Peter 3: 15

15 But sanctify the Lord God in your hearts; and always be ready to give an answer to everyone who asks you a reason concerning the hope that is in you, with humility and fear:

1 John 2: 28

28 Now, little children, remain in him, that when he appears, we may have boldness, and not be ashamed before him at his coming.

1 John 3: 2-3

2 Beloved, now we are children of God, and it is not yet revealed what we will be. But we know that, when he is revealed, we will be like him; for we will see him just as he is. 3 Everyone who has this hope set on him purifies himself, even as he is pure.

Man's choice

Deuteronomy 11: 26-28 (NASB)

26 "See, I am setting before you today a blessing and a curse: 27 the blessing, if you listen to the commandments of the Lord your God, which I am commanding you today; 28 and the curse, if you do not listen to the commandments of the Lord your God, but turn aside from the way which I am commanding you today, by following other gods which you have not known.

Deuteronomy 30: 19 (NASB)

19 I call heaven and earth to witness against you today, that I have set before you life and death, the blessing and the curse. So choose life in order that you may live, you and your descendants,,

Amos 5: 14-15 (NASB)

14 Seek good and not evil, that you may live; And thus may the Lord God of hosts be with you, Just as you have said! 15 Hate evil, love good, And establish justice in the gate! Perhaps the Lord God of hosts May be gracious to the remnant of Joseph.

Joshua 24: 15 (NASB)

15 If it is disagreeable in your sight to serve the Lord, choose for

yourselves today whom you will serve: whether the gods which your fathers served which were beyond the River, or the gods of the Amorites in whose land you are living; but as for me and my house, we will serve the Lord."

1 Kings 3: 6-14 (NASB)

6 Then Solomon said, "You have shown great lovingkindness to Your servant David my father, according as he walked before You in truth and righteousness and uprightness of heart toward You; and You have reserved for him this great lovingkindness, that You have given him a son to sit on his throne, as it is this day. 7 Now, O Lord my God, You have made Your servant king in place of my father David, yet I am but a little child; I do not know how to go out or come in. 8 Your servant is in the midst of Your people which You have chosen, a great people who are too many to be numbered or counted. 9 So give Your servant an understanding heart to judge Your people to discern between good and evil. For who is able to judge this great people of Yours?" 10 It was pleasing in the sight of the Lord that Solomon had asked this thing. 11 God said to him, "Because you have asked this thing and have not asked for yourself long life, nor have asked riches for yourself, nor have you asked for the life of your enemies, but have asked for yourself discernment to understand justice, 12 behold, I have done according to your words. Behold, I have given you a wise and discerning heart, so that there has been no one like you before you, nor shall one like you arise after you. 13 I have also given you what you have not asked, both riches and honor, so that there will not be any among the kings like you all your days. 14 If you walk in My ways, keeping My statutes and commandments, as your father David walked, then I will prolong your days."

Proverbs 16: 9

9 The mind of man plans his way, But the Lord directs his steps.

John 1: 9-13

9 The true light that enlightens everyone was coming into the world. 10 He was in the world, and the world was made through him, and the world didn't recognize him. 11 He came to his own, and those who were his own didn't receive him. 12 But as many as received him, to them he gave the right to become God's children, to those who believe in his name: 13 who were born not of blood, nor of the will of the flesh, nor of the will of man, but of God.

John 3: 36

36 One who believes in the Son has eternal life, but one who disobeys the Son won't see life, but the wrath of God remains on him."

John 15: 14-17

14 You are my friends, if you do whatever I command you. 15 No longer do I call you servants, for the servant doesn't know what his lord does. But I have called you friends, for everything that I heard from my Father, I have made known to you. 16 You didn't choose me, but I chose you, and appointed you, that you should go and bear fruit, and that your fruit should remain; that whatever you will ask of the Father in my name, he may give it to you. 17 "I command these things to you, that you may love one another.

Romans 9: 14-24

14 What shall we say then? Is there unrighteousness with God? May it never be! 15 For he said to Moses, "I will have mercy on whom I have mercy, and I will have compassion on whom I have compassion." 16 So then it is not of him who wills, nor of him who runs, but of God who has mercy. 17 For the Scripture says to Pharaoh, "For this very purpose I caused you to be raised up, that I might show in you my power, and that my name might be proclaimed in all the earth." 18 So then, he has mercy on whom he desires, and he hardens whom he desires. 19 You will say then to

me, "Why does he still find fault? For who withstands his will?" 20 But indeed, O man, who are you to reply against God? Will the thing formed ask him who formed it, "Why did you make me like this?" 21 Or hasn't the potter a right over the clay, from the same lump to make one part a vessel for honor, and another for dishonor? 22 What if God, willing to show his wrath, and to make his power known, endured with much patience vessels of wrath prepared for destruction, 23 and that he might make known the riches of his glory on vessels of mercy, which he prepared beforehand for glory, 24 us, whom he also called, not from the Jews only, but also from the Gentiles?

Philippians 1: 21-24

21 For to me to live is Christ, and to die is gain. 22 But if I live on in the flesh, this will bring fruit from my work; yet I don't know what I will choose. 23 But I am in a dilemma between the two, having the desire to depart and be with Christ, which is far better. 24 Yet, to remain in the flesh is more needful for your sake.

Hebrews 11: 24-29

24 By faith, Moses, when he had grown up, refused to be called the son of Pharaoh's daughter, 25 choosing rather to share ill treatment with God's people, than to enjoy the pleasures of sin for a time; 26 accounting the reproach of Christ greater riches than the treasures of Egypt; for he looked to the reward. 27 By faith, he left Egypt, not fearing the wrath of the king; for he endured, as seeing him who is invisible. 28 By faith, he kept the Passover, and the sprinkling of the blood, that the destroyer of the firstborn should not touch them. 29 By faith, they passed through the Red Sea as on dry land. When the Egyptians tried to do so, they were swallowed up.

2 Timothy 3: 1-7

1 But know this, that in the last days, grievous times will come. 2 For men will be lovers of self, lovers of money, boastful, arrogant,

blasphemers, disobedient to parents, unthankful, unholy, 3 without natural affection, unforgiving, slanderers, without self-control, fierce, not lovers of good, 4 traitors, headstrong, conceited, lovers of pleasure rather than lovers of God; 5 holding a form of godliness, but having denied its power. Turn away from these, also. 6 For some of these are people who creep into houses, and take captive gullible women loaded down with sins, led away by various lusts, 7 always learning, and never able to come to the knowledge of the truth.

1 Peter 1: 14-16

14 as children of obedience, not conforming yourselves according to your former lusts as in your ignorance, 15 but just as he who called you is holy, you yourselves also be holy in all of your behavior; 16 because it is written, "You shall be holy; for I am holy."

Judgment

Genesis 6: 5-8 (NASB)

5 Then the Lord saw that the wickedness of man was great on the earth, and that every intent of the thoughts of his heart was only evil continually. 6 The Lord was sorry that He had made man on the earth, and He was grieved in His heart. 7 The Lord said, "I will blot out man whom I have created from the face of the land, from man to animals to creeping things and to birds of the sky; for I am sorry that I have made them." 8 But Noah found favor in the eyes of the Lord.

Numbers 32: 20-24 (NASB)

20 So Moses said to them, "If you will do this, if you will arm yourselves before the Lord for the war, 21 and all of you armed men cross over the Jordan before the Lord until He has driven His enemies out from before Him, 22 and the land is subdued before the Lord, then afterward you shall return and be free of obligation toward the Lord and toward Israel, and this land shall be yours for a

possession before the Lord. 23 But if you will not do so, behold, you have sinned against the Lord, and be sure your sin will find you out. 24 Build yourselves cities for your little ones, and sheepfolds for your sheep, and do what you have promised."

Isaiah 13: 11 (NASB)

11 Thus I will punish the world for its evil And the wicked for their iniquity; I will also put an end to the arrogance of the proud And abase the haughtiness of the ruthless.

Jeremiah 18: 11-12 (NASB)

11 So now then, speak to the men of Judah and against the inhabitants of Jerusalem saying, 'Thus says the Lord, "Behold, I am fashioning calamity against you and devising a plan against you. Oh turn back, each of you from his evil way, and reform your ways and your deeds."' 12 But they will say, 'It's hopeless! For we are going to follow our own plans, and each of us will act according to the stubbornness of his evil heart.'

Amos 4: 12 (NASB)

12 "Therefore thus I will do to you, O Israel; Because I will do this to you, Prepare to meet your God, O Israel."

Matthew 13: 40-42 (NASB)

40 So just as the tares are gathered up and burned with fire, so shall it be at the end of the age. 41 The Son of Man will send forth His angels, and they will gather out of His kingdom all stumbling blocks, and those who commit lawlessness, 42 and will throw them into the furnace of fire; in that place there will be weeping and gnashing of teeth.

John 3: 17-18

17 For God didn't send his Son into the world to judge the world, but that the world should be saved through him. 18 He who believes in

him is not judged. He who doesn't believe has been judged already, because he has not believed in the name of the one and only Son of God.

John 3: 36

36 One who believes in the Son has eternal life, but one who disobeys the Son won't see life, but the wrath of God remains on him."

John 5: 21-24

21 For as the Father raises the dead and gives them life, even so the Son also gives life to whom he desires. 22 For the Father judges no one, but he has given all judgment to the Son, 23 that all may honor the Son, even as they honor the Father. He who doesn't honor the Son doesn't honor the Father who sent him. 24 "Most certainly I tell you, he who hears my word, and believes him who sent me, has eternal life, and doesn't come into judgment, but has passed out of death into life.

Romans 1: 18-21

18 For the wrath of God is revealed from heaven against all ungodliness and unrighteousness of men, who suppress the truth in unrighteousness, 19 because that which is known of God is revealed in them, for God revealed it to them. 20 For the invisible things of him since the creation of the world are clearly seen, being perceived through the things that are made, even his everlasting power and divinity; that they may be without excuse. 21 Because, knowing God, they didn't glorify him as God, neither gave thanks, but became vain in their reasoning, and their senseless heart was darkened.

1 Thessalonians 5: 1-10

1 But concerning the times and the seasons, brothers, you have no need that anything be written to you. 2 For you yourselves know well that the day of the Lord comes like a thief in the night. 3 For when

they are saying, "Peace and safety," then sudden destruction will come on them, like birth pains on a pregnant woman; and they will in no way escape. 4 But you, brothers, aren't in darkness, that the day should overtake you like a thief. 5 You are all children of light, and children of the day. We don't belong to the night, nor to darkness, 6 so then let's not sleep, as the rest do, but let's watch and be sober. 7 For those who sleep, sleep in the night; and those who are drunk are drunk in the night. 8 But let us, since we belong to the day, be sober, putting on the breastplate of faith and love, and, for a helmet, the hope of salvation. 9 For God didn't appoint us to wrath, but to the obtaining of salvation through our Lord Jesus Christ, 10 who died for us, that, whether we wake or sleep, we should live together with him

Romans 2: 1-11

1 Therefore you are without excuse, O man, whoever you are who judge. For in that which you judge another, you condemn yourself. For you who judge practice the same things. 2 We know that the judgment of God is according to truth against those who practice such things. 3 Do you think this, O man who judges those who practice such things, and do the same, that you will escape the judgment of God? 4 Or do you despise the riches of his goodness, forbearance, and patience, not knowing that the goodness of God leads you to repentance? 5 But according to your hardness and unrepentant heart you are treasuring up for yourself wrath in the day of wrath, revelation, and of the righteous judgment of God; 6 who "will pay back to everyone according to their works:" 7 to those who by perseverance in well-doing seek for glory, honor, and incorruptibility, eternal life; 8 but to those who are self-seeking, and don't obey the truth, but obey unrighteousness, will be wrath and indignation, 9 oppression and anguish, on every soul of man who does evil, to the Jew first, and also to the Greek. 10 But glory, honor, and peace go to every man who does good, to the Jew first, and also to the Greek. 11 For there is no partiality with God.

Romans 5: 1-21

1 Being therefore justified by faith, we have peace with God through our Lord Jesus Christ; 2 through whom we also have our access by faith into this grace in which we stand. We rejoice in hope of the glory of God. 3 Not only this, but we also rejoice in our sufferings, knowing that suffering produces perseverance; 4 and perseverance, proven character; and proven character, hope: 5 and hope doesn't disappoint us, because God's love has been poured out into our hearts through the Holy Spirit who was given to us. 6 For while we were yet weak, at the right time Christ died for the ungodly. 7 For one will hardly die for a righteous man. Yet perhaps for a righteous person someone would even dare to die. 8 But God commends his own love toward us, in that while we were yet sinners, Christ died for us. 9 Much more then, being now justified by his blood, we will be saved from God's wrath through him. 10 For if, while we were enemies, we were reconciled to God through the death of his Son, much more, being reconciled, we will be saved by his life. 11 Not only so, but we also rejoice in God through our Lord Jesus Christ, through whom we have now received the reconciliation. 12 Therefore as sin entered into the world through one man, and death through sin; and so death passed to all men, because all sinned. 13 For until the law, sin was in the world; but sin is not charged when there is no law. 14 Nevertheless death reigned from Adam until Moses, even over those whose sins weren't like Adam's disobedience, who is a foreshadowing of him who was to come. 15 But the free gift isn't like the trespass. For if by the trespass of the one the many died, much more did the grace of God, and the gift by the grace of the one man, Jesus Christ, abound to the many. 16 The gift is not as through one who sinned: for the judgment came by one to condemnation, but the free gift came of many trespasses to justification. 17 For if by the trespass of the one, death reigned through the one; so much more will those who receive the abundance of grace and of the gift of righteousness reign in life through the one, Jesus Christ. 18 So then

as through one trespass, all men were condemned; even so through one act of righteousness, all men were justified to life. 19 For as through the one man's disobedience many were made sinners, even so through the obedience of the one, many will be made righteous. 20 The law came in besides, that the trespass might abound; but where sin abounded, grace abounded more exceedingly; 21 that as sin reigned in death, even so grace might reign through righteousness to eternal life through Jesus Christ our Lord.

Romans 9: 22-23

22 What if God, willing to show his wrath, and to make his power known, endured with much patience vessels of wrath prepared for destruction, 23 and that he might make known the riches of his glory on vessels of mercy, which he prepared beforehand for glory,

Hebrews 10: 38-39

38 But the righteous will live by faith. If he shrinks back, my soul has no pleasure in him." 39 But we are not of those who shrink back to destruction, but of those who have faith to the saving of the soul.

Revelation 20: 15

15 If anyone was not found written in the book of life, he was cast into the lake of fire.

Parables to be grasped

The Parable of the Prodigal Son

Luke 15: 11-32

11 He said, "A certain man had two sons. 12 The younger of them said to his father, 'Father, give me my share of your property.' He divided his livelihood between them. 13 Not many days after, the younger son

The Parable of the Prodigal Son

gathered all of this together and traveled into a far country. There he wasted his property with riotous living. 14 When he had spent all of it, there arose a severe famine in that country, and he began to be in need. 15 He went and joined himself to one of the citizens of that country, and he sent him into his fields to feed pigs. 16 He wanted to fill his belly with the husks that the pigs ate, but no one gave him any. 17 But when he came to himself he said, 'How many hired servants of my father's have bread enough to spare, and I'm dying with hunger! 18 I will get up and go to my father, and will tell him, "Father, I have sinned against heaven, and in your sight. 19 I am no more worthy to be called your son. Make me as one of your hired servants."' 20 "He arose, and came to his father. But while he was still far off, his father saw him, and was moved with compassion, and ran, and fell on his neck, and kissed him. 21 The son said to him, 'Father, I have sinned against heaven, and in your sight. I am no longer worthy to be called your son.' 22 "But the father said to his servants, 'Bring out the best robe, and put it on him. Put a ring on his hand, and shoes on his feet. 23 Bring the fattened calf, kill it, and let us eat, and celebrate; 24 for this, my son, was dead, and is alive again. He was lost, and is found.' They began to celebrate. 25 "Now his elder son was in the field. As he came near to the house, he heard music and dancing. 26 He called one of the servants to him, and asked what was going on. 27 He said to him, 'Your brother has come, and your father has killed the fattened calf, because he has received him back safe and healthy.' 28 But he was angry, and would not go in. Therefore his father came out, and begged him. 29 But he answered his father, 'Behold, these many years I have served you, and I never disobeyed a commandment of yours, but you never gave me a goat, that I might celebrate with my friends. 30 But when this your son came, who has devoured your living with prostitutes, you killed the fattened calf for him.' 31 "He said to him, 'Son, you are always with me, and all that is mine is yours. 32 But it was appropriate to celebrate and be glad, for this, your brother, was dead, and is alive again. He was lost, and is found.'"

Author's Opinion

The *Parable of the Prodigal Son* tells us how God rejoices over a sinner's repentance, contrasting it with man's attitude of self-righteousness and the pride of good works. This parable was spoken to the Jewish religious leaders who were complaining that Jesus and His disciples were associating with sinners and people of low reputations. These outwardly religious people were jealous of the idea, and unable to believe that anyone other than mirror images of themselves could enter the Kingdom of God. Today like the Pharisees and Scribes of old, there are religious groups, by the virtue of their own reasoning, that preach salvation is automatic when a person joins their particular religious group. There are other churches that are so intensely proud of denominational traditions and complexities that they cannot see the value of simple repentance and humbling oneself, asking for mercy before Jesus. ₃*But I am afraid that somehow, as the serpent deceived Eve in his craftiness, so your minds might be corrupted from the simplicity that is in Christ. 2 Corinthians 11: 3* To worship Jesus in truth and spirit does not require a membership in an organized religious system or a superficial lifetime of good works, like the Prodigal son's brother. It does require personal circumspection and repentance as shown by the example of the Prodigal Son. We should enjoy the comfort and fellowship of others, within a Bible believing church, but Grace comes from our personal relationship with Christ – not a visible organization. Satan's cunning delusion has made this "membership" deception much easier to sell. Repentance means humbly regretting one's previous sinful ways, personally resolving to change those lifestyle patterns and forfeiting our self-centered will and trying to please God by trusting in Jesus exclusively. The Prodigal Son came to repentance when he said, "Father, I have sinned against heaven and before you. "We can only approach God through Christ. 6 *Jesus said to him, "I am the way, the truth, and the life. No one comes to the Father, except through me. John 14: 6* This example of gladness is also applicable today when a brother or sister who was dead now becomes alive in Christ Jesus; he or she was lost, but is now found.

Psalm 19: 14 (NASB)

> 14 Let the words of my mouth and the meditation of my heart Be acceptable in Your sight, O Lord, my rock and my Redeemer.

John 4: 21-24

> 21 Jesus said to her, "Woman, believe me, the hour comes, when neither in this mountain, nor in Jerusalem, will you worship the Father. 22 You worship that which you don't know. We worship that which we know; for salvation is from the Jews. 23 But the hour comes, and now is, when the true worshipers will worship the Father in spirit and truth, for the Father seeks such to be his worshipers. 24 God is spirit, and those who worship him must worship in spirit and truth."

Acts 17: 30-31

> 30 The times of ignorance therefore God overlooked. But now he commands that all people everywhere should repent, 31 because he has appointed a day in which he will judge the world in righteousness by the man whom he has ordained; of which he has given assurance to all men, in that he has raised him from the dead."

Ephesians 4: 14-15

> 14 that we may no longer be children, tossed back and forth and carried about with every wind of doctrine, by the trickery of men, in craftiness, after the wiles of error; 15 but speaking truth in love, we may grow up in all things into him, who is the head, Christ;

The Parable of the Unprofitable Servant

Luke 17: 7-10

> 7 But who is there among you, having a servant plowing or keeping sheep, that will say, when he comes in from the field, 'Come immediately and sit down at the table,' 8 and will not rather tell him, 'Prepare my supper, clothe yourself properly, and serve me, while I eat and drink. Afterward you shall eat and drink'? 9 Does he thank that servant because he did the things that were commanded? I think not. 10 Even so you also, when you have done all the things that are commanded you, say, 'We are unworthy servants. We have done our duty.'"

Author's Opinion

The *Parable of the Unprofitable Servant* is about the servant's proper attitude. We are unworthy servants, sinners approaching the great "I AM", God without beginning or end.

Philippians 3: 12-14 (NASB)

> 12 Not that I have already obtained, or am already made perfect; but I press on, that I may take hold of that for which also I was taken hold of by Christ Jesus. 13 Brothers, I don't regard myself as yet having taken hold, but one thing I do. Forgetting the things which are behind, and stretching forward to the things which are before, 14 I press on toward the goal for the prize of the high calling of God in Christ Jesus.

As Christians we must rededicate ourselves daily to the lowly position of servant, to Jesus our master. Emmanuel, God with us was the only person on earth that was equal with God. His Word invites us to "Come let us reason together" so that mankind can have life eternal with him in Heaven someday. We have access through Jesus, our mediator to

God, but we must not think we are equal with God. In *Luke 22: 42* Jesus set the example of a servant for us by praying ₄₂ *saying, "Father, if you are willing, remove this cup from me. Nevertheless, not my will, but yours, be done." In Mark 10: 45* Jesus also said ₄₅ *For the Son of Man also came not to be served, but to serve, and to give his life as a ransom for many."* On judgment day, only after we have performed our duty here on earth, will He promote us from unworthy servant to good and faithful servant. God loves true humility and abhors pride. It is not for us to think of ourselves as higher than we should.

Genesis 3: 22-24 (NASB)

₂₂ Then the Lord God said, "Behold, the man has become like one of Us, knowing good and evil; and now, he might stretch out his hand, and take also from the tree of life, and eat, and live forever" — ₂₃ therefore the Lord God sent him out from the garden of Eden, to cultivate the ground from which he was taken. ₂₄ So He drove the man out; and at the east of the garden of Eden He stationed the cherubim and the flaming sword which turned every direction to guard the way to the tree of life.

James 4: 10

₁₀ Humble yourselves in the sight of the Lord, and he will exalt you.

Philippians 2: 5-9

₅ Have this in your mind, which was also in Christ Jesus, ₆ who, existing in the form of God, didn't consider equality with God a thing to be grasped, ₇ but emptied himself, taking the form of a servant, being made in the likeness of men. ₈ And being found in human form, he humbled himself, becoming obedient to death, yes, the death of the cross. ₉ Therefore God also highly exalted him, and gave to him the name which is above every name;

The Parable of the Unforgiving Servant

Matthew 18: 23-35

23 Therefore the Kingdom of Heaven is like a certain king, who wanted to reconcile accounts with his servants. 24 When he had begun to reconcile, one was brought to him who owed him ten thousand talents. 25 But because he couldn't pay, his lord commanded him to be sold, with his wife, his children, and all that he had, and payment to be made. 26 The servant therefore fell down and knelt before him, saying, 'Lord, have patience with me, and I will repay you all!' 27 The lord of that servant, being moved with compassion, released him, and forgave him the debt. 28 "But that servant went out, and found one of his fellow servants, who owed him one hundred denarii, and he grabbed him, and took him by the throat, saying, 'Pay me what you owe!' 29 "So his fellow servant fell down at his feet and begged him, saying, 'Have patience with me, and I will repay you!' 30 He would not, but went and cast him into prison, until he should pay back that which was due. 31 So when his fellow servants saw what was done, they were exceedingly sorry, and came and told their lord all that was done. 32 Then his lord called him in, and said to him, 'You wicked servant! I forgave you all that debt, because you begged me. 33 Shouldn't you also have had mercy on your fellow servant, even as I had mercy on you?' 34 His lord was angry, and delivered him to the tormentors, until he should pay all that was due to him. 35 So my heavenly Father will also do to you, if you don't each forgive your brother from your hearts for his misdeeds."

Author's Opinion

The *Parable of the Unforgiving Servant* is ultimately about our being accountable to God for our actions. The first servant could not repay what he owed his master. He pleaded for mercy and was given complete forgiveness of his debt. This servant (that had been forgiven his debt) in turn went to a second servant and demanded payment in full for a smaller debt that the second servant owed to him. The second servant could not pay and was not given any mercy at all by the first servant. We all want and need the kind of mercy that wipes the slate clean of all our past and future sins. God's Grace is willing to forgive us, and blot out all records of sins. We should in turn be willing to completely forgive any offences from others. His mercy is pure and clean, never to be remembered again. We cannot have communion with God or even approach Him with hatred in our heart. With the same standard of forgiveness that He shows us, we are to have the grace to forgive others completely. We are to have a clean heart, love God, and love our neighbors as ourselves.

Matthew 7: 1-2

1 "Don't judge, so that you won't be judged. 2 For with whatever judgment you judge, you will be judged; and with whatever measure you measure, it will be measured to you.

Luke 6: 30-31

30 Give to everyone who asks you, and don't ask him who takes away your goods to give them back again. 31 "As you would like people to do to you, do exactly so to them.

Luke 6: 36

36 "Therefore be merciful, even as your Father is also merciful.

The Parable of the Ten Minas

Luke 19: 11-27

11 As they heard these things, he went on and told a parable,

because he was near Jerusalem, and they supposed that God's Kingdom would be revealed immediately. 12 He said therefore, "A certain nobleman went into a far country to receive for himself a kingdom, and to return. 13 He called ten servants of his, and gave them ten mina coins, and told them, 'Conduct business until I come.' 14 But his citizens hated him, and sent an envoy after him, saying, 'We don't want this man to reign over us.' 15 "When he had come back again, having received the kingdom, he commanded these servants, to whom he had given the money, to be called to him, that he might know what they had gained by conducting business. 16 The first came before him, saying, 'Lord, your mina has made ten more minas.' 17 "He said to him, 'Well done, you good servant! Because you were found faithful with very little, you shall have authority over ten cities.' 18 "The second came, saying, 'Your mina, Lord, has made five minas.' 19 "So he said to him, 'And you are to be over five cities.' 20 Another came, saying, 'Lord, behold, your mina, which I kept laid away in a handkerchief, 21 for I feared you, because you are an exacting man. You take up that which you didn't lay down, and reap that which you didn't sow.' 22 "He said to him, 'Out of your own mouth will I judge you, you wicked servant! You knew that I am an exacting man, taking up that which I didn't lay down, and reaping that which I didn't sow. 23 Then why didn't you deposit my money in the bank, and at my coming, I might have earned interest on it?' 24 He said to those who stood by, 'Take the mina away from him, and give it to him who has the ten minas.' 25 "They said to him, 'Lord, he has ten minas!' 26 'For I tell you that to everyone who has, will more be given; but from him who doesn't have, even that which he has will be taken away from him. 27 But bring those enemies of mine who didn't want me to reign over them here, and kill them before me.'"

Author's Opinion

The *Parable of the Ten Minas* is about being accountable to God as His servants. The money represents spiritual gifts that we are given. These gifts are to be used for the glory and benefit of God. Jesus was telling them that He (their king) was going to be gone for a time. He would be leaving His servant in charge with responsibilities. The servants that performed their duties were to be rewarded greatly. The servants that did nothing to benefit the master were judged harshly. The Master also destroyed His enemies who did not want Him as their ruler.

      The Jewish people of that day were hoping for a king as their Messiah who would bring a new triumphant government to them, replacing their Roman rulers. Because he was near Jerusalem, they supposed that God's Kingdom would be revealed immediately, having no idea that their Messiah and His kingdom was intended to rule in their hearts. This Parable is just as applicable today as it was back then. We have believers and religious leaders who are looking forward to the second coming of Christ, being productive for God's Kingdom. They are working diligently, preaching Christ crucified, equipping our heart to witness and worship, in truth and spirit. These servants (believers) who have clean hands and pure hearts, are looking forward to seeing their Lord and Redeemer. Sadly, there are also complacent church leaders that are reading their audiences, knowing their members do not want to hear about an exacting God ruling over them. *"We don't want this man to reign over us."* Consequently they are treating the church as a mere social gathering, avoiding any accountability issues and doing very little to serve God's Kingdom. He said to him, *"Out of your own mouth will I judge you, you wicked servant.* Christ's return and being held accountable is a fearful thing to *those enemies of mine who don't want me to reign over them."*

1 Timothy 4: 13

13 Until I come, pay attention to reading, to exhortation, and to teaching.

Acts 8: 21-22

21 You have neither part nor lot in this matter, for your heart isn't right before God. 22 Repent therefore of this, your wickedness, and ask God if perhaps the thought of your heart may be forgiven you.

The Parable of the Dragnet

Matthew 13: 47-50

47 "Again, the Kingdom of Heaven is like a dragnet, that was cast into the sea, and gathered some fish of every kind, 48 which, when it was filled, they drew up on the beach. They sat down, and gathered the good into containers, but the bad they threw away. 49 So will it be in the end of the world. The angels will come and separate the wicked from among the righteous, 50 and will cast them into the furnace of fire. There will be the weeping and the gnashing of teeth."

Author's Opinion

The *Parable of the Dragnet* is again about accountability. Man's human nature would like to think that a loving God would not hold us accountable for the choices we make during our lifetime. But that is not what the Bible tells us. God's wrath is on those who reject his offer of Grace. God's Word is very specific about what will happen at the end of the age; those who are steadfast, trusting only in Jesus's gift of Grace and not capitulating to Satan because of experiencing hard times will be rewarded greatly. This right choice has been described as difficult, a straight and narrow path that leads to Heaven's narrow gate. To do otherwise, God considers a wrong and a poor choice. The bad choices made by man have been described as a "wide and crooked path (that) leads to destruction." This Parable makes clear that choosing the wrong path will lead to unimaginable torment, in a furnace of fire, for all eternity. The idea that man can reject Jesus in this life and then be forgiven to enjoy the benefits of Heaven did not come from the scriptures, but by man's reason and Satan's lies. This Parable is telling us to plead for the mercy of God's Grace before the dragnet of accountability separates the evil from the righteous. Like it or not, we will give an account to God for our actions during our lifetime.

Luke 21: 34-36

> 34 "So be careful, or your hearts will be loaded down with carousing, drunkenness, and cares of this life, and that day will come on you suddenly. 35 For it will come like a snare on all those who dwell on the surface of all the earth. 36 Therefore be watchful all the time, praying that you may be counted worthy to escape all these things that will happen, and to stand before the Son of Man."

2 Corinthians 5: 10

> 10 For we must all be revealed before the judgment seat of Christ; that each one may receive the things in the body, according to what he has done, whether good or bad.

Chapter 7

Where are the right answers to be found?

Proverbs 8: 12-14 (NASB)

> 12 "I, wisdom, dwell with prudence, And I find knowledge and discretion. 13 "The fear of the Lord is to hate evil; Pride and arrogance and the evil way And the perverted mouth, I hate. 14 "Counsel is mine and sound wisdom; I am understanding, power is mine.

Psalm 18: 30-31 (NASB)

> 30 As for God, His way is blameless; The word of the Lord is tried; He is a shield to all who take refuge in Him. 31 For who is God, but the Lord? And who is a rock, except our God?

Psalm 103: 8-9 (NASB)

8 The Lord is compassionate and gracious, Slow to anger and abounding in lovingkindness. 9 He will not always strive with us, Nor will He keep His anger forever.

Psalm 19: 7-10 (NASB)

7 The law of the Lord is perfect, restoring the soul; The testimony of the Lord is sure, making wise the simple. 8 The precepts of the Lord are right, rejoicing the heart; The commandment of the Lord is pure, enlightening the eyes. 9 The fear of the Lord is clean, enduring forever; The judgments of the Lord are true; they are righteous altogether. 10 They are more desirable than gold, yes, than much fine gold; Sweeter also than honey and the drippings of the honeycomb.

Psalm 111: 10 (NASB)

10 The fear of the Lord is the beginning of wisdom; A good understanding have all those who do His commandments; His praise endures forever.

Psalm 119: 33-40 (NASB)

33 Teach me, O Lord, the way of Your statutes, And I shall observe it to the end. 34 Give me understanding, that I may observe Your law And keep it with all my heart. 35 Make me walk in the path of Your commandments, For I delight in it. 36 Incline my heart to Your testimonies And not to dishonest gain. 37 Turn away my eyes from looking at vanity, And revive me in Your ways. 38 Establish Your word to Your servant, As that which produces reverence for You. 39 Turn away my reproach which I dread, For Your ordinances are good. 40 Behold, I long for Your precepts; Revive me through Your righteousness.

Psalm 119: 88-91 (NASB)

88 Revive me according to Your lovingkindness, So that I may keep the testimony of Your mouth. 89 Forever, O Lord, Your word is settled

in heaven. 90 Your faithfulness continues throughout all generations; You established the earth, and it stands. 91 They stand this day according to Your ordinances, For all things are Your servants.

Psalm 145: 17-21 (NASB)

17 The Lord is righteous in all His ways And kind in all His deeds. 18 The Lord is near to all who call upon Him, To all who call upon Him in truth. 19 He will fulfill the desire of those who fear Him; He will also hear their cry and will save them. 20 The Lord keeps all who love Him, But all the wicked He will destroy. 21 My mouth will speak the praise of the Lord, And all flesh will bless His holy name forever and ever.

1 Corinthians 2: 14-16

14 Now the natural man doesn't receive the things of God's Spirit, for they are foolishness to him, and he can't know them, because they are spiritually discerned. 15 But he who is spiritual discerns all things, and he himself is judged by no one. 16 "For who has known the mind of the Lord, that he should instruct him?" But we have Christ's mind.

Ephesians 1: 15-18

15 For this cause I also, having heard of the faith in the Lord Jesus which is among you, and the love which you have toward all the saints, 16 don't cease to give thanks for you, making mention of you in my prayers, 17 that the God of our Lord Jesus Christ, the Father of glory, may give to you a spirit of wisdom and revelation in the knowledge of him; 18 having the eyes of your hearts enlightened, that you may know what is the hope of his calling, and what are the riches of the glory of his inheritance in the saints,

Author's Opinion

Answers for us today can be found in both the Old and New Testament. God's provision for man has not changed; Romans 2:11 tells us For there is no partiality with God. He is the same yesterday, today and tomorrow. There is a common misperception that the scriptures that were addressed to Israel in the Old Testament pertain exclusively to Israel. They may also pertain to all mankind.

Acts 10: 34-36

> 34 Peter opened his mouth and said, "Truly I perceive that God doesn't show favoritism; 35 but in every nation he who fears him and works righteousness is acceptable to him. 36 The word which he sent to the children of Israel, preaching good news of peace by Jesus Christ—he is Lord of all.

Ephesians 3: 6 (NASB)

> 6 that the Gentiles are fellow heirs, and fellow members of the body, and fellow partakers of his promise in Christ Jesus through the Good News.

The Abraham Covenant made Abraham the father of many nations, blessing all of Abraham's descendants that kept their part of the covenant, not just the Israelites. This is confirmed in *Galatians 3: 13-14* *13 Christ redeemed us from the curse of the law, having become a curse for us. For it is written, "Cursed is everyone who hangs on a tree," 14 that the blessing of Abraham might come on the Gentiles through Christ Jesus; that we might receive the promise of the Spirit through faith.*

    We cannot see God, but God has provided us with the right answers by His clear instruction form his Word of truth, the Bible. Jesus lets us choose to believe or not, we either welcome His offer of Grace or (by default) we are rejecting His precious love. The problem is that most people believe only what they want to believe and choose not to take the time to know God through His Scriptures. By choosing not to consider or take serious God's authority in our life, they are rebelling against Him and the blessing of being in the family of God.

Colossians 1: 26-28

> 26 the mystery which has been hidden for ages and generations. But now it has been revealed to his saints, 27 to whom God was pleased to make known what are the riches of the glory of this mystery among the Gentiles, which is Christ in you, the hope of glory; 28 whom we proclaim, admonishing every man and teaching every man in all wisdom, that we may present every man perfect in Christ Jesus;

In the quest to find God's wisdom, choosing a church can either be a great help, or a deterrent. Searching for spiritual answers from the Scriptures is far better than trusting answers that are unique and only come from a particular church or denomination. Answers not confirmed by Scripture are not from God's storehouse of wisdom and will fall short of what God intended for us. The visible churches and denominations can vary a great deal. Over time churches have developed their own priorities and style of governance. They have distinct personalities, worship patterns and traditions. These differences can be confusing. Do not let, even well intending religious leaders be your only guide that define, your relationship with Jesus. Remember the leaven. *(Matthew 13: 33)* Leaven is when man trusts in what seems right in his own eyes but can lead to false teachings and false church doctrine. Soul searching repentance and humble prayer for mercy, is what reconciles us to God. The unchanging Scriptures and the Holy Spirit guides us and will always pulls us back from the error, if we let Him. Christ is the head of the church, not man. There will always be some nonbelievers in every visible church, you can recognize good church congregations that are true to God! They will declare the preeminence of Christ, the inerrancy of the scriptures and produce fruit that glorifies God. Good churches have imperfect members but are trying to be spiritually separate from the nonbelieving world. That means living their lives, showing the love of God to others. Jesus' Word of Truth, describes the Church for us, in both the Old and New Testament.

Deuteronomy 4: 10 (NASB)

> 10 Remember the day you stood before the Lord your God at Horeb, when the Lord said to me, 'Assemble the people to Me, that I may let them hear My words so they may learn to fear Me all the days they live on the earth, and that they may teach their children.'

Matthew 16: 11-12

> 11 How is it that you don't perceive that I didn't speak to you concerning bread? But beware of the yeast of the Pharisees and Sadducees." 12 Then they understood that he didn't tell them to beware of the yeast of bread, but of the teaching of the Pharisees and Sadducees.

Colossians 1: 24-28

> 24 Now I rejoice in my sufferings for your sake, and fill up on my part that which is lacking of the afflictions of Christ in my flesh for his body's sake, which is the assembly; 25 of which I was made a servant, according to the stewardship of God which was given me toward you, to fulfill the word of God, 26 the mystery which has been hidden for ages and generations. But now it has been revealed to his saints, 27 to whom God was pleased to make known what are the riches of the glory of this mystery among the Gentiles, which is Christ in you, the hope of glory; 28 whom we proclaim, admonishing every man and teaching every man in all wisdom, that we may present every man perfect in Christ Jesus;

It is a strange thing that when Bibles and the preaching of the Gospel is abundantly available to people, searching for the right answers can have minimal value to them. But to others that do not have the Gospel available to them, sometimes go to great effort to hear His Word of truth, especially about God's love for them. If you ask for the right answers and desire wisdom, it will be given to you, as per James 1: 5-8.

Proverbs 1: 7 (NASB)

> 7 The fear of the Lord is the beginning of knowledge; Fools despise wisdom and instruction.

2 Timothy 3: 16-17

> 16 Every Scripture is God-breathed and profitable for teaching, for reproof, for correction, and for instruction in righteousness, 17 that the man of God may be complete, thoroughly equipped for every good work.

James 1: 5-8

> 5 But if any of you lacks wisdom, let him ask of God, who gives to all liberally and without reproach; and it will be given to him. 6 But let him ask in faith, without any doubting, for he who doubts is like a wave of the sea, driven by the wind and tossed. 7 For that man shouldn't think that he will receive anything from the Lord. 8 He is a double-minded man, unstable in all his ways.

Paradoxes to be examined

Church

Deuteronomy 4: 9-10 (NASB)

> 9 "Only give heed to yourself and keep your soul diligently, so that you do not forget the things which your eyes have seen and they do not depart from your heart all the days of your life; but make them known to your sons and your grandsons. 10 Remember the day you stood before the Lord your God at Horeb, when the Lord said to me, 'Assemble the people to Me, that I may let them hear My words so

they may learn to fear Me all the days they live on the earth, and that they may teach their children.'

Acts 2: 46-47

46 Day by day, continuing steadfastly with one accord in the temple, and breaking bread at home, they took their food with gladness and singleness of heart, 47 praising God, and having favor with all the people. The Lord added to the assembly day by day those who were being saved.

Acts 9: 31

31 So the assemblies throughout all Judea and Galilee and Samaria had peace, and were built up. They were multiplied, walking in the fear of the Lord and in the comfort of the Holy Spirit.

1 Corinthians 1: 10

10 Now I beg you, brothers, through the name of our Lord, Jesus Christ, that you all speak the same thing, and that there be no divisions among you, but that you be perfected together in the same mind and in the same judgment.

1 Corinthians 14: 33

33 for God is not a God of confusion, but of peace, as in all the assemblies of the saints.

Ephesians 1: 20-23 (NASB)

20 which He brought about in Christ, when He raised Him from the dead and seated Him at His right hand in the heavenly places, 21 far above all rule and authority and power and dominion, and every name that is named, not only in this age but also in the one to come. 22 And He put all things in subjection under His feet, and gave Him as head over all things to the church, 23 which is His body, the fullness of Him who fills all in all.

Ephesians 4: 11-16

11 He gave some to be apostles; and some, prophets; and some, evangelists; and some, shepherds and teachers; 12 for the perfecting of the saints, to the work of serving, to the building up of the body of Christ; 13 until we all attain to the unity of the faith, and of the knowledge of the Son of God, to a full grown man, to the measure of the stature of the fullness of Christ; 14 that we may no longer be children, tossed back and forth and carried about with every wind of doctrine, by the trickery of men, in craftiness, after the wiles of error; 15 but speaking truth in love, we may grow up in all things into him, who is the head, Christ; 16 from whom all the body, being fitted and knit together through that which every joint supplies, according to the working in measure of each individual part, makes the body increase to the building up of itself in love.

Ephesians 5: 26-27

26 that he might sanctify it, having cleansed it by the washing of water with the word, 27 that he might present the assembly to himself gloriously, not having spot or wrinkle or any such thing; but that it should be holy and without defect.

Hebrews 12: 22-24 (NASB)

22 But you have come to Mount Zion and to the city of the living God, the heavenly Jerusalem, and to myriads of angels, 23 to the general assembly and church of the firstborn who are enrolled in heaven, and to God, the Judge of all, and to the spirits of the righteous made perfect, 24 and to Jesus, the mediator of a new covenant, and to the sprinkled blood, which speaks better than the blood of Abel.

Inerrancy of Scriptures

Psalm 119: 160 (NASB)

160 The sum of Your word is truth,
And every one of Your righteous ordinances is everlasting.

Romans 16: 25-26 (NASB)

25 Now to Him who is able to establish you according to my gospel and the preaching of Jesus Christ, according to the revelation of the mystery which has been kept secret for long ages past, 26 but now is manifested, and by the Scriptures of the prophets, according to the commandment of the eternal God, has been made known to all the nations, leading to obedience of faith;

2 Peter 1: 19-21

19 We have the more sure word of prophecy; and you do well that you heed it, as to a lamp shining in a dark place, until the day dawns, and the morning star arises in your hearts: 20 knowing this first, that no prophecy of Scripture is of private interpretation. 21 For no prophecy ever came by the will of man: but holy men of God spoke, being moved by the Holy Spirit.

2 Timothy 3: 16-17

16 Every Scripture is God-breathed and profitable for teaching, for reproof, for correction, and for instruction in righteousness, 17 that the man of God may be complete, thoroughly equipped for every good work.

Hebrews 6: 17-20

17 In this way God, being determined to show more abundantly to the heirs of the promise the immutability of his counsel, interposed with an oath; 18 that by two immutable things, in which it is impossible for God to lie, we may have a strong encouragement,

who have fled for refuge to take hold of the hope set before us.
19 This hope we have as an anchor of the soul, a hope both sure and steadfast and entering into that which is within the veil; 20 where as a forerunner Jesus entered for us, having become a high priest forever after the order of Melchizedek.

John 1: 1-5

1 In the beginning was the Word, and the Word was with God, and the Word was God. 2 The same was in the beginning with God. 3 All things were made through him. Without him was not anything made that has been made. 4 In him was life, and the life was the light of men. 5 The light shines in the darkness, and the darkness hasn't overcome it.

Acts 28: 24-27

24 Some believed the things which were spoken, and some disbelieve 25 When they didn't agree among themselves, they departed after Paul had spoken one word, "The Holy Spirit spoke rightly through Isaiah, the prophet, to our fathers, 26 saying, 'Go to this people, and say, in hearing, you will hear, but will in no way understand. In seeing, you will see, but will in no way perceive. 27 For this people's heart has grown callous. Their ears are dull of hearing. Their eyes they have closed. Lest they should see with their eyes, hear with their ears, understand with their heart, and would turn again, and I would heal them.'

Revelation 22: 11-17 (NASB)

11 Let the one who does wrong, still do wrong; and the one who is filthy, still be filthy; and let the one who is righteous, still practice righteousness; and the one who is holy, still keep himself holy."
12 "Behold, I am coming quickly, and My reward is with Me, to render to every man according to what he has done. 13 I am the Alpha and the Omega, the first and the last, the beginning and the end."
14 Blessed are those who wash their robes, so that they may have

the right to the tree of life, and may enter by the gates into the city. 15 Outside are the dogs and the sorcerers and the immoral persons and the murderers and the idolaters, and everyone who loves and practices lying. 16 "I, Jesus, have sent My angel to testify to you these things for the churches. I am the root and the descendant of David, the bright morning star." 17 The Spirit and the bride say, "Come." And let the one who hears say, "Come." And let the one who is thirsty come; let the one who wishes take the water of life without cost.

Death

Ecclesiastes 12: 7

7 and the dust returns to the earth as it was, and the spirit returns to God who gave it.

Psalm 23: 1-6 (NASB)

1 The Lord is my shepherd, I shall not want. 2 He makes me lie down in green pastures; He leads me beside quiet waters. 3 He restores my soul; He guides me in the paths of righteousness For His name's sake. 4 Even though I walk through the valley of the shadow of death, I fear no evil, for You are with me; Your rod and Your staff, they comfort me. 5 You prepare a table before me in the presence of my enemies; You have anointed my head with oil; My cup overflows. 6 Surely goodness and lovingkindness will follow me all the days of my life, And I will dwell in the house of the Lord forever.

John 5: 24-27

24 "Most certainly I tell you, he who hears my word, and believes him who sent me, has eternal life, and doesn't come into judgment, but has passed out of death into life. 25 Most certainly, I tell you, the hour comes, and now is, when the dead will hear the Son of God's voice; and those who hear will live. 26 For as the Father has life in

himself, even so he gave to the Son also to have life in himself. 27 He also gave him authority to execute judgment, because he is a son of man.

Romans 8: 1-2

1 There is therefore now no condemnation to those who are in Christ Jesus, who don't walk according to the flesh, but according to the Spirit. 2 For the law of the Spirit of life in Christ Jesus made me free from the law of sin and of death.

Hebrews 2: 14-18

14 Since then the children have shared in flesh and blood, he also himself in the same way partook of the same, that through death he might bring to nothing him who had the power of death, that is, the devil, 15 and might deliver all of them who through fear of death were all their lifetime subject to bondage. 16 For most certainly, he doesn't give help to angels, but he gives help to the offspring of Abraham. 17 Therefore he was obligated in all things to be made like his brothers, that he might become a merciful and faithful high priest in things pertaining to God, to make atonement for the sins of the people. 18 For in that he himself has suffered being tempted, he is able to help those who are tempted.

Revelation 2: 9-11

9 "I know your works, oppression, and your poverty (but you are rich), and the blasphemy of those who say they are Jews, and they are not, but are a synagogue of Satan. 10 Don't be afraid of the things which you are about to suffer. Behold, the devil is about to throw some of you into prison, that you may be tested; and you will have oppression for ten days. Be faithful to death, and I will give you the crown of life. 11 He who has an ear, let him hear what the Spirit says to the assemblies. He who overcomes won't be harmed by the second death.

Satan

Isaiah 14: 12-15

12 How you have fallen from heaven, morning star, son of the dawn! How you are cut down to the ground, who laid the nations low! 13 You said in your heart, "I will ascend into heaven! I will exalt my throne above the stars of God! I will sit on the mountain of assembly, in the far north! 14 I will ascend above the heights of the clouds! I will make myself like the Most High!" 15 Yet you shall be brought down to Sheol, to the depths of the pit.

John 8: 42-47

42 Therefore Jesus said to them, "If God were your father, you would love me, for I came out and have come from God. For I haven't come of myself, but he sent me. 43 Why don't you understand my speech? Because you can't hear my word. 44 You are of your father, the devil, and you want to do the desires of your father. He was a murderer from the beginning, and doesn't stand in the truth, because there is no truth in him. When he speaks a lie, he speaks on his own; for he is a liar, and the father of lies. 45 But because I tell the truth, you don't believe me. 46 Which of you convicts me of sin? If I tell the truth, why do you not believe me? 47 He who is of God hears the words of God. For this cause you don't hear, because you are not of God."

Romans 16: 17-20

17 Now I beg you, brothers, look out for those who are causing the divisions and occasions of stumbling, contrary to the doctrine which you learned, and turn away from them. 18 For those who are such don't serve our Lord, Jesus Christ, but their own belly; and by their smooth and flattering speech, they deceive the hearts of the innocent. 19 For your obedience has become known to all. I rejoice therefore over you. But I desire to have you wise in that which is good, but innocent in that which is evil. 20 And the God of peace will quickly crush Satan under your feet. The grace of our Lord Jesus Christ be with you.

2 Corinthians 11: 13-15

13 For such men are false apostles, deceitful workers, masquerading as Christ's apostles. 14 And no wonder, for even Satan masquerades as an angel of light. 15 It is no great thing therefore if his servants also masquerade as servants of righteousness, whose end will be according to their works.

Ephesians 6: 12

12 For our wrestling is not against flesh and blood, but against the principalities, against the powers, against the world's rulers of the darkness of this age, and against the spiritual forces of wickedness in the heavenly places.

2 Thessalonians 2: 5-12

5 Don't you remember that, when I was still with you, I told you these things? 6 Now you know what is restraining him, to the end that he may be revealed in his own season. 7 For the mystery of lawlessness already works. Only there is one who restrains now, until he is taken out of the way. 8 Then the lawless one will be revealed, whom the Lord will kill with the breath of his mouth, and destroy by the manifestation of his coming; 9 even he whose coming is according to the working of Satan with all power and signs and lying wonders, 10 and with all deception of wickedness for those who are being lost, because they didn't receive the love of the truth, that they might be saved. 11 Because of this, God sends them a working of error, that they should believe a lie; 12 that they all might be judged who didn't believe the truth, but had pleasure in unrighteousness.

James 4: 7

7 Be subject therefore to God. Resist the devil, and he will flee from you.

1 Peter 5: 6-9

6 Humble yourselves therefore under the mighty hand of God, that he may exalt you in due time; 7 casting all your worries on him, because he cares for you. 8 Be sober and self-controlled. Be watchful. Your adversary, the devil, walks around like a roaring lion, seeking whom he may devour. 9 Withstand him steadfast in your faith, knowing that your brothers who are in the world are undergoing the same sufferings.

1 John 3: 7-8

7 Little children, let no one lead you astray. He who does righteousness is righteous, even as he is righteous. 8 He who sins is of the devil, for the devil has been sinning from the beginning. To this end the Son of God was revealed: that he might destroy the works of the devil.

1 John 5: 19-20

19 We know that we are of God, and the whole world lies in the power of the evil one. 20 We know that the Son of God has come, and has given us an understanding, that we know him who is true, and we are in him who is true, in his Son Jesus Christ. This is the true God, and eternal life.

Revelation 12: 7-12

7 There was war in the sky. Michael and his angels made war on the dragon. The dragon and his angels made war. 8 They didn't prevail, neither was a place found for them any more in heaven. 9 The great dragon was thrown down, the old serpent, he who is called the devil and Satan, the deceiver of the whole world. He was thrown down to the earth, and his angels were thrown down with him. 10 I heard a loud voice in heaven, saying, "Now the salvation, the power, and the Kingdom of our God, and the authority of his Christ has come; for the accuser of our brothers has been thrown down, who accuses them before our God day and night. 11 They overcame him because

of the Lamb's blood, and because of the word of their testimony. They didn't love their life, even to death. 12 Therefore rejoice, heavens, and you who dwell in them. Woe to the earth and to the sea, because the devil has gone down to you, having great wrath, knowing that he has but a short time."

Parables to be grasped

The Parable of the Growing Seed

Mark 4: 26-29

26 He said, "God's Kingdom is as if a man should cast seed on the earth, 27 and should sleep and rise night and day, and the seed should spring up and grow, though he doesn't know how. 28 For the earth bears fruit: first the blade, then the ear, then the full grain in the ear. 29 But when the fruit is ripe, immediately he puts in the sickle, because the harvest has come."

Author's Opinion

The *Parable of the Growing Seed* is about the Kingdom of God and how it grows in the believers' hearts. The Kingdom of God can be a mystery to man, but the earth will yield God's intended crop of believers. Man cannot go wrong in putting complete trust in the Word of God.

Psalm 1: 1-3 (NASB)

1 How blessed is the man who does not walk in the counsel of the wicked, Nor stand in the path of sinners, Nor sit in the seat of scoffers! 2 But his delight is in the law of the Lord, And in His law he meditates day and night. 3 He will be like a tree firmly planted by streams of water, Which yields its fruit in its season And its leaf does not wither; And in whatever he does, he prospers.

In another respect it might be said The Growing Seed is about a division of labor. It pleased God that *man should cast seed* or proclaim the Gospel to the people around him. Christians are to witness boldly and tenderly to all about His offer of grace to the glory of Jesus. After people have heard the Good News Gospel it is God's part to say who, where, when and how the word of God or *the seed should spring up and grow,* taking root in an individual's heart. The Word of God will not go out void and it will accomplish God's intended purpose. We may not be able to see or *know how,* this growth take place. This Parable also shows us that maturity in the Christian life takes time both in us personally and in other people. As we go about our lives (working and sleeping) trying to keep the faith, we develop different spiritual gifts that sprout and grow to His glory, over our lifetime. In the fullness of time, *when the fruit is ripe,* the Gospel message will have been spread to all the nations and peoples of the world He will gather the harvest into His Heavenly Kingdom.

Isaiah 55: 11

> 11 So is my word that goes out of my mouth; it will not return to me void, but it will accomplish that which I please, and it will prosper in the thing I sent it to do.

1 Peter 3: 15

> 15 But sanctify the Lord God in your hearts; and always be ready to give an answer to everyone who asks you a reason concerning the hope that is in you, with humility and fear:

1 Corinthians 15: 1-4

> 1 Now I declare to you, brothers, the Good News which I preached to you, which also you received, in which you also stand, 2 by which also you are saved, if you hold firmly the word which I preached to you—unless you believed in vain. 3 For I delivered to you first of all

that which I also received: that Christ died for our sins according to the Scriptures, 4 that he was buried, that he was raised on the third day according to the Scriptures,

Matthew 10: 23

23 But when they persecute you in this city, flee into the next, for most certainly I tell you, you will not have gone through the cities of Israel, until the Son of Man has come.

1 Corinthians 15: 20-26

20 But now Christ has been raised from the dead. He became the first fruits of those who are asleep. 21 For since death came by man, the resurrection of the dead also came by man. 22 For as in Adam all die, so also in Christ all will be made alive. 23 But each in his own order: Christ the first fruits, then those who are Christ's, at his coming. 24 Then the end comes, when he will deliver up the Kingdom to God, even the Father; when he will have abolished all rule and all authority and power. 25 For he must reign until he has put all his enemies under his feet. 26 The last enemy that will be abolished is death.

The Parable of the Unshrunk Cloth on Old Garment

Matthew 9: 16

16 No one puts a piece of unshrunk cloth on an old garment; for the patch would tear away from the garment, and a worse hole is made.

Author's opinion

The *Parable of the Unshrunk Cloth on an old Garment* is about pleasing God by faith and not by works. It is showing the incompatibility of the old covenant with Adam and Eve of works noted in Genesis 2; 15-17 and the new covenant of Grace. After the fall of man, as described in *Genesis 3: 14-21*, God created a new covenant of Grace, with Abraham where all the families of all the nations of the Earth can be blessed, through faith, as recorded in *Genesis 12: 1-3*. Mankind has always tried to please God through good works, bypassing the idea of repentance and simple faith in our Redeemer and Lord. *Genesis 22: 18* (Promises) 18 *All the nations of the earth will be blessed by your offspring, because you have obeyed my voice."* Good works alone without faith is like putting new cloth on an old garment, it will come apart, not passing the test of time. If we are guilty of just one law, we are still guilty in the sight of God's Law. The old covenant of works or trying to please God by keeping the law is impossible because of our sin nature. God in His mercy has given us this new covenant of Grace through faith in Jesus. When we reject Jesus as Lord we are choosing to reject the new covenant of faith. If man asks for justice before God, man will fail in his quest, because we are all guilty of sin. If man asks for mercy through faith in Jesus, God is faithful and merciful to forgiving our sins and welcoming us into his family.

Isaiah 59: 21 (NASB)

> 21 "As for Me, this is My covenant with them," says the Lord: "My Spirit which is upon you, and My words which I have put in your mouth shall not depart from your mouth, nor from the mouth of your offspring, nor from the mouth of your offspring's offspring," says the Lord, "from now and forever."

Romans 1: 16-17

> 16 For I am not ashamed of the Good News of Christ, because it is the power of God for salvation for everyone who believes; for the Jew first, and also for the Greek. 17 For in it is revealed God's righteousness from faith to faith. As it is written, "But the righteous shall live by faith."

Ephesians 2: 8-9

> 8 for by grace you have been saved through faith, and that not of yourselves; it is the gift of God, 9 not of works, that no one would boast.

The Parable of the New Wine in Old Wineskins.

Matthew 9: 17

> 17 Neither do people put new wine into old wine skins, or else the skins would burst, and the wine be spilled, and the skins ruined. No, they put new wine into fresh wine skins, and both are preserved."

Author's Opinion

The *Parable of the New Wine in Old Wineskins* is also about knowing that works without faith are futile. The people to whom Jesus spoke knew that putting new wine in to new wineskins stretches the wineskins in the fermentation processes. They also knew that putting new wine into old wineskins for a second time was foolish because it would break the old (already expanded) wine skins. The New Covenant of faith and the Old Covenant of Works are also incompatible with each other. God's New Covenant of faith is intended to replace and make void the Old Covenant of works, through our faith. This New Covenant of faith is based on Jesus Christ' atonement and righteousness, not on man's good works or self-righteousness. Either we submit to the free gift of Grace by faith and believe, or stand accountable to God's law. Christ paid the sacrificial price for our sin, so that sinful man could be reconciled with God.

2 Peter 3: 9

9 The Lord is not slow concerning his promise, as some count slowness; but is patient with us, not wishing that any should perish, but that all should come to repentance.

The Old Law Covenant guides us but also condemns us. Without faith, our sin makes us like old wineskins; we are stretched and ruined in the sight of the Lord. This parable of new wine in old wineskins is showing us that the New Covenant of Faith preserves both the righteousness of God and His believers. God sees no value in good works without faith; they are incompatible, but good works with faith brings glory to God.

Luke 22: 20

20 Likewise, he took the cup after supper, saying, "This cup is the new covenant in my blood, which is poured out for you.

Romans 8: 1-6

1 There is therefore now no condemnation to those who are in Christ Jesus, who don't walk according to the flesh, but according to the Spirit. 2 For the law of the Spirit of life in Christ Jesus made me free from the law of sin and of death. 3 For what the law couldn't do, in that it was weak through the flesh, God did, sending his own Son in the likeness of sinful flesh and for sin, he condemned sin in the flesh; 4 that the ordinance of the law might be fulfilled in us, who walk not after the flesh, but after the Spirit. 5 For those who live according to the flesh set their minds on the things of the flesh, but those who live according to the Spirit, the things of the Spirit. 6 For the mind of the flesh is death, but the mind of the Spirit is life and peace;

The Parable of the Two Sons

Matthew 21: 28-32

> 28 But what do you think? A man had two sons, and he came to the first, and said, 'Son, go work today in my vineyard.' 29 He answered, 'I will not,' but afterward he changed his mind, and went. 30 He came to the second, and said the same thing. He answered, 'I'm going, sir,' but he didn't go. 31 Which of the two did the will of his father?" They said to him, "The first." Jesus said to them, "Most certainly I tell you that the tax collectors and the prostitutes are entering into God's Kingdom before you. 32 For John came to you in the way of righteousness, and you didn't believe him, but the tax collectors and the prostitutes believed him. When you saw it, you didn't even repent afterward, that you might believe him.

Author's opinion

The *Parable of the Two Sons* tells us about two types of religious people. There is the person who says he is religious but in fact is not obedient to God's will. There is also the repentant person who does the will of the Father. We all come with a sin nature that is initially rebellious toward the gospel. Some people have a change of heart, having been converted and come to repent their actions and seek a right relationship with their Heavenly Father. The second type as described in this parable are the people that give lip service to and give the appearance of being religious and serving God, however their pride and self-righteousness prevents them from seeing their true sin nature and their need for reconciliation with God, They, in reality, have no intention of doing as the father asked. The father let the two sons make their own choices as to how they would serve him. Man's free choice to worship or not worship is part of the attributes of being created in

God's image. To the casual observer things are not always as they seem, but God knows who serves Him and who do not serve Him. The harlot and tax collector who believed are preferred over the proud and arrogant who do not truly believe, in spite of outward appearances. *17 For my eyes are on all their ways. They are not hidden from my face. Their iniquity isn't concealed from my eyes. Jeremiah 16: 17* God judges the heart of each person and asks him to believe in truth and spirit, giving his all to Jesus without holding anything back.

Jeremiah 17: 9-10 (NASB)

> 9 "The heart is more deceitful than all else And is desperately sick; Who can understand it? 10 "I, the Lord, search the heart, I test the mind, Even to give to each man according to his ways, According to the results of his deeds.

John 3: 36

> 36 One who believes in the Son has eternal life, but one who disobeys the Son won't see life, but the wrath of God remains on him."

Chapter 8

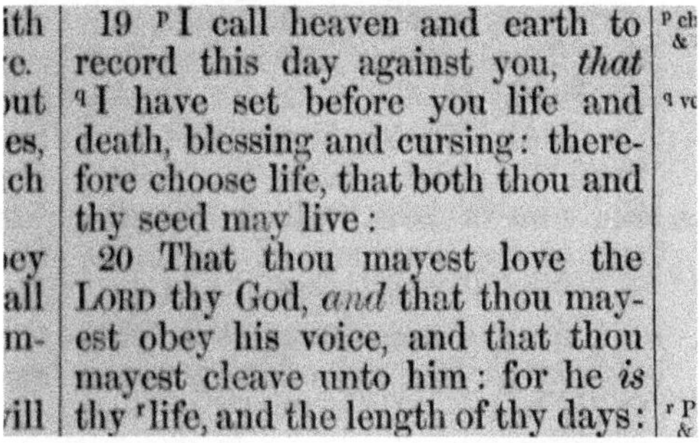

19 [p] I call heaven and earth to record this day against you, *that* [q] I have set before you life and death, blessing and cursing: therefore choose life, that both thou and thy seed may live:
20 That thou mayest love the LORD thy God, *and* that thou mayest obey his voice, and that thou mayest cleave unto him: for he *is* thy [r] life, and the length of thy days:

What choice do we have?

Genesis 2: 15-17 (NASB)

> **15** Then the Lord God took the man and put him into the garden of Eden to cultivate it and keep it. **16** The Lord God commanded the man, saying, "From any tree of the garden you may eat freely; **17** but from the tree of the knowledge of good and evil you shall not eat, for in the day that you eat from it you will surely die."

Genesis 22: 15-18 (NASB)

> **15** Then the angel of the Lord called to Abraham a second time from heaven, **16** and said, "By Myself I have sworn, declares the Lord, because you have done this thing and have not withheld your son, your only son, **17** indeed I will greatly bless you, and I will greatly multiply your seed as the stars of the heavens and as the sand which

is on the seashore; and your seed shall possess the gate of their enemies. 18 In your seed all the nations of the earth shall be blessed, because you have obeyed My voice."

Nehemiah 9: 17 (NASB)

17 "They refused to listen, And did not remember Your wondrous deeds which You had performed among them; So they became stubborn and appointed a leader to return to their slavery in Egypt. But You are a God of forgiveness, Gracious and compassionate, Slow to anger and abounding in lovingkindness; And You did not forsake them.

Psalms 86: 11-13 (NASB)

11 Teach me Your way, O Lord; I will walk in Your truth; Unite my heart to fear Your name. 12 I will give thanks to You, O Lord my God, with all my heart, And will glorify Your name forever. 13 For Your lovingkindness toward me is great, And You have delivered my soul from the depths of Sheol.

Joshua. 24: 15 (NASB)

15 If it is disagreeable in your sight to serve the Lord, choose for yourselves today whom you will serve: whether the gods which your fathers served which were beyond the River, or the gods of the Amorites in whose land you are living; but as for me and my house, we will serve the Lord."

Matthew 11: 28

28 "Come to me, all you who labor and are heavily burdened, and I will give you rest.

Romans 9: 24-33 (NASB)

24 even us, whom He also called, not from among Jews only, but also from among Gentiles. 25 As He says also in Hosea, "I will call those who were not My people, 'My people,' And her who was not

beloved, 'beloved.'" 26 "And it shall be that in the place where it was said to them, 'you are not My people,' There they shall be called sons of the living God." 27 Isaiah cries out concerning Israel, "Though the number of the sons of Israel be like the sand of the sea, it is the remnant that will be saved; 28 for the Lord will execute His word on the earth, thoroughly and quickly." 29 And just as Isaiah foretold, "Unless the Lord of Sabaoth had left to us a posterity, We would have become like Sodom, and would have resembled Gomorrah." 30 What shall we say then? That Gentiles, who did not pursue righteousness, attained righteousness, even the righteousness which is by faith; 31 but Israel, pursuing a law of righteousness, did not arrive at that law. 32 Why? Because they did not pursue it by faith, but as though it were by works. They stumbled over the stumbling stone, 33 just as it is written, "Behold, I lay in Zion a stone of stumbling and a rock of offense, And he who believes in Him will not be disappointed."

James 1: 22-25

22 But be doers of the word, and not only hearers, deluding your own selves. 23 For if anyone is a hearer of the word and not a doer, he is like a man looking at his natural face in a mirror; 24 for he sees himself, and goes away, and immediately forgets what kind of man he was. 25 But he who looks into the perfect law of freedom, and continues, not being a hearer who forgets, but a doer of the work, this man will be blessed in what he does.

1 John 2: 3-6

3 This is how we know that we know him: if we keep his commandments. 4 One who says, "I know him," and doesn't keep his commandments, is a liar, and the truth isn't in him. 5 But whoever keeps his word, God's love has most certainly been perfected in him. This is how we know that we are in him: 6 he who says he remains in him ought himself also to walk just like he walked.

Colossians 1: 21-22

21 You, being in past times alienated and enemies in your mind in your evil deeds, 22 yet now he has reconciled in the body of his flesh through death, to present you holy and without defect and blameless before him,

Psalms 81: 11-16 (NASB)

11 "But My people did not listen to My voice, And Israel did not obey Me. 12 "So I gave them over to the stubbornness of their heart, To walk in their own devices. 13 "Oh that My people would listen to Me, That Israel would walk in My ways! 14 "I would quickly subdue their enemies And turn My hand against their adversaries. 15 "Those who hate the Lord would pretend obedience to Him, And their time of punishment would be forever. 16 "But I would feed you with the finest of the wheat, And with honey from the rock I would satisfy you."

Revelation 16 10-11

10 The fifth poured out his bowl on the throne of the beast, and his kingdom was darkened. They gnawed their tongues because of the pain, 11 and they blasphemed the God of heaven because of their pains and their sores. They didn't repent of their works.

Revelation. 22: 17

17 The Spirit and the bride say, "Come!" He who hears, let him say, "Come!" He who is thirsty, let him come. He who desires, let him take the water of life freely.

Author's Opinion

We only have two choices that have eternal consequences. Either we repent and faithfully believe or disbelieve; that is the question that each of us must decide. In this world there are two unseen spiritual forces within man. Each person has two opposing voices trying to guide and dominate. Satan is always asking; What is in it for me? God is saying; Love your God and your neighbor and do unto others as you would have them do unto you. The people around us may not know the internal struggle that is raging within us, but we know. God and Satan know which master dominates our actions.

Deut. 30: 19 (NASB)

19 I call heaven and earth to witness against you today, that I have set before you life and death, the blessing and the curse. So choose life in order that you may live, you and your descendants,

Matthew 25: 40

40 "The King will answer them, 'Most certainly I tell you, because you did it to one of the least of these my brothers, you did it to me.

John 20: 31

31 but these are written, that you may believe that Jesus is the Christ, the Son of God, and that believing you may have life in his name.

Paradoxes to be examined

Pride

Psalm 10: 2-11 (NASB)

2 In pride the wicked hotly pursue the afflicted; Let them be caught in the plots which they have devised. 3 For the wicked boasts of his heart's desire, And the greedy man curses and spurns the Lord. 4 The wicked, in the haughtiness of his countenance, does not seek Him. All his thoughts are, "There is no God." 5 His ways prosper at all times; Your judgments are on high, out of his sight; As for all his adversaries, he snorts at them. 6 He says to himself, "I will not be moved; Throughout all generations I will not be in adversity." 7 His

mouth is full of curses and deceit and oppression; Under his tongue is mischief and wickedness. 8 He sits in the lurking places of the villages; In the hiding places he kills the innocent; His eyes stealthily watch for the unfortunate. 9 He lurks in a hiding place as a lion in his lair; He lurks to catch the afflicted; He catches the afflicted when he draws him into his net. 10 He crouches, he bows down, And the unfortunate fall by his mighty ones. 11 He says to himself, "God has forgotten; He has hidden His face; He will never see it."

Proverbs 13: 10

10 Pride only breeds quarrels, but with ones who take advice is wisdom.

Proverbs 16: 18

18 Pride goes before destruction, and a haughty spirit before a fall.

Isaiah 14: 12-15 (NASB)

12 How you have fallen from heaven, O star of the morning, son of the dawn! You have been cut down to the earth, You who have weakened the nations! 13 "But you said in your heart, 'I will ascend to heaven; I will raise my throne above the stars of God, And I will sit on the mount of assembly In the recesses of the north. 14 'I will ascend above the heights of the clouds; I will make myself like the Most High.' 15 "Nevertheless you will be thrust down to Sheol, To the recesses of the pit.

1 John 2: 15-17

15 Don't love the world or the things that are in the world. If anyone loves the world, the Father's love isn't in him. 16 For all that is in the world, the lust of the flesh, the lust of the eyes, and the pride of life, isn't the Father's, but is the world's. 17 The world is passing away with its lusts, but he who does God's will remains forever.

James 4: 6-10

6 But he gives more grace. Therefore it says, "God resists the proud, but gives grace to the humble 7 Be subject therefore to God. Resist the devil, and he will flee from you. 8 Draw near to God, and he will draw near to you. Cleanse your hands, you sinners; and purify your hearts, you double-minded. 9 Lament, mourn, and weep. Let your laughter be turned to mourning, and your joy to gloom. 10 Humble yourselves in the sight of the Lord, and he will exalt you.

Hypocrisy

Psalm 119: 113-115

113 I hate double-minded men, but I love your law. 114 You are my hiding place and my shield. I hope in your word. 115 Depart from me, you evildoers, that I may keep the commandments of my God.

Micah 4: 9-12 (NASB)

9 "Now, why do you cry out loudly? Is there no king among you, Or has your counselor perished, That agony has gripped you like a woman in childbirth? 10 "Writhe and labor to give birth, Daughter of Zion, Like a woman in childbirth; For now you will go out of the city, Dwell in the field, And go to Babylon. There you will be rescued; There the Lord will redeem you From the hand of your enemies. 11 "And now many nations have been assembled against you Who say, 'Let her be polluted, And let our eyes gloat over Zion.' 12 "But they do not know the thoughts of the Lord, And they do not understand His purpose; For He has gathered them like sheaves to the threshing floor.

Matthew 23: 25-28

25 "Woe to you, scribes and Pharisees, hypocrites! For you clean the outside of the cup and of the platter, but within they are full of extortion and unrighteousness. 26 You blind Pharisee, first clean the inside of the cup and of the platter, that its outside may become

clean also. 27 "Woe to you, scribes and Pharisees, hypocrites! For you are like whitened tombs, which outwardly appear beautiful, but inwardly are full of dead men's bones, and of all uncleanness. 28 Even so you also outwardly appear righteous to men, but inwardly you are full of hypocrisy and iniquity.

1 Peter 2: 1-3

1 Putting away therefore all wickedness, all deceit, hypocrisies, envies, and all evil speaking, 2 as newborn babies, long for the pure milk of the Word, that with it you may grow, 3 if indeed you have tasted that the Lord is gracious:

2 Peter 2: 17-22

17 These are wells without water, clouds driven by a storm; for whom the blackness of darkness has been reserved forever. 18 For, uttering great swelling words of emptiness, they entice in the lusts of the flesh, by licentiousness, those who are indeed escaping from those who live in error; 19 promising them liberty, while they themselves are bondservants of corruption; for a man is brought into bondage by whoever overcomes him. 20 For if, after they have escaped the defilement of the world through the knowledge of the Lord and Savior Jesus Christ, they are again entangled in it and overcome, the last state has become worse for them than the first. 21 For it would be better for them not to have known the way of righteousness, than, after knowing it, to turn back from the holy commandment delivered to them. 22 But it has happened to them according to the true proverb, "The dog turns to his own vomit again," and "the sow that has washed to wallowing in the mire."

1 John 2: 3-4

3 This is how we know that we know him: if we keep his commandments. 4 One who says, "I know him," and doesn't keep his commandments, is a liar, and the truth isn't in him.

Hell

Matthew 25: 46

46 These will go away into eternal punishment, but the righteous into eternal life."

Mark 9: 42-43 (NASB)

42 "Whoever causes one of these little ones who believe to stumble, it would be better for him if, with a heavy millstone hung around his neck, he had been cast into the sea. 43 If your hand causes you to stumble, cut it off; it is better for you to enter life crippled, than, having your two hands, to go into hell, into the unquenchable fire,

Luke 16: 25

25 "But Abraham said, 'Son, remember that you, in your lifetime, received your good things, and Lazarus, in the same way, bad things. But here he is now comforted, and you are in anguish.

2 Thessalonians 1: 8-9

8 punishing those who don't know God, and to those who don't obey the Good News of our Lord Jesus, 9 who will pay the penalty: eternal destruction from the face of the Lord and from the glory of his might,

Matthew 7: 13-14

13 "Enter in by the narrow gate; for wide is the gate and broad is the way that leads to destruction, and many are those who enter in by it. 14 How narrow is the gate, and restricted is the way that leads to life! Few are those who find it.

Matthew 13: 47-50

47 "Again, the Kingdom of Heaven is like a dragnet, that was cast into the sea, and gathered some fish of every kind, 48 which, when it was filled, they drew up on the beach. They sat down, and gathered the good into containers, but the bad they threw away. 49 So will it be in

the end of the world. The angels will come and separate the wicked from among the righteous, 50 and will cast them into the furnace of fire. There will be the weeping and the gnashing of teeth."

Revelations 19: 19-21

19 I saw the beast, and the kings of the earth, and their armies, gathered together to make war against him who sat on the horse, and against his army. 20 The beast was taken, and with him the false prophet who worked the signs in his sight, with which he deceived those who had received the mark of the beast and those who worshiped his image. These two were thrown alive into the lake of fire that burns with sulfur. 21 The rest were killed with the sword of him who sat on the horse, the sword which came out of his mouth. All the birds were filled with their flesh.

Revelation 14: 11

11 The smoke of their torment goes up forever and ever. They have no rest day and night, those who worship the beast and his image, and whoever receives the mark of his name.

Heaven

Isaiah 65: 16-19

16 so that he who blesses himself in the earth will bless himself in the God of truth; and he who swears in the earth will swear by the God of truth; because the former troubles are forgotten, and because they are hidden from my eyes. 17 "For, behold, I create new heavens and a new earth; and the former things will not be remembered, nor come into mind. 18 But be glad and rejoice forever in that which I create; for, behold, I create Jerusalem to be a delight, and her people a joy. 19 I will rejoice in Jerusalem, and delight in my people; and the voice of weeping and the voice of crying will be heard in her no more.

Isaiah 66: 1-2 (NASB)

1 Thus says the Lord, "Heaven is My throne and the earth is My footstool. Where then is a house you could build for Me? And where is a place that I may rest? 2 "For My hand made all these things, Thus all these things came into being," declares the Lord. "But to this one I will look, To him who is humble and contrite of spirit, and who trembles at My word.

1 Corinthians 2: 9-11

9 But as it is written, "Things which an eye didn't see, and an ear didn't hear, which didn't enter into the heart of man, these God has prepared for those who love him." 10 But to us, God revealed them through the Spirit. For the Spirit searches all things, yes, the deep things of God. 11 For who among men knows the things of a man, except the spirit of the man, which is in him? Even so, no one knows the things of God, except God's Spirit.

Matthew 6: 19-21

19 "Don't lay up treasures for yourselves on the earth, where moth and rust consume, and where thieves break through and steal; 20 but lay up for yourselves treasures in heaven, where neither moth nor rust consume, and where thieves don't break through and steal; 21 for where your treasure is, there your heart will be also.

John 14: 1-3

1 "Don't let your heart be troubled. Believe in God. Believe also in me. 2 In my Father's house are many homes. If it weren't so, I would have told you. I am going to prepare a place for you. 3 If I go and prepare a place for you, I will come again, and will receive you to myself; that where I am, you may be there also.

2 Corinthians 5: 1-8 (NASB)

1 For we know that if the earthly tent which is our house is torn down, we have a building from God, a house not made with hands, eternal in the heavens. 2 For indeed in this house we groan, longing to be clothed with our dwelling from heaven, 3 inasmuch as we, having put it on, will not be found naked. 4 For indeed while we are in this tent, we groan, being burdened, because we do not want to be unclothed but to be clothed, so that what is mortal will be swallowed up by life. 5 Now He who prepared us for this very purpose is God, who gave to us the Spirit as a pledge. 6 Therefore, being always of good courage, and knowing that while we are at home in the body we are absent from the Lord— 7 for we walk by faith, not by sight— 8 we are of good courage, I say, and prefer rather to be absent from the body and to be at home with the Lord.

Revelation 21: 1-4

1 I saw a new heaven and a new earth: for the first heaven and the first earth have passed away, and the sea is no more. 2 I saw the holy city, New Jerusalem, coming down out of heaven from God, prepared like a bride adorned for her husband. 3 I heard a loud voice out of heaven saying, "Behold, God's dwelling is with people, and he will dwell with them, and they will be his people, and God himself will be with them as their God. 4 He will wipe away every tear from their eyes. Death will be no more; neither will there be mourning, nor crying, nor pain, any more. The first things have passed away."

Parables to be grasped

The Parable of the Laborers

Matthew 20: 1-16

1 "For the Kingdom of Heaven is like a man who was the master of

a household, who went out early in the morning to hire laborers for his vineyard. 2 When he had agreed with the laborers for a denarius a day, he sent them into his vineyard. 3 He went out about the third hour, and saw others standing idle in the marketplace. 4 He said to them, 'You also go into the vineyard, and whatever is right I will give you.' So they went their way. 5 Again he went out about the sixth and the ninth hour, and did likewise. 6 About the eleventh hour he went out, and found others standing idle. He said to them, 'Why do you stand here all day idle?' 7 "They said to him, 'Because no one has hired us.' "He said to them, 'You also go into the vineyard, and you will receive whatever is right.' 8 When evening had come, the lord of the vineyard said to his manager, 'Call the laborers and pay them their wages, beginning from the last to the first.' 9 "When those who were hired at about the eleventh hour came, they each received a denarius. 10 When the first came, they supposed that they would receive more; and they likewise each received a denarius. 11 When they received it, they murmured against the master of the household, 12 saying, 'These last have spent one hour, and you have made them equal to us, who have borne the burden of the day and the scorching heat!' 13 "But he answered one of them, 'Friend, I am doing you no wrong. Didn't you agree with me for a denarius? 14 Take that which is yours, and go your way. It is my desire to give to this last just as much as to you. 15 Isn't it lawful for me to do what I want to with what I own? Or is your eye evil, because I am good?' 16 So the last will be first, and the first last. For many are called, but few are chosen."

Author's Opinion

The *Parable of the Laborers* is about gratitude for the Lord's gift of grace to us. He calls us into His kingdom at different ages and stages of life. Some have long and arduous times living the Christian life while others have it seemingly very easy. Mans' perspective of what is fair is not the same as

God's perspective. We are not in a position to negotiate with God, or tell Him how we think it ought to be. What do we have to offer Him? We should not be jealous or resentful of others, only grateful for His love to us in whatever station of life we find ourselves. *(Or is your eye evil because I am good?)* When Jesus knocks on the door, we must make the choice whether to let Him in our hearts or not. The cost of discipleship means resolving never to make complaints as to the terms and condition that follow. *('You also go into the vineyard, and you will receive whatever is right.')* God shows mercy and decides whatever is right for us whenever He pleases. Our blessings are not the result of our work but of His free gift of grace through faith in Jesus Christ.

Hebrews 12: 28-29

> 28 Therefore, receiving a Kingdom that can't be shaken, let us have grace, through which we serve God acceptably, with reverence and awe, 29 for our God is a consuming fire.

Colossians 1: 10-14

> 10 that you may walk worthily of the Lord, to please him in all respects, bearing fruit in every good work, and increasing in the knowledge of God; 11 strengthened with all power, according to the might of his glory, for all endurance and perseverance with joy; 12 giving thanks to the Father, who made us fit to be partakers of the inheritance of the saints in light; 13 who delivered us out of the power of darkness, and translated us into the Kingdom of the Son of his love; 14 in whom we have our redemption, the forgiveness of our sins;

The Parable of the Woman and the Judge

Luke 18: 1-8

> 1 He also spoke a parable to them that they must always pray, and

not give up, 2 saying, "There was a judge in a certain city who didn't fear God, and didn't respect man. 3 A widow was in that city, and she often came to him, saying, 'Defend me from my adversary!' 4 He wouldn't for a while, but afterward he said to himself, 'Though I neither fear God, nor respect man, 5 yet because this widow bothers me, I will defend her, or else she will wear me out by her continual coming.'" 6 The Lord said, "Listen to what the unrighteous judge says. 7 Won't God avenge his chosen ones, who are crying out to him day and night, and yet he exercises patience with them? 8 I tell you that he will avenge them quickly. Nevertheless, when the Son of Man comes, will he find faith on the earth?"

Author's Opinion

The Parable of the Woman and the Judge is about encouraging believers to be persistent in prayer. God is faithful. God hears our prayers and gives us assurance that He will be faithful in bringing about justice. This Parable tells us about a judge who is a civil servant who is not being responsible to the public trust that is indicative of his public office. He does not fear the people or God. But because a woman has chosen to be persistent in demanding justice, the judge relents and gives her protection from her opponent. God's love and faithfulness for us, His elect, is far beyond man's ability to imagine or describe. Our persistent prayer *(always pray, and not give up)* is our way of trusting and worshiping our Father in Heaven. The question about faith on earth when he returns is about having faith with a sense of urgency, not complacency. He is encouraging His disciples and us to be faithful in prayer, even to the end of the age.

Matthew 7: 7-12

7 "Ask, and it will be given you. Seek, and you will find. Knock, and it will be opened for you. 8 For everyone who asks receives. He who

seeks finds. To him who knocks it will be opened. 9 Or who is there among you, who, if his son asks him for bread, will give him a stone? 10 Or if he asks for a fish, who will give him a serpent? 11 If you then, being evil, know how to give good gifts to your children, how much more will your Father who is in heaven give good things to those who ask him! 12 Therefore whatever you desire for men to do to you, you shall also do to them; for this is the law and the prophets.

Luke 11: 5-8

5 He said to them, "Which of you, if you go to a friend at midnight, and tell him, 'Friend, lend me three loaves of bread, 6 for a friend of mine has come to me from a journey, and I have nothing to set before him,' 7 and he from within will answer and say, 'Don't bother me. The door is now shut, and my children are with me in bed. I can't get up and give it to you'? 8 I tell you, although he will not rise and give it to him because he is his friend, yet because of his persistence, he will get up and give him as many as he needs.

Galatians 4: 6-7 (NASB)

6 Because you are sons, God has sent forth the Spirit of His Son into our hearts, crying, "Abba! Father!" 7 Therefore you are no longer a slave, but a son; and if a son, then an heir through God.

Hebrews 11: 6

6 Without faith it is impossible to be well pleasing to him, for he who comes to God must believe that he exists, and that he is a rewarder of those who seek him.

The Parable of the Cost of Discipleship

Luke 14: 25-35

25 Now great multitudes were going with him. He turned and said to them, 26 "If anyone comes to me, and doesn't disregard his own

father, mother, wife, children, brothers, and sisters, yes, and his own life also, he can't be my disciple. 27 Whoever doesn't bear his own cross, and come after me, can't be my disciple. 28 For which of you, desiring to build a tower, doesn't first sit down and count the cost, to see if he has enough to complete it? 29 Or perhaps, when he has laid a foundation, and is not able to finish, everyone who sees begins to mock him, 30 saying, 'This man began to build, and wasn't able to finish.' 31 Or what king, as he goes to encounter another king in war, will not sit down first and consider whether he is able with ten thousand to meet him who comes against him with twenty thousand? 32 Or else, while the other is yet a great way off, he sends an envoy, and asks for conditions of peace. 33 So therefore whoever of you who doesn't renounce all that he has, he can't be my disciple. 34 Salt is good, but if the salt becomes flat and tasteless, with what do you season it? 35 It is fit neither for the soil nor for the manure pile. It is thrown out. He who has ears to hear, let him hear."

Author's Opinion

The *Parable of the Cost of Discipleship* is about making a clear choice, while knowing the difficulty of being a (servant) disciple of Jesus and resolving to publicly bear the cross of Jesus potentially at great personal cost *(for whoever of you does not forsake his own life also, he can't be my disciple.)* Jesus is not discouraging love of family, but is describing the priority of loyalty that a believer must have. In some societies, becoming a Christian means being ostracized from loved ones or even martyred. Jesus knows the difficulty that lies ahead for Himself and all his followers that will come in the future. Salt without flavor is useless. We are to let the light of Jesus shine through us so that men can see our good works to the glory of God. We must know that the straight and narrow way is difficult but the rewards are "out of this world great."

Matthew 10: 34-38

> 34 "Don't think that I came to send peace on the earth. I didn't come to send peace, but a sword. 35 For I came to set a man at odds against his father, and a daughter against her mother, and a daughter-in-law against her mother-in-law. 36 A man's foes will be those of his own household. 37 He who loves father or mother more than me is not worthy of me; and he who loves son or daughter more than me isn't worthy of me. 38 He who doesn't take his cross and follow after me, isn't worthy of me.

Luke 10: 27

> 27 He answered, "You shall love the Lord your God with all your heart, with all your soul, with all your strength, and with all your mind; and your neighbor as yourself."

Luke 6: 40

> 40 A disciple is not above his teacher, but everyone when he is fully trained will be like his teacher.

John 3: 16

> 16 For God so loved the world, that he gave his one and only Son, that whoever believes in him should not perish, but have eternal life.

1 Peter 5: 10

> 10 But may the God of all grace, who called you to his eternal glory by Christ Jesus, after you have suffered a little while, perfect, establish, strengthen, and settle you.

The Parable of the Rich Fool

Luke 12: 13-21

> 13 One of the multitude said to him, "Teacher, tell my brother to divide the inheritance with me." 14 But he said to him, "Man, who made

me a judge or an arbitrator over you?" 15 He said to them, "Beware! Keep yourselves from covetousness, for a man's life doesn't consist of the abundance of the things which he possesses." 16 He spoke a parable to them, saying, "The ground of a certain rich man produced abundantly. 17 He reasoned within himself, saying, 'What will I do, because I don't have room to store my crops?' 18 He said, 'This is what I will do. I will pull down my barns, and build bigger ones, and there I will store all my grain and my goods. 19 I will tell my soul, "Soul, you have many goods laid up for many years. Take your ease, eat, drink, be merry."' 20 "But God said to him, 'You foolish one, tonight your soul is required of you. The things which you have prepared – whose will they be?' 21 So is he who lays up treasure for himself, and is not rich toward God."

Author's Opinion

The *Parable of the Rich Fool* is about guarding against the greed of physical wealth of this world. Jesus would not be drawn into a dispute between two brothers over an inheritance. He warns them about the problem of covetousness. Jesus tells this parable about a successful and productive farmer. The farmer thinks to himself, "I will tear down my barns and build larger ones to store all that I possess." The rich fool thought his security was in his wealth. But God said, "Not so" You foolish one, tonight your soul is required of you. We can choose to see and lust for only the trivial things of this world thus denying the unseen mysteries of the ages and ignoring the spiritual blessings of God. But that would be the wrong way to understand the most important thing in this world. We should be seeking the gift of eternal life. The right answer is found in *Matthew 6: 33* 33 *But seek first God's Kingdom, and his righteousness; and all these things will be given to you as well.*

1 Timothy 6: 9-11

9 But those who are determined to be rich fall into a temptation and a snare and many foolish and harmful lusts, such as drown men in ruin and destruction. 10 For the love of money is a root of all kinds of evil. Some have been led astray from the faith in their greed, and have pierced themselves through with many sorrows. 11 But you, man of God, flee these things, and follow after righteousness, godliness, faith, love, perseverance, and gentleness.

James 1: 6-12

6 But let him ask in faith, without any doubting, for he who doubts is like a wave of the sea, driven by the wind and tossed. 7 For that man shouldn't think that he will receive anything from the Lord. 8 He is a double-minded man, unstable in all his ways. 9 But let the brother in humble circumstances glory in his high position; 10 and the rich, in that he is made humble, because like the flower in the grass, he will pass away. 11 For the sun arises with the scorching wind, and withers the grass, and the flower in it falls, and the beauty of its appearance perishes. So also will the rich man fade away in his pursuits.
12 Blessed is the man who endures temptation, for when he has been approved, he will receive the crown of life, which the Lord promised to those who love him.

The Parable of the Unjust Servant

Luke 16: 1-13 (NASB)

1 Now He was also saying to the disciples, "There was a rich man who had a *manager,* and this *manager* was to him as squandering his possessions. 2 And he called him and said to him, 'What is this I hear about you? Give an accounting of your management, for you can no longer be manager.' 3 The manager said to himself, 'What shall I do, since my master is taking the management away from me? I am not strong enough to dig; I am ashamed to beg. 4 I know

what I shall do, so that when I am removed from the management people will welcome me into their homes.' 5 And he summoned each one of his master's debtors, and he began saying to the first, 'How much do you owe my master?' 6 And he said, 'A hundred measures of oil.' And he said to him, 'Take your bill, and sit down quickly and write fifty.' 7 Then he said to another, 'And how much do you owe?' And he said, 'A hundred measures of wheat.' He *said to him, 'Take your bill, and write eighty.' 8 And his master praised the unrighteous manager because he had acted shrewdly; for the sons of this age are more shrewd in relation to their own kind than the sons of light. 9 And I say to you, make friends for yourselves by means of the wealth of unrighteousness, so that when it fails, they will receive you into the eternal dwellings. 10 "He who is faithful in a very little thing is faithful also in much; and he who is unrighteous in a very little thing is unrighteous also in much. 11 Therefore if you have not been faithful in the use of unrighteous wealth, who will entrust the true riches to you? 12 And if you have not been faithful in the use of that which is another's, who will give you that which is your own? 13 No servant can serve two masters; for either he will hate the one and love the other, or else he will be devoted to one and despise the other. You cannot serve God and wealth."

Author's Opinion

The *Parable of the Unjust Servant* is about choosing to use wealth honestly and wisely in a manner that is useful to the kingdom of God. The rich man represents God, who knows what is in the heart of man. The manager is a person who is given the responsibility to use God's resources honestly, to the benefit of the kingdom of God. The worldly people are the nonbelievers around us. In this parable the rich man sees and criticizes the unjust servant's use of his dishonest negotiating skills. The unjust servant negotiates at the expense of his employer to win future employment with the rich man's debtors. From a worldly point of view, looking to the future was a shrewd move, even if it took the form of dishonest behavior. *These sons of this age are more shrewd in relation to their own kind than the sons of light.* The parable is also telling us not to hoard but to use material things for the benefit of the kingdom of Heaven. Our Father will see our faithful service, and when it is completed, He will welcome us into His eternal rest. This Parable is hard to understand, because the rich man is speaking from a worldly perspective and not from a Godly perspective. It is not recommending dishonest behavior, but it is saying that it is prudent for a person to look to the future and try to make provision for his or her long-term (eternal) survival. This is similar to making a choice of believing in Jesus, which includes the future benefit of eternal joy in Heaven as opposed to choosing to live for yourself today without regard for the future. Hell fire and damnation is not a popular style of preaching today. But many a person came to know the Lord because of fear. Looking to the future in Heaven is a better choice even if it is made for purely selfish reasons. It is also telling us that a person who is honest with small things can be trusted with much more. *"No servant can serve two masters; for either he will hate the one and love the other, or else he will be devoted to one and despise the other. You cannot serve God and wealth."* If a person cannot be trusted with today's wealth or resources, who is going to trust a person in the future to handle their own property? We can serve only one master, *(if you have not been faithful in the use of unrighteous wealth)* the choices we make expose our heart. God will not let us have it both ways. We must choose our priority either our love for God or our love for money.

Psalm 24: 3-5 (NASB)

> 3 Who may ascend into the hill of the Lord? And who may stand in His holy place? 4 He who has clean hands and a pure heart, Who has

not lifted up his soul to falsehood And has not sworn deceitfully. 5 He shall receive a blessing from the Lord And righteousness from the God of his salvation.

Psalms 119: 119-120

119 You put away all the wicked of the earth like dross. Therefore I love your testimonies. 120 My flesh trembles for fear of you. I am afraid of your judgments.

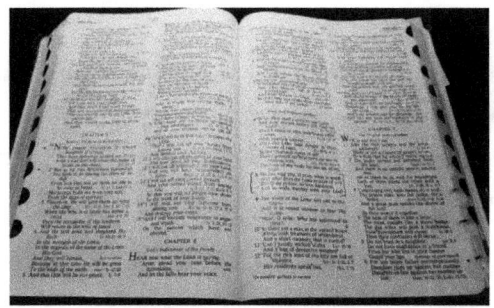

Chapter 9

9 ʳGod *is* faithful, by whom ye were called unto ˢthe fellowship of his Son Jesus Christ our Lord. 10 Now I beseech you, brethren, by the name of our Lord Jesus Christ, ᵗthat ye all speak the same thing, and *that* there be no †divisions among you; but *that* ye be perfectly joined together in the same mind and in the same judgment.

How do we know God is faithful?

Deuteronomy 7: 9 (NASB)

> 9 Know therefore that the Lord your God, He is God, the faithful God, who keeps His covenant and His lovingkindness to a thousandth generation with those who love Him and keep His commandments;

Psalm 51: 14-17 (NASB)

> 14 Deliver me from bloodguiltiness, O God, the God of my salvation; Then my tongue will joyfully sing of Your righteousness. 15 O Lord, open my lips, That my mouth may declare Your praise. 16 For You do not delight in sacrifice, otherwise I would give it; You are not pleased with burnt offering. 17 The sacrifices of God are a broken spirit; A broken and a contrite heart, O God, You will not despise.

Matthew 10: 21-22

21 "Brother will deliver up brother to death, and the father his child. Children will rise up against parents, and cause them to be put to death. 22 You will be hated by all men for my name's sake, but he who endures to the end will be saved.

Luke 6: 35-36

35 But love your enemies, and do good, and lend, expecting nothing back; and your reward will be great, and you will be children of the Most High; for he is kind toward the unthankful and evil 36 "Therefore be merciful, even as your Father is also merciful.

1 John 1: 3

3 that which we have seen and heard we declare to you, that you also man have fellowship with us. Yes, and our fellowship is with the Father, and with his Son, Jesus Christ.

1 John 4: 7-21

7 Beloved, let us love one another, for love is of God; and everyone who loves has been born of God, and knows God. 8 He who doesn't love doesn't know God, for God is love. 9 By this God's love was revealed in us, that God has sent his one and only Son into the world that we might live through him. 10 In this is love, not that we loved God, but that he loved us, and sent his Son as the atoning sacrifice for our sins. 11 Beloved, if God loved us in this way, we also ought to love one another. 12 No one has seen God at any time. If we love one another, God remains in us, and his love has been perfected in us.

13 By this we know that we remain in him and he in us, because he has given us of his Spirit. 14 We have seen and testify that the Father has sent the Son as the Savior of the world. 15 Whoever confesses that Jesus is the Son of God, God remains in him, and he in God. 16 We know and have believed the love which God has for us. God is love, and he who remains in love remains in God, and God remains

in him. 17 In this love has been made perfect among us, that we may have boldness in the day of judgment, because as he is, even so are we in this world. 18 There is no fear in love; but perfect love casts out fear, because fear has punishment. He who fears is not made perfect in love. 19 We love him, because he first loved us. 20 If a man says, "I love God," and hates his brother, he is a liar; for he who doesn't love his brother whom he has seen, how can he love God whom he has not seen? 21 This commandment we have from him, that he who loves God should also love his brother.

Romans 2: 5-13

5 But according to your hardness and unrepentant heart you are treasuring up for yourself wrath in the day of wrath, revelation, and of the righteous judgment of God; 6 who "will pay back to everyone according to their works:" 7 to those who by perseverance in well-doing seek for glory, honor, and incorruptibility, eternal life; 8 but to those who are self-seeking, and don't obey the truth, but obey unrighteousness, will be wrath and indignation, 9 oppression and anguish, on every soul of man who does evil, to the Jew first, and also to the Greek. 10 But glory, honor, and peace go to every man who does good, to the Jew first, and also to the Greek. 11 For there is no partiality with God. 12 For as many as have sinned without the law will also perish without the law. As many as have sinned under the law will be judged by the law. 13 For it isn't the hearers of the law who are righteous before God, but the doers of the law will be justified

1 Corinthians 1: 9

9 God is faithful, through whom you were called into the fellowship of his Son, Jesus Christ, our Lord.

Matthew 5: 14-16

14 You are the light of the world. A city located on a hill can't be hidden. 15 Neither do you light a lamp, and put it under a measuring basket, but on a stand; and it shines to all who are in the house.

> 16 Even so, let your light shine before men; that they may see your good works, and glorify your Father who is in heaven.

Romans 8: 30

> 30 Whom he predestined, those he also called. Whom he called, those he also justified. Whom he justified, those he also glorified.

1 Corinthians 10: 13

> 13 No temptation has taken you except what is common to man. God is faithful, who will not allow you to be tempted above what you are able, but will with the temptation also make the way of escape, that you may be able to endure it.

1 Thessalonians 5: 24

> 24 He who calls you is faithful, who will also do it.

2 Thessalonians 3: 3

> 3 But the Lord is faithful, who will establish you, and guard you from the evil one.

Philippians 1: 6

> 6 being confident of this very thing, that he who began a good work in you will complete it until the day of Jesus Christ.

2 Timothy 2: 13

> 13 If we are faithless, he remains faithful. For he can't deny himself."

Hebrews 4: 15

> 15 For we don't have a high priest who can't be touched with the feeling of our infirmities, but one who has been in all points tempted like we are, yet without sin

Hebrews 10: 23

> 23 let us hold fast the confession of our hope without wavering; for he who promised is faithful.

1 Peter 5: 10

> 10 But may the God of all grace, who called you to his eternal glory by Christ Jesus, after you have suffered a little while, perfect, establish, strengthen, and settle you.

Author's Opinion

God is faithful and loves those who believe in Christ Jesus and His wrath is sure to fall on those who do not believe. Not everyone believes and understands all of the predictions and prophecies that are written in the Bible. But none of Biblical history and prophecies has been proven wrong. The heart of man is deceitful and does not begin to understand the concept of complete and undefiled faithfulness. God is true to himself and man. To lie is not within God's nature as He is in total control. What would motivate God to be anything but straight forward and truthful with us? God is pure, just and without blemish. God has no limits. We think of God, Jesus and the Holy Spirit as having no beginning or no end. God said to Moses, "I AM WHO I AM." God also said "He is faithful"; therefore He is faithful. Man cannot wholly conceive the magnitude of God's faithfulness and holiness.

1 Corinthians 1: 9

> 9 God is faithful, through whom you were called into the fellowship of his Son, Jesus Christ, our Lord.

Isaiah 55: 8-9 (NASB)

> 8 "For My thoughts are not your thoughts, Nor are your ways My ways," declares the Lord. 9 "For as the heavens are higher than the earth, So are My ways higher than your ways And My thoughts than your thoughts.

Hebrews 7: 3

3 without father, without mother, without genealogy, having neither beginning of days nor end of life, but made like the Son of God), remains a priest continually.

Deuteronomy 32: 4

4 The Rock, his work is perfect, for all his ways are just. A God of faithfulness who does no wrong, just and right is he.

Proverbs 30: 5 (NASB)

5 Every word of God is tested; He is a shield to those who take refuge in Him.

Psalm 18: 30 (NASB)

30 As for God, His way is blameless; The word of the Lord is tried; He is a shield to all who take refuge in Him.

Psalm 19: 9 (NASB)

9 The fear of the Lord is clean, enduring forever;
The judgments of the Lord are true; they are righteous altogether.

Isaiah 45: 19 (NASB)

19 "I have not spoken in secret, In some dark land; I did not say to the offspring of Jacob, 'Seek Me in a waste place'; I, the Lord, speak righteousness, Declaring things that are upright.

Acts 9: 31 (NASB)

31 So the church throughout all Judea and Galilee and Samaria enjoyed peace, being built up; and going on in the fear of the Lord and in the comfort of the Holy Spirit, it continued to increase.

Romans 3: 21-31

21 But now apart from the law, a righteousness of God has been revealed, being testified by the law and the prophets; 22 even the

righteousness of God through faith in Jesus Christ to all and on all those who believe. For there is no distinction, 23 for all have sinned, and fall short of the glory of God; 24 being justified freely by his grace through the redemption that is in Christ Jesus; 25 whom God sent to be an atoning sacrifice, through faith in his blood, for a demonstration of his righteousness through the passing over of prior sins, in God's forbearance; 26 to demonstrate his righteousness at this present time; that he might himself be just, and the justifier of him who has faith in Jesus. 27 Where then is the boasting? It is excluded. By what kind of law? Of works? No, but by a law of faith. 28 We maintain therefore that a man is justified by faith apart from the works of the law. 29 Or is God the God of Jews only? Isn't he the God of Gentiles also? Yes, of Gentiles also, 30 since indeed there is one God who will justify the circumcised by faith, and the uncircumcised through faith. 31 Do we then nullify the law through faith? May it never be! No, we establish the law.

Paradoxes to be examined

Redemption

Psalm 19: 14 (NASB)

14 Let the words of my mouth and the meditation of my heart Be acceptable in Your sight, O Lord, my rock and my Redeemer.

Psalm 49: 6-9

6 Those who trust in their wealth, and boast in the multitude of their riches— 7 none of them can by any means redeem his brother, nor give God a ransom for him. 8 For the redemption of their life is costly, no payment is ever enough, 9 that he should live on forever, that he should not see corruption.

Psalm 130: 7 (NASB)

7 O Israel, hope in the Lord; For with the Lord there is lovingkindness, And with Him is abundant redemption.

Matthew 9: 13

13 But you go and learn what this means: 'I desire mercy, and not sacrifice,' for I came not to call the righteous, but sinners to repentance."

Luke 4: 18

18 "The Spirit of the Lord is on me, because he has anointed me preach good news to the poor. He has sent me to heal the broken hearted, to proclaim release to the captives, recovering of sight to the blind, to deliver those who are crushed,

Luke 21: 25-28

25 There will be signs in the sun, moon, and stars; and on the earth anxiety of nations, in perplexity for the roaring of the sea and the waves; 26 men fainting for fear, and for expectation of the things which are coming on the world: for the powers of the heavens will be shaken. 27 Then they will see the Son of Man coming in a cloud with power and great glory. 28 But when these things begin to happen, look up, and lift up your heads, because your redemption is near."

Romans 3: 23-25

23 for all have sinned, and fall short of the glory of God; 24 being justified freely by his grace through the redemption that is in Christ Jesus; 25 whom God sent to be an atoning sacrifice, through faith in his blood, for a demonstration of his righteousness through the passing over of prior sins, in God's forbearance;

Romans 5: 8

8 But God commends his own love toward us, in that while we were yet sinners, Christ died for us.

Romans 8: 22-23

22 For we know that the whole creation groans and travails in pain together until now. 23 Not only so, but ourselves also, who have the first fruits of the Spirit, even we ourselves groan within ourselves, waiting for adoption, the redemption of our body.

Ephesians 1: 7-9

7 in whom we have our redemption through his blood, the forgiveness of our trespasses, according to the riches of his grace, 8 which he made to abound toward us in all wisdom and prudence, 9 making known to us the mystery of his will, according to his good pleasure which he purposed in him

Ephesians 1: 13-14

13 In him you also, having heard the word of the truth, the Good News of your salvation—in whom, having also believed, you were sealed with the promised Holy Spirit, 14 who is a pledge of our inheritance, to the redemption of God's own possession, to the praise of his glory.

Ephesians 4: 30-32

30 Don't grieve the Holy Spirit of God, in whom you were sealed for the day of redemption. 31 Let all bitterness, wrath, anger, outcry, and slander, be put away from you, with all malice. 32 And be kind to one another, tender hearted, forgiving each other, just as God also in Christ forgave you.

Hebrews 9: 11-14

11 But Christ having come as a high priest of the coming good things, through the greater and more perfect tabernacle, not made with hands, that is to say, not of this creation, 12 nor yet through the blood of goats and calves, but through his own blood, entered in once for all into the Holy Place, having obtained eternal redemption. 13 For if the blood of goats and bulls, and the ashes of a heifer

sprinkling those who have been defiled, sanctify to the cleanness of the flesh: 14 how much more will the blood of Christ, who through the eternal Spirit offered himself without defect to God, cleanse your conscience from dead works to serve the living God?

Salvation

1 Chronicles 16: 23 (NASB)

23 Sing to the Lord, all the earth; Proclaim good tidings of His salvation from day to day.

Psalm 3: 8 (NASB)

8 Salvation belongs to the Lord; Your blessing be upon Your people!

Psalm 98: 2 (NASB)

2 The Lord has made known His salvation; He has revealed His righteousness in the sight of the nations.

Isaiah 30: 18 (NASB)

18 Therefore the Lord longs to be gracious to you, And therefore He waits on high to have compassion on you. For the Lord is a God of justice; How blessed are all those who long for Him.

Joel 2: 27-32 (NASB)

27 "Thus you will know that I am in the midst of Israel, And that I am the Lord your God, And there is no other; And My people will never be put to shame. 28 "It will come about after this That I will pour out My Spirit on all mankind; And your sons and daughters will prophesy, Your old men will dream dreams, Your young men will see visions. 29 "Even on the male and female servants I will pour out My Spirit in those days. 30 "I will display wonders in the sky and on the earth, Blood, fire and columns of smoke. 31 "The sun will be turned into darkness And the moon into blood Before the great and

awesome day of the Lord comes. 32 "And it will come about that whoever calls on the name of the Lord Will be delivered; For on Mount Zion and in Jerusalem There will be those who escape, As the Lord has said, Even among the survivors whom the Lord calls.

Luke 2: 28-32

28 then he received him into his arms, and blessed God, and said, 29 "Now you are releasing your servant, Master, according to your word, in peace; 30 for my eyes have seen your salvation, 31 which you have prepared before the face of all peoples; 32 a light for revelation to the nations, and the glory of your people Israel."

John 10: 9

9 I am the door. If anyone enters in by me, he will be saved, and will go in and go out, and will find pasture.

Acts 4: 11-12

11 He is 'the stone which was regarded as worthless by you, the builders, which has become the head of the corner.' 12 There is salvation in none other, for neither is there any other name under heaven, that is given among men, by which we must be saved!"

2 Corinthians 6: 2 (NASB)

2 for He says, "At the acceptable time I listened to you, and on the day of salvation I helped you." Behold , Now is "the acceptable time " Behold now is "the day of salvation"

2 Thessalonians 2: 13

13 But we are bound to always give thanks to God for you, brothers loved by the Lord, because God chose you from the beginning for salvation through sanctification of the Spirit and belief in the truth;

Hebrews 2: 3

3 how will we escape if we neglect so great a salvation—which at the first having been spoken through the Lord, was confirmed to us by those who heard;

Born again

John 3: 3-7

3 Jesus answered him, "Most certainly, I tell you, unless one is born anew, he can't see God's Kingdom." 4 Nicodemus said to him, "How can a man be born when he is old? Can he enter a second time into his mother's womb, and be born?" 5 Jesus answered, "Most certainly I tell you, unless one is born of water and spirit, he can't enter into God's Kingdom. 6 That which is born of the flesh is flesh. That which is born of the Spirit is spirit. 7 Don't marvel that I said to you, 'You must be born anew.'

Zechariah 2: 3-13 (NASB)

3 And behold, the angel who was speaking with me was going out, and another angel was coming out to meet him, 4 and said to him, "Run, speak to that young man, saying, 'Jerusalem will be inhabited without walls because of the multitude of men and cattle within it. 5 For I,' declares the Lord, 'will be a wall of fire around her, and I will be the glory in her midst.'" 6 "Ho there! Flee from the land of the north," declares the Lord, "for I have dispersed you as the four winds of the heavens," declares the Lord. 7 "Ho, Zion! Escape, you who are living with the daughter of Babylon." 8 For thus says the Lord of hosts, "After glory He has sent me against the nations which plunder you, for he who touches you, touches the apple of His eye. 9 For behold, I will wave My hand over them so that they will be plunder for their slaves. Then you will know that the Lord of hosts has sent Me. 10 Sing for joy and be glad, O daughter of Zion; for behold I am coming and I will dwell in your midst," declares the Lord. 11 "Many

nations will join themselves to the Lord in that day and will become My people. Then I will dwell in your midst, and you will know that the Lord of hosts has sent Me to you. 12 The Lord will possess Judah as His portion in the holy land, and will again choose Jerusalem. 13 "Be silent, all flesh, before the Lord; for He is aroused from His holy habitation."

John 8: 31-32

31 Jesus therefore said to those Jews who had believed him, "If you remain in my word, then you are truly my disciples. 32 You will know the truth, and the truth will make you free."

2 Corinthians 5: 17-19

17 Therefore if anyone is in Christ, he is a new creation. The old things have passed away. Behold, all things have become new. 18 But all things are of God, who reconciled us to himself through Jesus Christ, and gave to us the ministry of reconciliation; 19 namely, that God was in Christ reconciling the world to himself, not reckoning to them their trespasses, and having committed to us the word of reconciliation.

Spirit

Matthew 1: 20-21

20 But when he thought about these things, behold, an angel of the Lord appeared to him in a dream, saying, "Joseph, son of David, don't be afraid to take to yourself Mary, your wife, for that which is conceived in her is of the Holy Spirit. 21 She shall give birth to a son. You shall call his name Jesus, for it is he who shall save his people from their sins."

John 16: 13-15

13 However when he, the Spirit of truth, has come, he will guide you into all truth, for he will not speak from himself; but whatever he hears, he will speak. He will declare to you things that are coming. 14 He will glorify me, for he will take from what is mine, and will declare it to you. 15 All things whatever the Father has are mine; therefore I said that he takes of mine, and will declare it to you.

Romans 8: 5-11

5 For those who live according to the flesh set their minds on the things of the flesh, but those who live according to the Spirit, the things of the Spirit. 6 For the mind of the flesh is death, but the mind of the Spirit is life and peace; 7 because the mind of the flesh is hostile towards God; for it is not subject to God's law, neither indeed can it be. 8 Those who are in the flesh can't please God. 9 But you are not in the flesh but in the Spirit, if it is so that the Spirit of God dwells in you. But if any man doesn't have the Spirit of Christ, he is not his. 10 If Christ is in you, the body is dead because of sin, but the spirit is alive because of righteousness. 11 But if the Spirit of him who raised up Jesus from the dead dwells in you, he who raised up Christ Jesus from the dead will also give life to your mortal bodies through his Spirit who dwells in you.

Galatians 4: 6-7

6 And because you are children, God sent out the Spirit of his Son into your hearts, crying, "Abba, Father!" 7 So you are no longer a bondservant, but a son; and if a son, then an heir of God through Christ.

Ephesians 1: 13-14

13 In him you also, having heard the word of the truth, the Good News of your salvation—in whom, having also believed, you were sealed with the promised Holy Spirit, 14 who is a pledge of our inheritance, to the redemption of God's own possession, to the praise of his glory.

Ephesians 4: 4-6

4 There is one body, and one Spirit, even as you also were called in one hope of your calling; 5 one Lord, one faith, one baptism, 6 one God and Father of all, who is over all, and through all, and in us all.

Proverbs 20: 27 (NASB)

27 The spirit of man is the lamp of the Lord, Searching all the innermost parts of his being.

1 Corinthians 2: 8-12 (NASB)

8 the wisdom which none of the rulers of this age has understood; for if they had understood it they would not have crucified the Lord of glory; 9 but just as it is written, "Things which eye has not seen and ear has not heard, And which have not entered the heart of man, All that God has prepared for those who love Him." 10 For to us God revealed them through the Spirit; for the Spirit searches all things, even the depths of God. 11 For who among men knows the thoughts of a man except the spirit of the man which is in him? Even so the thoughts of God no one knows except the Spirit of God. 12 Now we have received, not the spirit of the world, but the Spirit who is from God, so that we may know the things freely given to us by God,

2 Corinthians 7: 1

1 Therefore, since we have these promises, dear friends, let us purify ourselves from everything that contaminates body and spirit, perfecting holiness out of reverence for God.

1 John 4: 1-6

1 Beloved, don't believe every spirit, but test the spirits, whether they are of God, because many false prophets have gone out into the world. 2 By this you know the Spirit of God: every spirit who confesses that Jesus Christ has come in the flesh is of God, 3 and every spirit who doesn't confess that Jesus Christ has come in the flesh is not of God, and this is the spirit of the Antichrist, of whom

you have heard that it comes. Now it is in the world already. 4 You are of God, little children, and have overcome them; because greater is he who is in you than he who is in the world. 5 They are of the world. Therefore they speak of the world, and the world hears them. 6 We are of God. He who knows God listens to us. He who is not of God doesn't listen to us. By this we know the spirit of truth, and the spirit of error.

Parables to be grasped

The Parable of the Talents

Matthew 25: 14-30

14 "For it is like a man, going into another country, who called his own servants, and entrusted his goods to them. 15 To one he gave five talents, to another two, to another one; to each according to his own ability. Then he went on his journey. 16 Immediately he who received the five talents went and traded with them, and made another five talents. 17 In the same way, he also who got the two gained another two. 18 But he who received the one talent went away and dug in the earth, and hid his lord's money. 19 "Now after a long time the lord of those servants came, and reconciled accounts with them. 20 He who received the five talents came and brought another five talents, saying, 'Lord, you delivered to me five talents. Behold, I have gained another five talents besides them.' 21 "His lord said to him, 'Well done, good and faithful servant. You have been faithful over a few things, I will set you over many things. Enter into the joy of your lord.' 22 "He also who got the two talents came and said, 'Lord, you delivered to me two talents. Behold, I have gained another two talents besides them.' 23 "His lord said to him, 'Well done, good and faithful servant. You have been faithful over a few things, I will set you over many things. Enter into the joy of your

lord.' 24 "He also who had received the one talent came and said, 'Lord, I knew you that you are a hard man, reaping where you did not sow, and gathering where you did not scatter. 25 I was afraid, and went away and hid your talent in the earth. Behold, you have what is yours.' 26 "But his lord answered him, 'You wicked and slothful servant. You knew that I reap where I didn't sow, and gather where I didn't scatter. 27 You ought therefore to have deposited my money with the bankers, and at my coming I should have received back my own with interest. 28 Take away therefore the talent from him, and give it to him who has the ten talents. 29 For to everyone who has will be given, and he will have abundance, but from him who doesn't have, even that which he has will be taken away. 30 Throw out the unprofitable servant into the outer darkness, where there will be weeping and gnashing of teeth.'

Author's Opinion

The *Parable of the Talents* is about accountability to an all-knowing and just God. There are three servants given talents (or gifts) to be used to the glory and benefit of the master (God) who has traveled to a distant land. On return the master finds that two of his servants have invested one hundred percent of their gifts and received back in return from their wise investments one hundred percent gain plus their initial investments. These two servants received great reward commensurate with their faithfulness. But the third lazy, unproductive servant admitted to being afraid and hiding the one talent that was given to him. The master took the one gift from the unprofitable servant who lacked faith and gave the gift of this talent to the faithful first servant. To the wicked and unfaithful servant, the master said, "You should have put the talent that I gave you to use with others so that when I returned I would have received at least some benefit." God punished the servant severely by separating him from all

God's love that we take for granted.

Today, this parable is telling us that the Master's judgment is certain and can be severe, holding each one of us responsible to worship and glorify Him. Many people are afraid to speak up and witness to friends. Our witness may be the one small gift or talent that the master has given us. Think of how many people are choosing to be like the complacent *unprofitable servant.* They are hiding their gifts not using their talents to benefit the kingdom of God, living only for themselves. Like it or not, we cannot hide from God. It will be futile to say *"Lord, I knew you that you are a hard man,* the thought of eternal punishment was too hard and unbelievable for me to think about, *I was afraid, and went away and hid your talent."*

Psalms 98: 6-9 (NASB)

> 6 With trumpets and the sound of the horn Shout joyfully before the King, the Lord. 7 Let the sea roar and all it contains, The world and those who dwell in it. 8 Let the rivers clap their hands, Let the mountains sing together for joy 9 Before the Lord, for He is coming to judge the earth; He will judge the world with righteousness And the peoples with equity.

Matthew 10: 32-33

> 32 Everyone therefore who confesses me before men, him I will also confess before my Father who is in heaven. 33 But whoever denies me before men, him I will also deny before my Father who is in heaven.

Matthew 16: 25

> 25 For whoever desires to save his life will lose it, and whoever will lose his life for my sake will find it.

Matthew 25: 31-34

31 "But when the Son of Man comes in his glory, and all the holy angels with him, then he will sit on the throne of his glory. 32 Before him all the nations will be gathered, and he will separate them one from another, as a shepherd separates the sheep from the goats. 33 He will set the sheep on his right hand, but the goats on the left. 34 Then the King will tell those on his right hand, 'Come, blessed of my Father, inherit the Kingdom prepared for you from the foundation of the world

John 20: 29

29 Jesus said to him, "Because you have seen me, you have believed. Blessed are those who have not seen, and have believed."

The Parable of the Persistent Friend

Luke 11: 5-13

5 He said to them, "Which of you, if you go to a friend at midnight, and tell him, 'Friend, lend me three loaves of bread, 6 for a friend of mine has come to me from a journey, and I have nothing to set before him,' 7 and he from within will answer and say, 'Don't bother me. The door is now shut, and my children are with me in bed. I can't get up and give it to you'? 8 I tell you, although he will not rise and give it to him because he is his friend, yet because of his persistence, he will get up and give him as many as he needs. 9 "I tell you, keep asking, and it will be given you. Keep seeking, and you will find. Keep knocking, and it will be opened to you. 10 For everyone who asks receives. He who seeks finds. To him who knocks it will be opened. 11 "Which of you fathers, if your son asks for bread, will give him a stone? Or if he asks for a fish, he won't give him a snake instead of a fish, will he? 12 Or if he asks for an egg, he won't give him a scorpion, will he? 13 If you then, being evil, know how to give good gifts to your children, how much more will your heavenly Father give the Holy Spirit to those who ask him?"

Author's Opinion

The *Parable of the Persistent Friend* is about how we are to pray to the Father. Jesus, just before these verses, taught His disciples to pray the Lord's prayer. This parable is telling us to be persistent, in asking for the things that we need.

1 Peter 5: 6-7

> 6 Humble yourselves therefore under the mighty hand of God, that he may exalt you in due time; 7 casting all your worries on him, because he cares for you.

God knows our needs, and He will be faithful to provide them. This type of prayer is evidence of our faithful trust and worship of our Heavenly Father. We are His children and we must not lose faith, but know that all good things come from God. His Holy Spirit will never leave or forsake us when we trust Him.

Romans 8: 24-29

> 24 For we were saved in hope, but hope that is seen is not hope. For who hopes for that which he sees? 25 But if we hope for that which we don't see, we wait for it with patience. 26 In the same way, the Spirit also helps our weaknesses, for we don't know how to pray as we ought. But the Spirit himself makes intercession for us with groanings which can't be uttered. 27 He who searches the hearts knows what is on the Spirit's mind, because he makes intercession for the saints according to God. 28 We know that all things work together for good for those who love God, to those who are called according to his purpose. 29 For whom he foreknew, he also predestined to be conformed to the image of his Son, that he might be the firstborn among many brothers

Philippians 1: 3-11

> 3 I thank my God whenever I remember you, 4 always in every request of mine on behalf of you all, making my requests with joy, 5 for your

partnership in furtherance of the Good News from the first day until now; 6 being confident of this very thing, that he who began a good work in you will complete it until the day of Jesus Christ. 7 It is even right for me to think this way on behalf of all of you, because I have you in my heart, because, both in my bonds and in the defense and confirmation of the Good News, you all are partakers with me of grace. 8 For God is my witness, how I long after all of you in the tender mercies of Christ Jesus. 9 This I pray, that your love may abound yet more and more in knowledge and all discernment; 10 so that you may approve the things that are excellent; that you may be sincere and without offense to the day of Christ; 11 being filled with the fruits of righteousness, which are through Jesus Christ, to the glory and praise of God.

The Parable of the Lost Coin

Luke 15: 8-10 (NASB)

> 8 "Or what woman, if she has ten silver coins and loses one coin, does not light a lamp and sweep the house and search carefully until she finds it? 9 When she has found it, she calls together her friends and neighbors, saying, 'Rejoice with me, for I have found the coin which I had lost!' 10 In the same way, I tell you, there is joy in the presence of the angels of God over one sinner who repents."

Author's Opinion

The *Parable of the Lost Coin* is telling us that every person is of value to God. There is great joy in Heaven when one sinner repents and comes humbly before the throne of God. We individually, and the Church corporately, are to *light a lamp and sweep the house and search carefully* and tenderly, to find the lost. We should rejoice and be grateful in our salvation and have a sense of urgency in our witness to others for the glory of God. While we were sinners, God loved us first. Jesus' Atonement at Calvary and His resurrection on the third day, speak to God's faithfulness and Love for man. 27 *"Now my soul is troubled. What shall I say? 'Father, save me from this time?' But for this cause I came to this time.* 28 *Father, glorify your name!" Then there came a voice out of the sky, saying, "I have both glorified it, and will glorify it again."* John 12: 27-28 Christ not only paid the ransom for our sins; He also searches for all that will come to Him. The joy in Heaven over even one lost soul who repents and is converted, confirms God's love and faithfulness to man.

Hebrews 1: 8-9

8 But of the Son he says, "Your throne, O God, is forever and ever. The scepter of uprightness is the scepter of your Kingdom. 9 You have loved righteousness, and hated iniquity; therefore God, your God, has anointed you with the oil of gladness above your fellows."

Hebrews 12: 1-2

1 Therefore let us also, seeing we are surrounded by so great a cloud of witnesses, lay aside every weight and the sin which so easily entangles us, and let us run with perseverance the race that is set before us, 2 looking to Jesus, the author and perfecter of faith, who for the joy that was set before him endured the cross, despising its shame, and has sat down at the right hand of the throne of God.

The Parable of the Creditor and Two Debtors

Luke 7: 41-43

41 "A certain lender had two debtors. The one owed five hundred denarii, and the other fifty. 42 When they couldn't pay, he forgave them both. Which of them therefore will love him most?" 43 Simon answered, "He, I suppose, to whom he forgave the most." He said to him, "You have judged correctly."

Author's Opinion

The *Parable of the Creditor and Two Debtors* is about gratitude. It is questioning who is likely to love God more. We literally have nothing of value except our love and gratitude to repay God for his forgiveness of our sin. We are in His debt for his gift of grace that is extended to us. Which of the two debtors should love God more, the person who has led not a perfect life, but a good life or a person that has led a very bad and rebellious life? The assurance of forgiveness or salvation is not in question here. But we all have memory of a lifetime of past sins. We know how indebted we are and the great disparity between our sin and God's Grace. *15 And let the peace of God rule in your hearts, to which also you were called in one body; and be thankful. Colossians 3: 15* This can translate proportionally into how much gratitude and love we show God in return. The man who wrote the song Amazing Grace had been a slave trading ship captain in his youth. He knew all too well the depth of his grievous sins and heights of God's Grace that wiped all record of his sins clean, never to be remembered again. Amazing Grace was his expression of gratitude and love to God. Even when we feel far from God and laden with guilt, He is still faithfully telling us; "He is the way, the truth and the life. Come unto me."

Psalm 107; 1-3 (NASB)

> 1 Oh give thanks to the Lord, for He is good, For His lovingkindness is everlasting. 2 Let the redeemed of the Lord say so, Whom He has redeemed from the hand of the adversary 3 And gathered from the lands, From the east and from the west, From the north and from the south.

Colossians 1: 12-14

> 12 giving thanks to the Father, who made us fit to be partakers of the inheritance of the saints in light; 13 who delivered us out of the power of darkness, and translated us into the Kingdom of the Son of his love; 14 in whom we have our redemption, the forgiveness of our sin.

Everyone has a need to know that Jesus saves!

Holy is His name, Faithful, Good Shepherd, Jehovah, Lamb of God, Mediator, Messiah, Physician, Prince of Peace, Redeemer, Savior, Servant, Teacher, Yahweh, the way, and the Word. Please know that Jesus (The King of Kings and Lord of Lords) humbled Himself by coming to earth, to die on the cross and give us the free gift of His Grace. His offer of Grace proves God is faithful. The sinful man cannot please God without a child-like faith in Jesus. His words of truth were given to us so that we would know Him, His precepts and His commandments. Jesus' Parables are a special gift to those people who truly seek to understand, (Matthew 13: 10-15). I am reminded of the statement a doctor made to his mental patient, "You certainly see things that other people do not see." It is hoped that the reader will see the spiritual value in the scriptures and come to understand their personal significance, even if other people do not.

1 Corinthians 1: 21-25

> 21 For seeing that in the wisdom of God, the world through its wisdom didn't know God, it was God's good pleasure through the foolishness of the preaching to save those who believe. 22 For Jews ask for signs, Greeks seek after wisdom, 23 but we preach Christ crucified; a stumbling block to Jews, and foolishness to Greeks, 24 but to those who are called, both Jews and Greeks, Christ is the power of God and the wisdom of God. 25 Because the foolishness of God is wiser than men, and the weakness of God is stronger than men.

In looking at the forty parables, there are numerous recurring themes. Speaking in very general terms, ten of the parables speak of being accountable to the Father and His authority in our life. Six of the parables make it clear that Jesus is the author of the Bible, and without exception, we are to believe His Word of Truth. Five parables stress the need for all people to come to repentance. There are several parables that instructed us to be persistent in our prayer and to witness to God's Words of truth, both inside and outside the church, and to beware of Satan's leaven, the distortion of doctrine. We are admonished to love one another, be grateful for God's Grace and warned against disbelief, hypocrisy, greed, self-righteousness, having an unforgiving spirit and of an unproductive complacency. Jesus' Word and His Parables show that we are all sinners, but we are still very important to God. God values every individual and has no desire that any should perish.

We are coming close to the end of our journey to find God's wisdom from His Word in *All Authority*. Very little has been said about the paradoxes that we have examined from the Bible. Here the paradoxes and precepts stand alone, with only scripture verses as their witness. These paradoxes are only a small part of the unseen mysteries of the ages that can be seen by man through Jesus' word of truth. Our future wellbeing depends on our approaching God and His scriptures with an attitude of hope and faith. Faith is not a form of superstition or ignorance. It cherishes the love and wisdom that God has provided for us. Searching the scriptures to see God more clearly can pay dividends for today and all eternity. *(Romans 8: 6-8* (NASB)*)* 6 *For the mind of the flesh is death, but the mind of the Spirit is life and peace;* 7 *because the mind of the flesh is hostile towards God; for it is not subject to God's law, neither indeed can it be.* 8 *Those who are in the flesh can't please God.* The mysteries of God and the fear of God are all a part of our faith in God. Rebellion from God and his word can take many forms. One way is to ignore or deny God's existence altogether. Another way is to try to reduce Jesus and His word of truth to man's level, by refuting His word to accommodate man's intellect.

Acts 20: 26-27

> 26 Therefore I testify to you today that I am clean from the blood of all men, 27 for I didn't shrink from declaring to you the whole counsel of God.

The author's opinions, our questions and the parables have not always been uplifting or flattering to man's sin nature or church complacency. It is hard to embrace the idea that our loving God is also capable of dispensing everlasting punishment when we reject Jesus' authority in our life. By necessity, the tone of our search for answers has not catered to man's ego or tried to lure the reader with the seductive music of cheap Grace (faith without personal commitment). *Declaring to you the whole counsel of God* accurately sometimes requires treading on harsh and stony ground, compassionately without being unduly provocative. To some people, any religious issue is provocative. God has placed before man, a clear choice, either we believe and receive God's blessing or by denying His authority we receive His curse. It is hard to understand why anyone would choose God's curse.

Deuteronomy 30: 19

> 19 I call heaven and earth to witness against you today, that I have set before you life and death, the blessing and the curse. Therefore choose life, that you may live, you and your descendants;

Luke 24: 46-47

> 46 He said to them, "Thus it is written, and thus it was necessary for

the Christ to suffer and to rise from the dead the third day, 47 and that repentance and remission of sins should be preached in his name to all the nations, beginning at Jerusalem.

All Authority has focused on Jesus' words of truth, as recorded in the Bible. It makes clear Christ's authority, our accountability to God, the cost of discipleship and also showing the glorious hope and joy of Christ's promise of Grace. The Holy Spirit will choose who sees God's love and purpose, taking to heart, what the scriptures, are telling us. God gives each one of us the free will to choose what we want to believe. We cannot serve two masters. Repentance must come before we can be forgiven. Repentance is the feeling of sorrow for our sin nature and the very opposite of rebellion. Within the heart rebellion and repentance cannot occupy the same space, it is ether one or the other. Remission of sin is another way of saying our sins have been paid for and forgiven. We cannot have forgiveness if we are harboring rebellion in our heart. He is the Potter and we are the clay. If the clay is not responsive to the potter, the clay will be discarded.

2 Timothy 2: 20

20 Now in a large house there are not only vessels of gold and of silver, but also of wood and of clay. Some are for honor, and some for dishonor.

2 Timothy 2: 25

25 in gentleness correcting those who oppose him: perhaps God may give them repentance leading to a full knowledge of the truth,

The Questions, Paradoxes and Parables within *All Authority* looked at many issues. Please note; some of Jesus' parables have reoccurring themes. If any of these issues or themes are confusing you because the shoe fits uncomfortably, it call's for you to think carefully about it. Don't ignore troubling issues.

Search the scriptures for the right answers. Circumspection is how the Holy Spirit convicts us of our rebellion. It is better to be convicted and return to the family of God, than to be convicted as a nonbeliever on the day of accountability.

Luke 22: 31-32

> 31 The Lord said, "Simon, Simon, behold, Satan asked to have all of you, that he might sift you as wheat, 32 but I prayed for you, that your faith wouldn't fail. You, when once you have turned again, establish your brothers."

Have you heard the old saying and half-truth "knowledge is power"? Many people are always learning, but never able to come to the saving knowledge of the truth. Knowledge can only be turned into power, if you are willing to use that knowledge to your advantage. Sadly there is another familiar verse that is very true: 14 *"For Many are called but few chosen" Matthew 22: 14.* Many are called, but not everyone wants to be chosen. Many people hear about spiritual knowledge from sermon after sermon, but few are willing to submit themselves, as a living sacrifice holy acceptable to God.

Romans 12: 1-2

> 1 Therefore I urge you, brothers, by the mercies of God, to present your bodies a living sacrifice, holy, acceptable to God, which is your spiritual service. 2 Don't be conformed to this world, but be transformed by the renewing of your mind, so that you may prove what is the good, well-pleasing, and perfect will of God.

Good churches exalt the preeminence of Christ. Finding a church in which to worship and fellowship requires discrimination. Beware of Satan's stumbling blocks. The true church is governed as a theocracy! God requires obedience. *Today's church leadership must not capitulate to worldly traditions and procedures that clearly violate and makes a mockery of scripture for God is not a God of confusion.* The true Church is where the unseen mysteries of ages and riches of wisdom are revealed. The Church is God's gift of sanctuary, the guardian of truth and the habitation of God's spirit. It is a place of hope, knowledge, fellowship, comfort and discipline.

People often relate to God and religion by focusing on their visible local church. This fact puts tremendous responsibility on church leaders and their congregations to glorify Jesus and faithfully preach of the words of truth from the scriptures with a sense of urgency, not complacency. *2 Corinthians 6: 2* Tells us that *...now is the day of salvation.* The vision and purpose of our visible local churches vary tremendously, but there is only one great commission which is to go out and make disciples, preaching the Good News Gospel. Making disciples means daring to speak up and not being afraid to ask people to see their need to accept Jesus as Lord and Savior.

The Church you choose is very important. It is there to teach and comfort with Jesus' words of truth. It is a refuge where individuals and families can grow and mature in their walk with the Lord. A person may come to the saving knowledge of Christ before or after joining the church or in some cases, come to know the Lord in spite of the church. But the visible church environment and their church denominations are simply not the deciding factor in the most important question man will ever face. John 4: 23-24 Records Jesus' personal invitation. *23 But the hour comes, and now is, when the true worshipers will worship the Father in spirit and truth, for the Father seeks such to be his worshipers. 24 God is spirit, and those who worship him must worship in spirit and truth."* Do you have Christ in you? Have you asked Christ into your heart to stay? If the answer is yes, you will forever be in the family of God. He will never leave or forsake you. Jesus Christ is the Alpha and Omega, the beginning and the end, our Lord God Almighty.

Hebrews 1: 1-3

1 God, having in the past spoken to the fathers through the prophets at many times and in various ways, 2 has at the end of these days spoken to us by his Son, whom he appointed heir of all things, through whom also he made the worlds. 3 His Son is the radiance of his glory, the very image of his substance, and upholding all things by the word of his power, who, when he had by himself purified us of our sins, sat down on the right hand of the Majesty on high;

Hebrews 12: 2

2 looking to Jesus, the author and perfecter of faith, who for the joy that was set before him endured the cross, despising its shame, and has sat down at the right hand of the throne of God.

Revelation 21: 6

6 He said to me, "I have become the Alpha and the Omega, the Beginning and the End. I will give freely to him who is thirsty from the spring of the water of life.

The joy in Heaven is well documented, ten thousand tongues singing the Hallelujah Chorus, when one sinner repents. Please know that our God in three persons are united in offering today the saving knowledge of His Grace to all that will bow down and worship Jesus Christ, our rock and redeemer.

1 Corinthians 14: 33 (NASB)

33 for God is not a God of confusion but of peace, as in all the churches of the saints.

Ephesians 5: 25-26 (NASB)

25 Husbands, love your wives, just as Christ also loved the church and gave Himself up for her, 26 so that He might sanctify her, having cleansed her by the washing of water with the word,

In the all too near future the lights will be turned out. We will have to go home alone to our Father. On bended knee we all will confess Christ as Lord and have to stand in judgment, giving an account. Do you hear the Holy Spirit calling you today?

Ecclesiastes 12: 7

> 7 and the dust returns to the earth as it was, and the spirit returns to God who gave it.

Philippians 2: 10-11

> 10 that at the name of Jesus every knee should bow, of those in heaven, those on earth, and those under the earth, 11 and that every tongue should confess that Jesus Christ is Lord, to the glory of God the Father.

Chapter 10

> 9 That ʰif thou shalt confess with thy mouth the Lord Jesus, and shalt believe in thine heart that God hath raised him from the dead, thou shalt be saved.
> 10 For with the heart man believeth unto righteousness; and with the mouth confession is made unto salvation.

What must I do to be saved?

Acts 16: 29-31

> 29 He called for lights, sprang in, fell down trembling before Paul and Silas, 30 brought them out, and said, "Sirs, what must I do to be saved?" 31 They said, "Believe in the Lord Jesus Christ, and you will be saved, you and your household."

John 6: 47-48

> 47 Most certainly, I tell you, he who believes in me has eternal life. 48 I am the bread of life.

Romans 10: 8-11

> 8 But what does it say? "The word is near you, in your mouth, and in your heart"; that is, the word of faith, which we preach: 9 that if you will confess with your mouth that Jesus is Lord, and believe in your heart that God raised him from the dead, you will be saved. 10 For with the heart, one believes unto righteousness; and with the mouth confession is made unto salvation. 11 For the Scripture says, "Whoever believes in him will not be disappointed."

1 Corinthians 1: 9 (NASB)

> 9 God is faithful, through whom you were called into fellowship with His Son, Jesus Christ our Lord.

Author's Opinion

Please join me in noting eleven of the most beautiful words ever spoken to man.

Jeremiah 30: 22

> 22 You shall be My people, And I will be your God.

Amen

Appendix

Parables in alphabetical order

The Parable of the absent householder	153
The Parable of the Barren Fig Tree	59
The Parable of the Cost of Discipleship	226
The Parable of the Creditor and Two Debtors	256
The Parable of the Dragnet	185
The Parable of the Expedient Servant	81
The Parable of the Faithful Servant	125
The Parable of the fig tree	150
The Parable of the foolish man who builds his house on the sand	147
The Parable of the Good Samaritan	80
The Parable of the Great Supper	58
The Parable of the Growing Seed	203
The Parable of the Hidden Treasure	32
The Parable of the householder	145
The Parable of the Laborers	222
The Parable of the Lamp and Salt	76
The Parable of the Leaven	53
The Parable of the Lost Coin	255
The Parable of the Lost Sheep	77
The Parable of the Marriage Feast	83
The Parable of the Mustard Seed	27
The Parable of the New Wine in Old Wineskins	207
The Parable of the Pearl of Great Price	32
The Parable of the Pharisee and the Tax Collector	116
The Parable of the Persistent Friend	253
The Parable of the Prodigal Son	175
The Parable of the Rich Fool	228
The Parable of the Rich Man and Lazarus	30
The Parable of the Sower	50
The Parable of the Talents	250

The Parable of the Ten Minas 182
The parable of the Ten Virgins 129
The Parable of the Two Sons. 209
The Parable of the Unforgiving Servant. 181
The Parable of the Unjust Servant. 230
The Parable of the Unprofitable Servant 179
The Parable of the Unshrunk Cloth on Old Garment. 205
The Parable of the Wheat and Tares 118
The Parable of the Wicked Vinedressers 55
The Parable of the Woman and the Judge 224

Paradoxes in alphabetical order

Born again. 246
Church 193
Creation. 41
Death. 198
Divisions 109
Eternal Life 138
Fairness of God's Law 140
Faith 72
Fall or depravity of man. 111
False Teaching 43
Grace. 23
Heaven 220
Hell 219
Hope 164
Hypocrisy 217
Inerrancy of Scriptures 196
Judgment 170
Man's choice. 166
Man's sin nature 112
One God in three persons. 15
Predestination 70

Pride	215
Redemption	241
Repentance	160
Resurrection	143
Salvation	244
Satan	200
Scandal (Shame)	48
Soul	74
Spirit	247
Stumbling Blocks	45
The Word	18
Worship	67
Virgin birth	21

Manufactured in the United States of America

www.ingramcontent.com/pod-product-compliance
Lightning Source LLC
Chambersburg PA
CBHW061633040426
42446CB00010B/1397